T3-BNW-611

QUALITY IN INSTRUCTIONAL TELEVISION

THE EAST-WEST CENTER—formally known as "The Center for Cultural a Technical Interchange Between East and West"—was established in Haw. by the United States Congress in 1960. As a national educational insti tion in cooperation with the University of Hawaii, the Center's mandated goal is ' promote better relations and understanding between the United States and the r tions of Asia and the Pacific through cooperative study, training, and researcl

Each year about 2,000 men and women from the United States and some countries and territories of Asia and the Pacific area work and study together witl multi-national East-West Center staff in wide-ranging programs dealing with pr lems of mutual East-West concern. Participants are supported by federal scholarsh and grants, supplemented in some fields by contributions from Asian/Pacific gove. ments and private foundations.

Center programs are conducted by the East-West Communication Institute, East-West Culture Learning Institute, the East-West Food Institute, the East-W Population Institute, and the East-West Technology and Development Institute. Op Grants are awarded to provide scope for educational and research innovation, cluding a program in humanities and the arts.

East-West Center Books are published by The University Press of Hawaii further the Center's aims and programs.

Quality in Instructional Television

edited by
Wilbur Schramm

contributors

C. Ray Carpenter
Max Egly
Gerald S. Lesser
Arthur A. Lumsdaine
Rolf Lundgren
Edward Palmer
Wilbur Schramm

An East-West Center Book
The University Press of Hawaii
Honolulu

Library of Congress Catalog Card Number 72-90004
ISBN 0-8248-0255-1
Manufactured in the United States of America

CONTENTS

I

THE PRODUCER'S VIEW

One of the authors of this book tells the story of certain biologists who are reputed to have cross-bred a crocodile and an abalone in hopes of producing an abadile. This had never been done before, and something went wrong: The product turned out to be a crocoblone.

In the last week of January, 1972, 17 broadcasters and scholars in the field of instructional television met at the East-West Center in Hawaii to try to do something else that had never (or at least seldom) been done before: to accomplish a full and frank exchange of ideas between producers and researchers on what are the qualities of an effective instructional television program. The product, insofar as it could be captured on paper, was this book.

In many ways it was an extraordinary meeting. The environment of Hawaii contributed something to the uncommon quality of it: For example, how many conferences can adjourn for an evening to watch 160 Polynesian dancers, or spend a coffee break with a 350-pound sumo champion who just happened to be visiting? But perhaps the most remarkable thing about the meeting was that it happened at all.

It has been far from usual for program people and researchers to work together on problems of program quality, and when that has occurred, it has usually been focused on a particular task like the making of Sesame Street or The Electric Company, or a high-cost television commercial. But in Hawaii, some of the world's most distinguished producers of instructional television programs and some of the scholars who have contributed most to the research on teaching by television came together to talk about general principles rather than a specific task. They came from eight countries of Europe, Africa, Asia, the Americas, and the South Pacific, and from some of the best-known ITV projects in the world. They came as scholars and broadcasters to share their different kinds of professionalism in quest of tentative answers to the question of what in an instructional television program makes for effectiveness, -- and, consequently, in search of a firmer foundation for the kind and quality of instructional television all of us hope to see in the future.

We tend to talk mostly to our colleagues. Scholars expect appreciation and criticism mostly from their fellow professionals; broadcasters from their fellow professionals. Scholars write papers for other scholars; when a producer puts on a program, he is expecially happy if applause comes from the best of his fellow producers. All too seldom does a broadcaster have the experience of hearing from a scholar: a very nice program, but how do you know it had any effect? Or a scholar hear from a broadcaster: a very nice finding, but what does it mean practically to me? The 17 participants in the Hawaii conference had that experience.

Furthermore, they had a set of ITV programs to keep the discussion realistic. One of the most useful features of the meeting was the viewing and discussion of a number of broadcast programs, many of them winners of awards in the Japan Prize competition, and graciously made available by NHK and the Japan Prize organization, whose Secretary General was in the group. Other programs came from places and projects whose programs are much talked about but not often seen outside their own coverage areas -- Niger, for example, Samoa, El Salvador, Ghana, Japan, Singapore, Hungary -- these in addition to examples from Western Europe and North America, including, among others, a program from the British Open University and a new program of The Electric Company. These programs provided a common ground for discussion: Why did the producer do that? and what do we know that would let us say whether it was a good or bad thing to do? The programs thus contributed to a healthy combination of practicality and generality.

Neither this introduction nor the papers that follow pretend to summarize the conference. It was too rich for that. Rather, they should be read as a coda -- something reflective of a piece of music in which all the themes were previously announced and developed.

The Two Points of View

The focus of discussion was the program, rather than its use. It was assumed that television would serve as a component of a unified instructional system. It was assumed that the television would be efficiently delivered to the classroom, displayed adequately, and woven into a web of learning activities. The discussion began with the question, what is a good television program? -- not bothering to define "good" too closely.

From the beginning, the two points of view were easily distinguishable. Most of the broadcasters tended to talk of a "good" program in terms of quality; most of the scholars, in terms of effectiveness. They sparred a bit, as conferees always do, from their respective viewpoints. But they established common ground much more easily than might have been anticipated of a group divided between art and science. Obviously, the broadcasters were deeply concerned with the effect and effectiveness to be expected from different kinds and levels of quality, and the researchers with the quality or qualities that make for effectiveness. More important, a little discussion uncovered confidence limits on each side that somewhat surprised the other side. The scholars were unwilling to speak with as much assurance as the broadcasters anticipated, and the broadcasters were equally cautious about generalizing on their insights and experience. They shared common uncertainties and uneasiness, and "How little we really know about this question!" became an unspoken refrain of the conference.

Two Papers by Broadcasters

Let us begin, as the conference did, with two notable papers by broadcasters, which are presented in the following pages.

They could hardly have come from situations more unlike. Rolf Lundgren, the author of the first paper, is Director of the Instructional Programming Unit of the Swedish Broadcasting Corporation. Max Egly, author of the second paper, was until recently Director of Tele-Niger. Lundgren thus makes instructional television and radio for a country that has one of the highest percentages of educated persons in Europe, where there is a long tradition of the use of educational broadcasting, and where both broadcasters and teachers have become highly sophisticated in its use. Egly was head of a French team sent to Niger, a sparsely settled country on the edge of the Sahara, where there was no television, only a short history of the use of broadcasting for instruction, and a scarcity of educated persons even at the primary level. Lundgren thus spoke for a long national experience with ITV; Egly, from the experience of introducing ITV into a situation where it was completely new. Yet, both the instructional programs from Sweden and those from Niger have attracted world-wide interest and acclaim.

Lundgren's paper is sensitive and insightful, stating a number of propositions derived from Sweden's long experience in the field. One of the features of his presentation that most interested the conferees was what he had to report about Sweden's way of assigning an educational task to television rather than to other media. Sweden can afford to worry about this sort of problem because its schools are so rich in audio-visual equipment; there is no problem exactly parallel to this in Niger. Yet every developing country faces the problem whether to introduce television or use radio for instruction, whether to expand television or use less costly media. Therefore, the conferees kept Lundgren talking a long time about the principles behind this choice, and looked closely at the programs with which he illustrated it.

Some of this material is in his paper that follows. For example, in a social science class when the subject is juvenile delinquency, television is used to make a concrete presentation of a case by means of a TV play; radio is then used to discuss what happened and what was said in the play. In addition, printed study materials are used as a kind of "steering wheel" to focus interest on key points. In teaching English, ITV is used to present language material in situations; radio, to drill on the structures introduced in the TV program, and printed material to let the student see the language, to provide further drills and guide revision. Because Swedish schools have the necessary audio-visual equipment, the radio programs are often recorded for repetition and individual study. Furthermore, radiovision (radio plus filmstrips) is often used -- for example, to comment in greater detail on individual pictures seen on the television, or to substitute for television when movement is not essential.

Beyond the history of the Nigerien project itself, the part of Egly's presentation that attracted most interest was what he had to say about the use of television for making active learners. The programs in Niger have been described by almost all visitors as being phenomenally effective in creating motivation to learn and active participation in learning. Dropouts, absenteeism have been practically eliminated in the experimental classrooms, and students typically make up their own playlets and games, after the television, to practice the skills taught in the program. A rather remarkable experiment was carried out after television had been in use three years. The teachers (monitors) were withdrawn from a classroom for a week, and television expanded to carry more directions on what post-television activities might be appropriate. Without teachers, the classes went on, throughout the week, the students devising their own practice and choosing "game masters." There was no disciplinary problem and almost no absenteeism.

Egly was asked how he went about achieving a result like this. In the first place, he said, television was conceived, not as something for optional use by a teacher as an "illustration" within his course, but as direct communication with the students. Furthermore, the temptation was resisted, so far as possible, to use television as an "illustrated textbook" -- that is, to present a filmed course with a teacher. The broadcasts were thought of as "shows" for students, not "model lessons" taught by a "super teacher," and this made things easier for the classroom teacher who did not feel himself in a competition in which he would have been at a disadvantage from the start. Rather than focusing on a teacher, teaching through the television tube, the student found himself always in the presence of multiple performers, doing things that he, too, might do. The performers were friendly, and enjoyed doing what was broadcast. The program was so designed that the students, too, could be relaxed and enjoy the television. They were permitted to talk if they so wished, to ask questions or make a comment. During the first two years, the context of the broadcasts was borrowed from scenes near at hand, and situations familiar to all the students. In the third year, the programs began to introduce images of the "outside" world -- cities, different geographies, foreign countries. It was possible in a framework like this to teach all the subject matter of the primary school, although, as Egly frankly admitted, it is not easy: It requires sustained imagination and talent, and it must resist outside pressure to "teach the syllabus" in the usual blocks of content, rather than the much freer patterns used on television.

The two papers, by Lundgren and Egly, which follow, are excellent representations of the viewpoints of experienced and successful producers toward the problems of building quality into instructional television -- the former drawing conclusions from a long and ongoing project, the latter citing some lessons to be learned by future projects from an exciting experiment which has been at least temporarily interrupted.

WHAT IS A GOOD INSTRUCTIONAL PROGRAM

By Rolf Lundgren, Director of the Instructional Programming Unit, Swedish Broadcasting Corporation

I have been asked to try and put down on paper what I consider as a good instructional program. The question has been put to me 25 years too late. If I had been asked in 1947, after two years' experience of instructional radio programming, I should probably, very cocksure, have answered the question with great confidence. Now, after 27 years' experience of instructional radio and television, I do not know the answer.

In fact, it is an impossible question. But still, I will try to answer it and intend to start with a few general remarks about factors outside instructional programming, then give examples of various roles that ITV can play in multi-media projects, and finally take up a number of aspects that are important for the quality of the individual program. Of course, it will not be possible to enlarge on any of the points. They are only touched upon very briefly, as must be the case in this kind of paper.

Good cannot be defined in general terms. What is a good program, depends on what job it is intended to do, and that in its turn depends on the general situation in which it is produced and consumed, i.e., what educational need it is meant to meet. Furthermore, you may have a mental picture of what you think is the perfect ITV program, but that ideal will always have to be modified according to the hard facts of life, such as budgets and technical and staff facilities. Thus, good is always relative to the resources at hand. It is also obvious that a program that is a component in a package consisting of e.g., 2 programs, 6 radio programs, a facts-giving booklet and a work pamphlet for the pupils, and a teachers' guide, will probably look different from an ITV program that has to do all the job itself. The general mass media situation of the country also affects our ideas of what is a good ITV program. The conventional program forms of a country's general radio and television influence our opinion on instructional programs. To be considered good an instructional program cannot differ too much from what is considered a good general program (which does not necessarily mean that in the United States instructional programs should be in the form of Westerns).

Youngsters who are spoiled by having access to first-class shows in their leisure time will frown on ITV programs that are considerably under the technical standard of such shows. By this I do not mean that we need all the money, personnel, and technical facilities that go into the production of a commercial show that draws big crowds of viewers. Instructional programs are normally smaller in their format, but within that format they should be professional. The technical facilities used should be the same as in general television, good actors used whenever possible, etc. After all, there is a constant (unintentional) competition for the interest of the audience between what they come across in their leisure time and what they have to work with in school hours. Schoolbooks cannot any longer be considerably less attractive than other books for young people. Nor can instructional programs on television and radio be remarkably less attractive than general children's and youth programs. At least, this goes for programs that are offers to the schools and not musts, but even in the case of a must bad quality is apt to cause frowns and negative attitudes.

In short, ITV programs must, I think, be of the same professional standard as the country's general programs.

But not only must the ITV programs compare reasonably well with general programs, they must also -- and this is more important to teachers and educational administrators -- be in keeping with the principles that guide the work carried out by the educational institutions concerned. What then are those principles? I can, of course, only answer for my own country. The key words of the practical everyday work in Swedish schools are -- according to the official curriculum of the compulsory nine-year school -- motivation, activity, concretization, individualization, and cooperation. Now, this is a lucky situation to produce instructional programs in. The first three words -- motivation, activity, and concretization -- could be written as principal guidelines for ITV program producers, and the last two -- individualization and cooperation -- are certainly key words for the editors of the pupils' printed material which steers the follow-up work after the broadcast (or listening to -- viewing -- the tape). Thus, the fundamental principles guiding the work in Swedish classrooms are very much in accordance with what we as producers of instructional programs on radio and television and their ancillary material want to do.

From this point of view, then, I think, a good program is one that helps teachers and pupils put one or more of those fundamental principles into practice.

In order to be able to produce a program that his audience

considers good, a producer must know the situation of that audience. In this an instructional-program producer is in a favorable position in comparison with general-program producers. If it is a school program the producer knows what age his viewers are and roughly what they know before they sit down to watch his product, what they expect of it, etc. The school curriculum gives him a reasonably precise brief. Even producers of adult educational programs whose audience is far more heterogeneous know that people watching his programs at least have one thing in common: They have an active interest in the subject matter which made them switch on his program of their own accord. A good program must always meet the demands of its specific target audience, and an ITV producer, then, is in a favorable position in that he can reasonably well define those demands. He knows comparatively well the conditions of his audience and he must make use of that knowledge, so that he can present the matter in such a way that his viewers feel it is something that concerns them.

It has struck me how little general-program producers can sometimes care about their audience. This, of course, is a nasty thing to say, but I have often found that that is one of the fundamental differences between general broadcasting and instructional broadcasting. An instructional-program producer must always care for what happens at the consumer's end, so to speak. I do not dare to say that he always does -- sufficiently. General programs are more often than not remarkably "content centered" or "performer centered," i.e., they have the ambition to present all the stuff there is in a certain question whether the viewers can follow or not, or they have the obvious purpose of showing to all the world what a good man the performer and/or producer of the program is. All right, this attitude has given us a great many wonderful programs, there is no denying that fact, but it is all wrong as a starting point for instructional programs. In producing ITV programs your main concern must always be with your viewers. What will happen among the students if I do this, what will happen if I do that, etc.

From this point of view, then, I think a good ITV program is one where the production team has all the way through paid heed to what happens at the receiving end.

What is a good program also varies according to the educational context in which it is to be used. In a broader sense that context is set by the curriculum, as has been indicated above, but in a narrower sense the context is set by the production team. An ITV program is never a self-contained unit. It is always intended to be part of some kind of educational work which can vary very much in quantity and quality. It can be a matter of very informal follow-up discussions among grown-up viewers around a cafe table, and it can be a matter of quite complicated classroom work with a multi-media package of which the TV program is part.

Television in a Multi-media Package

The role of an ITV program in a multi-media package can vary very much, and this is a subject that could be worth a paper for itself. Let me here just very briefly indicate what sort of roles they could be, and I will choose examples from multi-media projects we have produced in Sweden. The roles of television, radio, and printed material were in the cases I have in mind in these broad terms, but I would like to stress that we have no hard and fast rules about the division of labor between the three media and we have hardly any research results to fall back upon. We are still experimenting and empirically trying to find out what kinds of roles the media can play.

Example no. 1: civics

The story of a juvenile delinquent. TV gave the concrete presentation of the case in a documentary film, showing how a young man was let out of prison, how he tried to find somewhere to live, how he immediately found himself in a vicious circle (he could not find a place to live because he had no job, and he could not get a job because he had no permanent address), and how he finally went back to his gang and the kind of life that had led to his imprisonment.

Radio discussed what happened, interviewed people having to deal with this kind of problem, like probation officers, etc. The message was purely verbal now, and that is why radio was used instead of television.

Printed material acted as a steering wheel for the work of the students, structuring the subject matter and focusing interest on certain points.

Example no. 2: geography -- The British Isles

TV here gave motivation. It was its job to create an interest in the subject matter, and again TV gave concrete presentations of the milieu, both geographically and socially.

Radio gave more subject matter in the form of interviews and comments and posed a number of problems for the students to consider, i.e., gave food for thought. It was also used to comment on projected pictures (radiovision).

Printed material gave some fundamental information and acted as a base for the radio programs, and again steered the work in the classroom. (In fact, it practically always takes on the last-mentioned job.)

<u>Example no. 3: music for grade 2</u>

TV here showed teachers and pupils how to work in the classroom (singing, playing, moving). The TV programs were mainly intended as methodological hints for teachers but could also be watched in class.

Radio gave full music lessons, presenting musical material and drilling it. Students were expected to be musically active during the broadcast. (That is always so in musical radio lessons.)

Printed material gave the base of the work (scores, texts, teachers' guidelines).

<u>Example no. 4: geography</u>

In some cases radio programs have been meant for group work and TV for classwork. It has then been recommended either that the TV program is used for motivation in the beginning of the work with the project or that it is used as a starting point for the reporting to the whole class of the work done in the groups. That reporting is usually the weak point in group-work methodology, and the TV program can give the reporting a good start. The various groups will then be "specialists" on the various segments of the TV program and be able to comment on them for the benefit of their classmates.

<u>Example no. 5: elementary language course</u>

TV was used to present language material in concrete situations.

Radio was used to drill structures introduced in TV programs.

Printed material gave language material in print, exercises for further drill work and revision.

The philosophy behind this division of labor is very simple. Learning a new language is a matter of creating new conditioned reflexes, and that is a job that takes a lot of drilling which is normally executed in the form of questions and answers. In our program unit TV is usually 11 times as expensive as radio. At the cost of one TV question and answer we can get 11 radio questions and answers, then. Thus, for drilling purposes radio is the better medium, once the structure has been properly understood through the combined visual-verbal presentation on TV. Thus, TV is far too costly to be used for drill purposes. Let it do only the presentation work where it is at its best.

Example no. 6: pollution -- lives in danger

Here I will leave the above model of presentation and describe the series in a different way.

The series (intended for grade nine) started with a TV program giving a general survey of various kinds of pollution, the examples mainly taken from Sweden but also from other countries. Then three radio programs described more fully (a) water pollution, (b) air pollution, (c) soil pollution. Next a TV program described the effects on one place in Sweden of the various kinds of pollution, and a third TV program gave examples of possible future solutions, speculated about possible technological and scientific development that will help us solve our problems, etc. Then regional radio programs were added, two in each of the 11 regions of the Swedish Broadcasting Corporation. The first of the two regional programs gave very concrete information about pollution problems in the region and suggested that the students should propose measures to be taken against them -- using the printed material and what they had learned from the TV and radio programs as a base for their concrete suggestions. In the second regional program some of the suggestions of students in the region were described and discussed. We consider this series (which has been broadcast several years) most successful, and what is principally interesting in it is the fact that we used four media: printed material as a base and steering wheel as usual, TV, national radio, and regional radio, and the important job of regional radio was to increase the interest in the whole project by making it more concrete and down-to-earth to all parts of the country. Students in far-off places suddenly realized, "This does not concern only Stockholmers, but damn it all, it concerns us."

From this point of view, then, I think a good program is one that does the job it has been given to do as a component of a multi-media package.

So far I have tried to show that an ITV program should be judged in relation to other TV programs, to the prevalent pedagogical principles of the receiving institutions, to what it gives rise to in those institutions, and to what its role is intended to be as compared with other media involved.

Some Principles of Good Programming

But let us now leave these more general considerations and look at the individual program as such and see if we can then make up our minds what is good. Even if they are bricks in a big building constructed according to all the rules of the prevalent school of thinking in educational technology, the bricks must be good bricks by themselves. It is no use making big beautiful constructions without assuring the standard of the individual components of those constructions. A wonderfully well thought-out pedagogical project where on the planning table the blocks and arrows and what have you form a most beautiful design, may in practice fall to pieces because one or two components are so dull and uninspiring that pupils and teachers just give it all up, having lost all interest in the project.

Speaking of the individual programs, I am not going to discuss technical questions such as using the screen to its full potential, such as working with close-ups that are close enough (it seems to be one of the beginner's most common mistakes to stop halfway when zooming in for close-ups, so apparently it takes a lot of experience before a producer dares come close enough to what he wants to demonstrate), such as using the so-called subjective camera when showing, for example, chemical experiments that the viewers are expected to learn to make themselves, such as following the rules of classical painting and drawing in composing your picture so as to give prominence to what is the main information you want your picture to impart, etc. Let me take up just one point of this kind, which is a hobby-horse of mine I just cannot refrain from riding, namely, insisting on full coordination between what is said and what is shown in a program. I just cannot accept as good ITV a program where you show one thing while you are talking about another. This is where the influence of the conventional forms of general programming can be very bad for instructional programming. In news programs -- in Sweden as in other countries -- it is very common that you illustrate the news items with film sequences that may, that is true, be about the same thing as the telegram that is just being read, but there is no coordination whatsoever. For example, any news telegram that has to do with road traffic -- whether it is the latest statistics of road accidents or a government proposal to introduce speed limits all over the country -- is illustrated by sequences of motor traffic on a Stockholm bridge, etc. In the worst cases of misuse of the medium you have to close your eyes in order to be able to follow and understand what is said, as the pictures just act as distractors. If you point out this sort of reaction, some broadcasters will go so far as to maintain very stubbornly that a viewer can take in two pieces of information at the same time, one through his ears and the other through his eyes. If the younger generation really has that kind of multicapacity, it is to be congratulated, because it opens up fantastic vistas, not least for education -- just fancy learning Chinese through pictures at the same time as you are learning Russian the audio way!

That was a joke, of course. But let me say most emphatically that if there is not complete coordination between the video and the audio, one will act as a distractor of the other.

Therefore, in ITV we must insist on full coordination between the two. The best part of news broadcasts in our country is very often the weather forecasts, I think. In them the meteorologist does talk about what he shows us. He even points to details on his map and uses expressions such as "The low pressure we can see here between Scotland and Norway is moving eastwards -- like this -- and is expected to pass Stockholm tomorrow in the afternoon or evening." This is simple, unsophisticated television, and from our point of view, I think, good television!

But to the point, then, what is a good ITV program (presupposing that there are at least pupils' pamphlets to go with them)? Now, this is probably something that can hardly be verbalized. Whether you consider an individual program good or not in itself, is rather a matter of "Fingerspitsgefühl," something you have somewhere in you without being able to express it in words. But in spite of that, let me try to make a few points here as a basis for further discussion.

The first point I would like to make then is that by and large instructional television is often at its best when it does not instruct. You can of course argue that this is a matter of definition. It all depends on how you define the word instruct. But let me say then that an ITV program should avoid teaching in the traditional meaning of the word. A teacher's job is no longer to inform in the first place -- nor is ITV's. The strong point of a TV program is seldom to give factual information but rather to give the human aspects of the matter. If it is a question of giving students facts and people, let the printed material give them the facts, and television the people. Suppose we want to give the students an idea of what the Swedish society does to take care of its alcoholics. Information on how many alcoholics there are, where in the country there are special clinics for them, how much they cost the taxpayers, etc., all those kinds of facts could be better given in printed form than in a program. In the program we could follow an alcoholic's normal day, thus giving the student a moving document of the seamy side of the welfare state. Let the printed material take care of the cognitive aspects and the program of the emotional aspects of the matter. This, as a matter of fact, can be a very important contribution to the emotional development of a student in a school situation that has so far been and still is too much concerned with his intellectual development, maybe at the expense of the development of other aspects of his personality. In the example mentioned -- which is part of a multimedia project we produced a couple of years ago -- the TV program gave the students the case of an unfortunate fellowman and they could not help being affected by what they saw; in the classroom discussions that followed they could generalize their program impressions with the help of the factual information given them in the pupil's pamphlet.

Thus, I think an ITV program should avoid instructing in the sense of telling pupils a lot of facts. There is a risk in using the mass media to drown audiences in facts. The problem in our schools today is no longer primarily the acquisition of information, but to sort out the material available, to structure it so that the children will find contexts and causal connections, to create an ability in the students to analyze critically what they see and hear, and to help them find their own way to knowledge. In this respect, both the radio and television, and the teachers themselves, are guilty of an unfortunate predilection to tell the students all they know, without establishing whether the students want or are able to absorb it. Far too many programs in Sweden and elsewhere have simply poured facts over defenseless students, and their very natural and sound reaction has then been to switch off their attention, letting the TV receiver preach to deaf ears.

Thus, what a good ITV program does is to give students emotional experiences and food for thought, i.e., something to work with.

A good program should therefore stimulate students. That is why, by and large, I am skeptical about showing classroom situations on the screen. That is fine if it is a methodological program for teachers. Then you should show your viewers how the ideas you want them to adopt work in the classroom. But it is generally no use showing pupils in a classroom to pupils in other classrooms. One of the fundamental jobs of school television is to take its viewers out of the classroom situation. There is also, I think, a psychological reason. A class in the studio will create a teacher-pupil relationship between the ITV teacher and his studio class, and they will sort of perform in front of the viewers, who will be just viewers and not participants. Far more important is to create some kind of interaction between the TV teacher and his viewers, and that is more easily achieved without the studio class when the speaker on the screen talks directly to the viewers.

To stimulate students, that also means that an ITV program should start them working one way or another. It should free creative energy within the students. It should therefore be open-ended, and there should preferably be a number of open-ends that could be used as starting points for all kinds of work among the students. The work started by the program is more often than not mental work: thinking, discussing, desiring to find out more about the matter, etc., but programs can also start physical activities. Now, starting activities does not necessarily mean that students should be made physically active during the broadcast. In this respect I find radio infinitely superior to television. During a radio program students can easily be made to perform a lot of actions like moving about in the room (in a language lesson), filling in figures in the pamphlet, choosing the right answer among a number of alternatives, finding a detail in a picture in their pamphlet, etc., etc. During a TV broadcast you can of course ask questions of the viewers and expect them to answer you. In fact, that can often create that human relationship between the TV teacher and his audience that I briefly touched upon above.

But do not expect your viewers to perform more complicated actions during the TV broadcast. I will never forget the mistake we made in that respect in the first multi-media project we produced in school programs. It was a series on rhythmical movement for grade two, and the plan was to give teachers sketches of the movements in their guidebook, to show the children the movements and start them practicing by means of TV programs, and to give them chances to practice more through radio programs. It was all right to show the kids the movements, but when they were told to make the same movements in front of the TV receiver they more or less broke their necks by trying to watch the TV screen at the same time as they tried to make the movements they were asked to make. The radio programs on the other hand worked all right.

My next point is the choice of TV teacher or presenter in the kind of ITV program that -- in spite of what I have said so far -- is a presentation of facts, i.e., a TV lesson. First of all, should there be a presenter at all or should we use off voices for the spoken text? I do not want to be dogmatic about this, and I must confess that in our Instructional Program Department we do both. Let me mention here, though, an experiment carried out by German colleagues. They made three versions of a mathematics program: (a) a trick film with an off speaker, (b) a presenter in a studio with models, animations, etc., (c) a teacher with a class in the studio, but I think that even in this case there was a certain amount of animations, etc. They then measured the teaching effects of the three versions and there was no doubt whatsoever that version (b) was the most effective in that viewing pupils had learned more from it than from the other two versions.

If we are to use a presenter on camera, then, and in most cases that is probably to be recommended, the choice of person is most important. In fact, I wonder if that is not the most important thing of all in the production of a program. What are the characteristics of a good presenter? Again we are up against something that is hard to verbalize.

It is so much a question of personality. We must accept the fact that there are such things as radio personality and TV personality. From my own experience as a radio producer -- ages ago -- I could cite examples of French radio teachers who just said "Bonjour, mesdames," "Bonjour, mesdemoiselles," "Bonjour, messieurs," and that was enough for everybody to prick up their ears and listen with full attention, whereas others could say the most interesting things without anybody caring to follow their train of thought. How can that be? I do not know, and I am not going to speculate about it either, although it might be tempting to do so. Let me just stress again that I think the choice of presenter is the most important thing in the production of a program. If you choose a beginner in the game, that will always be something of a lottery. Nobody is at his best the first time in front of a TV camera, and it is a question of judging whether the person tried has the potential to become a good presenter or not. Sometimes we draw blanks, but experienced producers will draw more winning tickets than blanks.

How important the choice of presenter is was drastically illustrated to me a couple of years ago when colleagues in another European country were starting instructional television. Their courses had been planned and written in collaboration with the best psychological, pedagogical, sociological, and what have you logical expertise of the country, and everything was just wonderful -- on paper. But in their choice of presenters they made awful mistakes, and I for one was inclined to switch off the programs after two minutes.

What sort of person should the presenter be then? Well, he should have the right sort of personality -- which cannot be expressed in words. He should be a prepossessing kind of person who has a great interest in and likes what he is talking about, and he should be able to transmit at least some of his own feelings about the subject to his audience. He must also be a brave person. Why brave? Oh yes, he must have the courage to risk being criticized by his expert colleagues for oversimplifying matters, for leaving out most important things, for telling half-lies, etc.

I will always remember a German senior high school teacher whose class I visited 15 years ago. He taught literature, and had picked out a classical Greek drama, a Shakespeare drama, a Molière drama, a Schiller drama, and a few others. That was his way of treating the history of literature. When I asked him whether they did not study the history of literature in the traditional form also, his answer was "Man muss den Mut haben, Lücken zu lassen." (You must have the courage to leave holes.) He was the sort of person who could make a good TV presenter. All teaching means choosing within an unlimited material, and one of the characteristics of the good teacher has always been that he has made a good choice of subject matter. This goes for the TV presenter, too, only even more so, I think.

The presenter must also have the courage to make things seem simpler than they really are, particularly in broadcasts for the lower grades. Naturally, I could quote here another teacher -- a Swede this time -- who used to tell his pupils "Now in junior high I tell you a lot of lies, but that is to make you able to understand the truths I am going to tell you in senior high." He was also the right sort of person to make a good TV presenter.

Two more points about the presenter. He must not be what the Germans call a "Besserwisser" (Mr. Know-all). Our natural reaction is to dislike a "Besserwisser," and a presenter must be liked by his audience, and he must be the kind of person we believe in.

A good ITV program, I think then, is a program that has the kind of presenter possessing all the good qualities described above, and possibly a lot more, but do not ask me where to find him, please. It is quite remarkable, though, how often a good and experienced producer does find him!

Very near to what has been said about the simplicity of the presentation is the simplicity of the language used in the program. One of the main jobs of the producer is to see to it that all those taking part in the program express themselves in a way that is understandable for the target audience. This is so obvious that it may seem ridiculous to mention it here, and yet, it is an elementary rule that is sinned against daily. It is my experience that TV producers who have started in radio often are more particular about the form of the verbal message of a TV program than TV producers who lack radio experience.

Nowadays we usually recruit our school-TV producers from among our school-radio producers.

A good ITV program, then, uses a language that its audience can understand.

My next point is that a good ITV program should have an element of humor. I have heard colleagues from other countries in all earnestness maintain that instructional programs should not be humorous, and I have heard teachers ask whether we should be allowed to make jokes in school-radio programs. I have never seen the point in having a dull time if you can have a good time, and this certainly goes for instructional programs as well. It can easily be said to be a superficial attitude to education, but I have myself always preferred studying with a smile on my lips than with tears in my eyes, and I am not very abnormal in that, am I? So why should we not watch ITV programs with a smile on our lips as well?

Of course, I realize that you cannot bring in jokes everywhere, and I certainly warn producers not to exaggerate and produce guffaws in the classes. There can, of course, also be different opinions on what is fun and what is just ridiculous.

But, please, ITV producers, do try to make us smile sometimes during your programs. One of my most vivid impressions of the instructional programs taking part in the famous Japan Prize Contest (where I have twice been honored with the job of a jury member) is that the teachers and instructional-program makers of the world must be an extremely dull lot. There were all sorts of good pedagogical tricks in their programs, and there was often every reason to be impressed, but it was very seldom indeed that one had reason to smile, and in the few cases when it did happen, that was certainly felt as a great relief.

If one of the jobs of instructional television is to motivate students, then ITV producers should certainly try to use all the tricks of the trade, and one of the tricks is using humor. I think this is particularly important in a long series. Pupils will get to like a presenter who makes them smile now and then, and they will want to come back to the next program, and the next, and the next, etc. And liking the presenter, is not that a kind of motivation not only for further viewing but also for follow-up work?

How far can you go then in humorous presentation? I do not mean to say that you should use farcical tricks like throwing cream cakes into the face of your partner, but a quiet humor allowing for an unexpected choice of simile, a surprising phrase, etc., will be appreciated by your audience. And you could sometimes try using a well-known comedian instead of a subject expert as your presenter. In fact, we have done that in a number of cases, knowing that the pupils will listen very attentively to people who are favorites of theirs from variety shows, even if what they say is not terribly funny. We think the experiments we have made in this respect have been successful, but when we have played this kind of program to colleagues from other countries (who do not have the same associations when they hear the names of comedians unknown to them), they have usually been rather skeptical. (One important point should be made here. If you use a comedian or any other actor as a presenter, he should not be made to appear as an expert. Everybody knows he is not, so be careful how you phrase his text.)

A good ITV program, then, is one where you have reason to smile -- at least once -- I think.

Another characteristic of a good ITV program is that it makes good use of musical and sound effects. And this is certainly a field of activity where a lot more could be done. In fact, it is my impression that the audio side of TV programs is often not up to the standard of the video side. Please, notice that when I say musical effects I do mean musical <u>effects</u> and not the bad habit of having background music to every film insert. That is an old movie tradition that can often just be a distractor. Getting the right kind of musical effects that underline the important parts of your message is of course often a matter of money (if you have to have special music written for you). But you can often enough do with simpler things than that. It is actually the question of creating the right sort of sensitivity to music and other effects in the producers. It can also often be effective to repeat information in the form of a simple song with a catchy tune. I am not too keen on quoting examples from my own activities as a radio producer, but I will mention here one of the grammar-drilling songs I wrote for an English beginners' course I gave on the radio 20 years ago. The simple philosophy was this. A well-known catchy tune often sticks in your head for hours after you have heard it -- which can be a nuisance. If there is a text to the tune and that text drills something you want your students to drill, that nuisance can be turned into something most positive. Thus, e.g., the present-tense ending -<u>s</u> in the third person singular was drilled with this text to the well-known tune of "Clementine."

I like coffee,
You like coffee,
He likes tea,
And she likes me.

We say "I and you and we and they like."
After "he, she, it: We must say likes."

Again referring to experiences from the Japan Prize Contest, it was another striking fact how seldom music was used in a really meaningful way. The programs of the host organization, NHK, used to be outstanding exceptions.

This again is a point that is hard to express in words, but what I want to say is that a good ITV program should make good use of music and sound effects.

It is also the job of a good ITV program to present unique stuff and/or present well-known stuff in unique forms. This may sound like big words, so let me phrase it otherwise and say that we should try to present stuff in forms that are typical of the medium and different from the forms in which subject matter is otherwise presented to students. The case study of the alcoholic mentioned above is a point in case here. There it was the question of meeting a person, meeting "real life" if you like. I have already said that one of the jobs of instructional television is to take students out of the classroom. Bringing society into the classroom, and forming as many links as possible between the work of the classroom and life outside, that is what we should do. Take chemistry programs, for instance. The demonstration of a laboratory experiment in the studio should whenever possible be connected with film inserts taking students to visit industries, so that they can see principles made clear through experiments in the lab in their industrial applications.

Another obvious example of the point we are discussing now is bringing topical matters into the classroom. Current affairs programs seem to be important parts of the ITV output in most countries — if the school curricula allow for that kind of subject matter, of course. Not only should we help teachers and students discuss the political events of today -- like the situation in Vietnam and the Middle East -- but it should also be one of our ambitions to be "the last page of the student's textbook." In most subjects, i.e., give him "the latest," that which has not yet found its way into his books.

A good ITV program, I think, then, makes use of the unique possibilities of the medium, i.e., tries to give the students subject matter that they would otherwise not get and tries to use forms of presentation that they do not otherwise meet.

In some respects the ITV producer has a far more favorable situation than the classroom teacher. That is true about some of the points made so far. It is certainly true about my next point, which is that of the varied repetition.

One of the principles of classical teaching is that the stuff should be repeated, and that the form in which it comes back should be varied. Naturally the team producing an ITV broadcast has far more possibilities for variation at its disposal than a teacher normally has in his everyday work. It has more time at its disposal for preparation, and it has the resources of the production center to play about with. Even the smallest production center will have more means of variation than a teacher in a classroom.

A good ITV program, then, says the same thing twice in different ways.

Like a good teacher the good ITV presenter links up with the situation and the experience of his audience. This is easy enough in some cases -- like an introduction to chemistry, where you could describe the normal day of a seventh-grade girl and look at what she meets during the day from the point of view of chemistry, i.e., analyzing in an elementary way the powder she puts on her nose, the food she has for breakfast, the cloth of her dress, etc. It is more difficult when the subject matter is a long way from the experience of the students, but this is really where ITV can be at its best because here the principle of concretization comes in. Subject matter that would otherwise be very theoretical can be made concrete through ITV presentations where students meet people and milieus that are completely unknown to them. The obvious examples are, of course, geography programs, but concretizing unknown milieus can be useful also in other contexts. Danish colleagues took their school audience to Iceland in beautiful films on Icelandic scenery as an introduction to classical Icelandic literature (which is still studied in Scandinavian schools). I have no doubt that students who had watched those TV programs read the old sagas with so much more interest and appreciation.

I have made a number of points here as to what a good ITV program could and should do. One thing that it should not do is this: It should not press ready-made opinions on its viewers. This is unfortunately a trap that we often fall into, both as teachers and as TV producers. It is very often just a question of how we express ourselves. There is, for example, a lot of difference between saying "This is a marvelous piece of music," and "I think this is a marvelous piece of music." Students should be made to draw their own conclusions and to form their own opinions -- that is one of the most important objectives of our school. Therefore, always present something beautiful in a way that will make the students think it is beautiful by themselves. You may prompt them by giving them your own opinion, but never tell them as a fact that it is beautiful.

I have a vivid memory of this kind of thing myself. When I was 13, I heard on the radio a man, who was known to me as one of the leading musical experts in the country, say about the first theme of César Franck's Symphony in D Minor that in his opinion that was the most beautiful thing ever composed. The way he said that made such an impression on me that that symphony still is one of my musical favorites. Of course, we can say that he pressed his opinion on me, but mind you, he did so through his own enthusiasm and the way he expressed it, and he did not try to give me the idea that this was objectively beautiful. Maybe I am dealing with nuances now that are of no importance to many people. To me they do make a lot of difference, though. And to me that man was certainly a good presenter!

If you have made a program that meets all or most of the demands above, then you have probably succeeded in making a very good ITV program. But the remarkable thing is that you can violate most of the "rules" I have tried to lay down here, and yet the result can be something that is felt to be a good program. If so, you are probably a genius, and such have their own rules.

THE END OF A PERIOD FOR TELE-NIGER (1964-1971): SOME OBSERVATIONS FOR FUTURE PROJECTS

By Max Egly, former Director of Tele-Niger

The lines that follow attempt to pull together some personal reflections at the end of my participation in Tele-Niger and of the six months of renewed contact with foreign organizations specializing in audio-visual teaching and, more especially, educational television.

There are few studies published up to the present on Tele-Niger. Besides some brief articles in specialized journals, there is only one study from the International Institute of Educational Planning (IIEP), done by UNESCO in the framework of the Ivory Coast project, plus the report given at the Congress of the European Broadcasting Union (Paris, 1967). A general report is being prepared at the initiative of the Secretary of State for Foreign Affairs for Cooperation (*Secrétariat d'Etat aux Affaires étrangères chargé de la Coopération*).

The present remarks are basically structured around the following themes:

(a) One can do much more and go much further in the use of educational broadcasting than what was done by Tele-Niger.

(b) At the moment that educational television seems able to really "take off" (that is, on a large scale and with systematic use), we are encountering some general misgivings about using educational television (as a particular element of broadcasting).

(c) At present there are more material and educational resources available than can "materially" and "psychologically" be absorbed by teaching systems. An even larger gap separates the practical possibilities of tomorrow from their chances of implementation.

We are talking about the convergence of personal impressions. These need to be nuanced and adjusted by the contribution of precise information on numerous projects with which I am only slightly acquainted.

A Summary of Some of the Facts about Tele-Niger

-- The audience: formal education; primary level; age: 6 to 11 years; 22 classes; 40 students per class.

-- Programs: four broadcasts a day (14 minutes each). The core elements of instruction; entirely in French; local production; video taped for rebroadcast.

-- Teachers: one monitor per class; primary level education; two-and-one-half months training; one daily supporting broadcast.

-- Support documents: "Fiches pédagogiques" (seven a day) basically for the monitors.

-- Hardware: four studios in Niamey; one 50-watt transmitter; battery-operated TV receivers.

-- Team: 115 people (53 technical assistants) take care of conception, production, and transmission of broadcasts and written documents, as well as the maintenance of all equipment and the training and continuing retraining of the monitors.

-- Financing: coverage of continuing needs assured by French bilateral aid; average cost of a broadcast (14 minutes): $800.

-- Orientation: initially planned to give schooling over ten years to 200,000 students, the operation remained at an experimental level. At the beginning it was a question of having a short cycle of four years not resulting in any kind of degree. Currently a fifth year is being created to prepare students for the entrance exam for "sixth" year (secondary).

Positive Aspects of Tele-Niger

We gather here in an unordered way the things that seem to us most significant and capable of being useful to future projects:

1. Broadcasts addressed directly to students

The broadcasts were conceived of, from the very beginning, as addressed directly to the isolated student, or to a group of students, or to a class; but not as something of optional use to a teacher within the structure of his "course." Thus, we wanted to maximize our chances that the message would effectively reach its target audience. Students quickly became aware of this intention (numerous remarks witness this: "and its television that is speaking to us," "the programs are stories (sic) made up by the people at the station to teach children").

The period of familiarization with audio-visual forms of expression was brief (one month on the average). It was helped by a concern among producers and directors to make a progressive introduction. By the third year, a large number of students could distinguish filmed from studio portions of broadcasts.

During the first month, the types of images most easily understood were, in order:

(1) images with moving persons live from the studio
(2) animated films
(3) cartoons
(4) animated stills
(5) drawings
(6) still photos

During the first two years, the context of the broadcasts, their general framework, was essentially borrowed from the environment of the students' life: people, countryside, objects; situations were consciously chosen from the rural environment in which students lived.

By the beginning of the third year, we began to present images of the "outside" world (urban surroundings, foreign countries, different geographies and climatic zones). The understanding of programs that referred to an unknown cultural context was facilitated by constant reminders of the familiar context and by the presentation of differences as such, ordered into common themes by the method of the "variation series."

2. Educational spectacle

From 1963, at the time of the first studies, we had planned to use to the maximum the potentialities of expression by television; that is, to make the program an attractive whole, dramatically structured, while refusing to make a filmed course of a teacher and the "illustrated textbook" (where the ideas are interrelated by rhetoric as in a treatise and the image comes in only to evoke each of the ideas). We have to point out that this option was, in fact, only partially carried out. Basically for two reasons: in the first place, because this type of program is very hard to do well, demanding producers and directors endowed with a considerable (and sustained) imagination; secondly, because the external pressure from traditional educational demands (the necessity every year of teaching too much content from the regular school curriculum) led naturally to the usual "chopping up" of content into subject matter.

The point needs to be emphasized that the broadcasts allowed treatment, without exception, of all the disciplines, including writing and reading. This conviction was shared by all of the members of the Tele-Niger team, so strongly among some that they asked how one could teach anything again without television.

We will come back later to some interesting aspects of the option of "educational spectacle" and the educational richness of some possible developments. One can see here in this perspective the polyvalent nature of broadcasting and that its functions are multiple:

- presentation of new things;
- facilitation of learning;
- stimulation to investigate, development of curiosity

3. An operation in "real dimensions"

Sometimes it has been pointed out that one of the greatest merits of Tele-Niger is to have operated for seven years, and to continue to do so. It is no less interesting to point out that this operation took place in real conditions; that is, without artificial external intervention: The students had in no way been specially chosen, the teachers actually had no more than a primary degree and had never taught before, and more than one operator, formed "on the job," ruined his lens when trying to make some daring repair. A number of visitors saw that each of the 22 classes could be visited every day. This concern to "play the game," to take into account the reality of Niger, was the guarantee for possible effective expansion. If this had taken place, it would not have created a qualitative lowering in results nor would it have caused notable disturbances.

4. Reducing the role of the teacher

The importance given to the role of broadcasts in the system and the simultaneous reduction in the role of the teacher are the direct results of the situation in Niger: absence of qualified teachers (96 in the whole country in 1963), the impossibility of forming within an acceptable time a sufficient number of capable teachers. If one wanted to spread the system rapidly, one had to use the only resources at hand; that is, the young Nigeriens with some schooling, armed with a primary degree and out of work.

A posteriori, this inevitable reduction in the teacher's role appeared to us to be beneficial for a number of reasons:

-- Never having taught, the monitors of Tele-Niger accepted the changes without opposition or difficulty.

-- Since they were conscious of their lack of training, they had to learn their job by working at it and thus found themselves in a situation of permanent learning. Faced with an unforeseen problem, they would call for help from the training group of Niamey instead of falling back on worn-out principles of an archaic pedagogy.

-- The less able and less active among them were happy to make an approximate application of advice and thereby minimize the disturbance of the process of student learning.

-- The broadcasts were thought of as "shows" and not as "model lessons" given as an example by a "super teacher," and so the monitors did not feel themselves in a competition in which they would have been disadvantaged from the start.

We can, however, note two paradoxical phenomena. We found that, by the second year, classes could get along even when the teacher was absent and by the fourth, that some of the more talented students had surpassed their teachers.

These two discoveries led us in June, 1971, to carry out, on an experimental level, a project of open listening. During a certain week the 20 classes in the rural network carried on from morning until night without teachers. Special broadcasts (from 10 to 80 minutes long) were prepared for this purpose, the TV set was on all day long, and the succession of events was overseen by a "game master." Special educational forms were prepared for the use of students; the students came to the schools as usual without abseenteeism or any lowering of usual classroom discipline. On the contrary, they showed a real enthusiasm for pursuing their own learning.

This experiment gave us some indications about the form of broadcasts for open listening, about the way to present the programs, the whole set of indispensable conventions and acquired habits for such listening, the possible evolution of student groups exposed to this type of teaching (by the constitution of micro-groups according to affinities, tastes, capacities, and by the emergency of pressure groups and of leaders).

5. The positive relation of television

There is an old prejudice always hanging on that says the intensive use of television in the school will deprive the student of important human relations with his teacher and reduce him to a mechanized state. Talking with a Tele-Niger student for a few minutes will be enough to dispel this false impression. It seems that far from dehumanizing the relation between the student and learning, television establishes an array of new relations and that these are not without appropriate affective traits between teacher and student, with this difference, however, that these relations are never negative. Thanks to television, the student is never in the presence of just one person, but of multiple performers and actors. These are always friendly (they don't stop when the student comes in late). Moreover, the television always gives the students the freedom to talk during the broadcasts (something never allowed during a "course"); it allows some to ask questions, others to explain, and for each to make remarks about the program in much the same way as one would write notes on the margin of his workbook. Television's role is basically different and it has the great advantage of always being available. A student who was asked whether he would prefer the TV set or the teacher responded: "The set is also a teacher; it helps the students. But if you have to choose between the teacher and the set, I choose the teacher because it's he who has a heart and breathes. The set does not breathe."

6. Programming by "series"

The whole of the programming was not conceived of as a series of independent broadcasts, each a whole unto itself, but as a series of related reinforcing elements which divided complex ideas into their basic elements. This educational policy was determined both by the decision to use the approach of an educational "spectacle," as well as by the educational principle of integrating teachers, and by the reduced possibility of the teacher's intervention. An outstanding teacher can always take advantage of a highly concentrated audio-visual program (he explains the difficult points, mobilizes the necessary memories, and establishes the relationships where others find only juxtaposition). The teachers of Tele-Niger were not able to carry out this work, and so it happened that the broadcasts became a daily link in a long chain of very important repetitions for them. This perspective had the great advantage of making producers and directors think in general themes, each theme being partially developed in several broadcasts. The textbook custom of treating each idea just one time was thus left further behind, and we could approach the real conditions of learning and develop over time, by successive approaches, the elements for acquiring new ideas.

The team responsible for idea development was frequently inspired by programmed instruction, but it never had the necessary means for putting this into real practice.

7. The opposition of tradition and innovation

In the preceding lines we have tried to make a rapid inventory of the principal innovative elements which seem to us the most characteristic of Tele-Niger. The question that we often get is under what conditions were we able to carry out this set of innovations.

If we go back to the period of preparation (1963-1964), we are forced to admit that the present system is much less innovative than was the original plan. Other than the educational "spectacle," imperfectly realized as we have said, certain aspirations were abandoned, particularly those touching on the introduction to logic, modern mathematics, and the integration of the culture of customs and African behavior at the level of production and reception.

On the other hand, if one were to compare the actual state of things in the 22 classes of Tele-Niger with the problems encountered of getting other projects off the ground, it might be thought that Tele-Niger was graced with particularly favorable conditions. Two questions may be asked: "What are these conditions?" and "Can they be brought together at the beginning of other projects?"

At the first level of favorable factors, we should note the isolation of the operation. Geographical isolation (Niamey isn't even an important stopping-off place), political isolation (the project, considered sometimes as a risk, sometimes as an adventure, sometimes as a Utopia, benefited at the beginning from the great discretion of its promoters), institutional isolation (from the side of French aid, it was a special program; from the side of the Nigerien authorities, the operation did not demand a general reform of teaching). One can also conceive of the little credit given to the project at the beginning as contributing not a little to its ultimate success. The pessimistic incredulity of some, leading to comments such as "let them do themselves in, the project will fail by itself," also stiffened into an attitude of "nonintervention."

A closed system, developed on the edge of the traditional world of education, Tele-Niger benefited from a rare freedom of action permitting it to take numerous risks in the area of innovation. But

this isolation and all of the innovative elements such a condition could provide were at the same time the obstacles to extending the system and added to the major problems of finance and politics.

It is worth pointing out, however, that with the passing years, the advantages of isolation gradually diminished and the external pressure of traditional education did not cease to mount. It would be worth devoting a whole study to this phenomenon, to lay out the causes and their manifestations. Strictly from the local point of view, it appeared useful, as the students began to approach the end of their studies, to let them compete on equal terms with the students of the traditional system (this obliged us to introduce much more content and traditional "exercises"). From a general point of view, we can think of this as the attempted absorption of a foreign group by the official school system. This latter had never made room for the "media," nor would it accept a system of tele-education that so diminished its distinguishing characteristics. It would only accept the familiar, the similar. The more the television school resembled the traditional school (by external signs as well as in fundamental principles), the more it would be assimilable.

Added Remarks

We have made certain observations about the team of Tele-Niger. It is strange that really in studies of tele-education projects basically the only things that concern us are the financing, the hardware, the planning, the institutionalization, and the content. We often pass over in silence a very important factor, the human factor. Everything goes ahead as if the problems of conception and execution could be solved quantitatively (once we have hired five directors, fifteen teachers, and four designers). This attitude implies at once the existence of these specialists and, to go no further, the existence of a proven technique for giving form to educational audio-visual messages. The reality unfortunately contradicts this optimism and there still remains much to do to form specialists and to develop effective messages. On the other hand, the very great responsibility of creators in the work of tele-education implies that one gives such problems particular attention. Airline companies choose and follow their flight pilots in their professional capacities, their physical health, and their psychological balance.

We are only making some comments here where we ought to undertake a serious investigation, or perhaps write a novel.

1. Anonymous production

The Tele-Niger team has grown (from 1964 to 1971) from three to six directors, from two to eighteen teachers, from one to two photographers, from none to four designers and one decorator. The broadcasts were never signed. Each member of the team was notified of this at the moment of his hiring and gave up his rights as an author. Each broadcast was the result of the common effort of a small group made up according to the demands of the program. According to personal affinities, certain groups had the tendency to become stabilized, but the small number of the team and the diversity of the programs obliged frequent changes (on the average of every two months). This mobility also permitted a more equitable distribution of satisfying work (directors were not tied to a single series; teachers were not contributors to only one director). Over the years, or even from season to season, certain series were in vogue or out of fashion, certain techniques much used or much neglected. We are trying at the present time to focus on the process and to separate out what was for different team members the prototype image of a good broadcast.

One of the great problems was to establish and maintain the balance between the demands of planned production (as much as possible) and those of a permanent invention of creators (four broadcasts had to be made every day). Clearly this ideal balance was never attained but one can plainly see that on the one hand, it was promoted by the necessity of treating programs in series (dividing themes up as we have said above), and on the other hand, the anonymity of the final product did not dampen the inventiveness at all; it even was one of the determining elements of the work in teams. The proof was the fact that when on the occasion of a colloquium the names of the creators of the tapes presented were announced, there followed protests and reactions of jealousy, something that up to that time had never surfaced in the group.

2. Human problems

We can only mention here the even more important question of people working in foreign countries, in technical assistance, practically separated from their native environment. The question here is: "How do you set up a team?"

We have said above that the anonymity of the production even helped the forming of a team; at the very least it helped avoid bickering among its members. Another very positive factor was the possibility we had of recruiting almost all of the personnel by co-optation. Each year a small number of the heads of sections was able to interview the candidates (French and Nigerien) for their new jobs. Recruiting the secretary for the head of the project was no exception to the rule. In the case where the choice turned out badly (which happened sometimes), the responsibility could not be placed on any outside organism.

The isolation of Tele-Niger, its operation within a closed system, along with the indifference and scepticism (occasionally even hostility) from the outside, brought the team together by creating a spirit of an oppressed minority, and we noted that on certain critical occasions a number of team members showed that they felt personally responsible for the project.

This point brings up another question: "Why was it that a good number of team members did much more than was expected of them?"

If we objectively put into relation the working conditions of technical assistance personnel and the work produced, we see that they far surpassed the usual level of output. Indeed, these workers did not have any of the usual satisfactions (credits for their productions or the protection of copyright, overtime pay) and besides, the trustee agencies remained ignorant of this fact. It seems that a number of diverse motivations must explain this somewhat rare behavior: a bet with one-self that he would succeed, awareness that one was participating in an exceptional project, attraction of teamwork, concern for the success of one's students, a desire to give the lie to external criticism. Thus, during the first years of the operation, a complex mythology was developed and was variously considered by observers as a fine team spirit, a naive "boy scoutism," or an "effete snobbism." Whatever the reason for it, the overtime work of many of the Tele-Niger members corresponded to an important affective investment. It generated some painful group problems, and it cannot simply be taken as a guide for other projects without certain qualifications.

For all of the difficulties that we have seen, the situation of isolation and, above all, of exile from homeland were, nevertheless, favorable to innovation. A common criticism of some detractors was that the "people of Tele-Niger came to Niamey to do what they couldn't do in Paris." A more objective spirit on the contrary should have congratulated them for "doing in Niger something else than what was being done in France." The concern to adapt to a milieu unknown to practically the whole of the team, the desire to be inventive, the possibility given to each team member to see the results of his work, these all coincided with the somewhat rare opportunities for production in a center small in size but entirely devoted to educational programming.

Impressions on Some Differences between Tele-Niger and Other Systems

1. The centralization

One of the characteristics of Tele-Niger most often cited was its centralized and highly directed structure. A single center in the capital of the country made and distributed all of the messages. These were received and used by all of the classes at the same time by all of the students of the same grade level. This "Napoleonic" aspect of the system was often criticized: by reason of the absence of feedback (though it was not specifically excluded), in the name of the liberty of the teacher in the classes (but should one not consider whether the lack of materials and intellectual training of the Nigerien monitors provided a real condition for the use of their liberty?), by reason of the risk of conditioning the students (yet is it certain that the traditional school, which uses fixed schedules, completely escapes the techniques of conditioning?).

Whatever it was in itself, the Tele-Niger system remains in many minds tied to this image of a centralized distribution system. In this sense, it is placed in a radically different perspective (if not one actually opposed) from most of the present-day tendencies which look, on the contrary, for greater diversity, an expansion of the possibilities of choice, and the maximum individualization of services.

2. Utilization of broadcasting in an underdeveloped country

If it is possible, as it is often written, that the world crisis in education affects all countries, that the problems are basically the same in well-equipped countries as those on the way to development, it is not at all certain that the solution of these problems is the same for the two types of countries. The reason is so simple as to be almost banal: It relates to the lack of means (above all human and material) of developing countries.

This is why we think that broadcasting (the transmission of radio broadcasts and, especially, of television) could play a key role in the solution of educational problems of developing countries, with regard to the simplest and most effective of these means now available. All of the other means in fact demand conditions that these countries can in no way carry out on a large scale. These other solutions demand either highly qualified (and numerous!) personnel, or the regular distribution of documents to a large number of distribution points (most of them hardly accessible), or the storage in each place of considerable materials, or all of these conditions at once. It seems that people are again forgetting very quickly the possibility cited in all of the basic texts on audio-visual teaching: that television allows the diffusion of a great variety of images (including the flannelboard) and in order to obtain these and their accompanying sound, all one has to do is turn a button. Is it necessary to recall this other obvious fact: that the diffusion by air waves has certain advantages in countries where roads are difficult, muddy, sand-filled, or simple nonexistent? It is strange to note that at the very moment when the means are available to reach effectively all of the points in a country, thanks to diffusion by satellite, the use of this system is being seriously questioned.

3. Big hardware and individualized instruction

Since Tele-Niger was not able to expand, it might be considered as only a "model" and consequently not really important on the level of broadcast projects of a large scale.

These latter seem less and less in favor among the "rich" and well-equipped countries, who seem to be seeking a solution to their educational problems in the individualization of learning. This concept contains different elements: concern for a more developed adaptation to the capabilities of the student, to his interests, to his objective needs, a change in the relationship between the student and his sources of learning.

This movement goes along with the appearance of new techniques that are the basis of grand hopes:

-- individual machines (from simple machines to teaching by computer);

-- cheap video tape recorders;

-- cassettes and videodiscs;

-- multi-media systems;

-- systems for delayed broadcast (here the example of Sweden is significant: The schools do not use direct reception of the broadcasts of Swedish Radio but copy these broadcasts on tapes).

It is not possible to discuss here the merits of individualization and the technology it is spawning. Let us only point out that the rich countries have (relatively) the means to try these experiments. The other problem will be to try to make clear the deeper reasons for questioning the approach of broadcasting.

From Tele-Niger to Future Systems

1. The need to anticipate new systems

Most changes in the world of teaching take place by small successive modifications, focused on a particular sector (methods, programs, institutions, examinations, use of the media. . .). One of the unique characteristics of Tele-Niger was that a team thought up a complete system and was completely in charge of bringing it into existence. The team chose its methods, made its broadcasts, and printed materials, trained its teachers and placed them in schools. Few educators have had the chance to enjoy at one and the same time all of these possibilities and the freedom to use them over a period of years.

It is also rare to find the elaboration, even on a theoretical level, of complete systems. People seem to prefer thinking in the categories of improvement or of reform. One of the disadvantages of this approach is that in this case innovation can only grow on the solid foundation of archaic structures. One thinks of developing the automobile of tomorrow by putting a rotary motor under the hood, when one ought to build a Hovercraft.

The educational world has opened its doors to projections to economic studies and to persons relatively new like planners who are quite well received. In the same way, there is a push to introduce the techniques of modern management and organization, and more than one innovative educator has dreamed of a program as exact and reliable as those that managers of the space programs could develop and execute.

Up to this point in the tentative remarks we have failed to take into account certain entire areas or groups of problems, commonly considered as self-evident; this involves "a priori" educators, moral and social, who continually imbue the world of teaching, shape the foundations of the traditional school and still are involved with a good number of innovative projects without the promoters of these even being aware of it. Education is like Euclidian geometry, considered in ancient times as unique and perfectly adapted to the external world.

In fact, education itself has to revise its axioms and postulates, and it is the burden of educators to create in the near future, departing from new postulates, non-Euclidian pedagogies. These should allow the effective use of the media while deciding on the best application of each one of them. But it is difficult at present to make clear the a priori elements of traditional education and to deduce their relations to the present systems. Along with the analysis of systems, it would be good to gather a group of researchers to make a kind of "psychoanalysis" of educational systems.

2. Directions

In an empirical way and essentially concentrating on developing countries, we might suggest that future systems of tele-education would benefit from the following elements:

(a) reduction of costs by the use of transnational programming. If we think of effective utilization of satellite broadcasting, it seems possible to produce a series of programs very widely useful without their being necessarily impoverished or too rigidly structured.

(b) improving quantitatively and qualitatively the means for freeing the audience. This could be accomplished by the suppression of the "animator" (or classroom "presenter"); we are thinking here not only of the week of "free" listening sponsored by Tele-Niger last year, but above all of the success of similar series, of which the best-known example is Sesame Street. In another way, one could free the audience by institutionalizing a "digressive" use of the teacher (that is, a system in which each day the teacher devotes two hours of his time to beginners, an hour and a half to students of second grade, an hour to third grade). From an economic point of view, one could expand the system without greatly expanding the costs. From an educational perspective, one allows the teacher to play only his essential role as educator.

(c) facilitating production by developing techniques of automatic production. Production, which has remained largely in the craft stage, could greatly benefit both by these educational advances and by the choice and the ordering of images, from possibilities offered by computers or video-recorders with memory.

3. Advent of new forms of programming

Among the areas ordinarily considered as "self-evident" is one of the most important elements of the television system: program production. We generally think that the problem has been solved once a director has been hired. On the contrary, it is at this point that the problems are posed.

It is strange to note that the instructional film and the educational broadcast on the whole have not evolved in any significant way during the past 20 years. Putting aside several exceptional productions, educational broadcasting has not yet defined its own styles. A number of reasons can account for this state of affairs:

- the lack of economic incentive in this area (the best directors being held by the higher salaries in commercial broadcasting and advertising);

- the widely shared opinion that educational production is a "minor genre";

- the real problem of creating audio-visual programming (it is at least as difficult to a well-made mathematical demonstration on the screen as it is to stage a crime of passion);

- the pressure of the "a priori" elements of traditional education, of which we have spoken before.

We would like to dwell a little upon this last point. It is, in our view, one of the basic reasons for the stagnation of educational production in two principal genres: "the illustration" and the "transcription from the textbook." In the first case, the broadcast is considered as an interesting element capable of being integrated, at the will of the teacher, into any moment of his course. We can appreciate in this kind of program its descriptive and concrete contribution and above all the perfect control that the teacher maintains over its usage. This latter attitude is certainly at the bottom of the favorable response that the different cassette systems have received, even before they are available. A reassuring and perfectly controlled instrument, the illustrative broadcast, does not demand a particularly innovative production: It is enough to show as many things as possible and to show them well. It does not threaten the security of the teacher and it accommodates itself to all methods of exploitation.

The broadcast of the "transcription from the textbook" witnesses another kind of "domestication" of television. Certainly it pays homage to the powers of audio-visual expression, but at the same time it does not permit these to be fully activated. We are not talking here about a filmed course by a teacher which is limited to the recording in a classroom of the ordinary lesson, but rather to those programs that in one or several broadcasts try to deal with a single section of the matter to be taught. But, we find that these programs, even if they apparently treat their subject in a way satisfactory to their producers or the groups running the education system, reveal themselves as not very effective at all on the level of student acceptance. Here one finds again another manifestation of the pedagogical "a priori." In fact, these broadcasts do not actually treat their real subject matter: "Such and such a set of concepts that the students ought to learn," but only that set of concepts "that is explained in the textbook." Stated in another way, they do not attack the reality but only its bookish expression. The camera is used as an "extension," or a means of visualizing a rhetorical piece (written or spoken) when it could be an instrument of exploration, of deciphering reality and its educational problematic and by that means making available a much more direct access to it. We do not have the space available here to develop this point in a concrete way, but let us simply point out that it is easier to understand it if one reflects, for example, on the nature of the linkages that relate the pedagogical sequences and above all the ellipses that they imply. One can also ask himself why when the fiction film excels in dealing with nuances of very complex moral, social, and psychological problems, the audio-visual educational documentary practically never touches on these subjects in their same complexity, whether scientific or philosophical. Is it perhaps that in order to do, recourse to feature-length treatment is called for? As far as we know, we can only cite one attempt of this kind, a very interesting one indeed: the animation film "Of Stars and Men" and the project of a French group to film in full length, wide screen, and color Descartes' "Discourse on Method." In the two cases, it was not a question of making a reportage on a famous work, but of attacking with all of the powers of audio-visual expression the problems (in this case philosophical ones). Too often, the director of educational broadcasts (or of films) behaves like an amateur painter who confounds the beauty of the model with the beauty of the picture. Excellent reproduction of a chapter from the textbook does not result in high-quality educational broadcasting. Excellence in teaching is not tied to this kind of transcription.

We would like to emphasize in conclusion how little these broadcasts of illustration or simple transcription take into account the real situation of the spectator. It is often said that it would be good to make architects live in the houses they build. In the same way, it would be interesting to oblige directors and producers of educational programs to do their studies with the help of programs similar to ones they have created. Without waiting for the arrival of a Frank Lloyd Wright or a Le Corbusier of audio-visual education, one can wish for a greater concern given to the student-spectator, who should be thought of as a real, living being, struggling with various problems. It is not a question in this case of aesthetic consideration, but only of the desire that the audio-visual education production fully benefit from the best understanding of the act of learning. Recent research in this area leads us to hope that a group of investigations could be developed so as to constitute a kind of "micro-teaching" of audio-visual education.

(English translation by Emile G. McAnany)

II

THE SCHOLAR'S VIEW

Lundgren said modestly that the propositions cited in his paper were merely "some very personal ideas" of what makes for quality in ITV. Arthur A. Lumsdaine, Professor of Psychology in the University of Washington, considered those propositions against 20 years of research on instructional technology. He said they sounded like very reasonable ideas with which he was strongly tempted to agree. "But when I look at them," he said, "either there is no real evidence from the experimental literature to support or refute them; or else the evidence is so thin and so particularized that the amount we need to know to include these in a science of instruction lies far in the future."

One proposition before the conference said that "instructional television is at its best when it does not instruct" (i.e., when it teaches indirectly). It was noted that this is reminiscent of Alexander Pope's maxim,

> "Men must be taught as if you taught them not,
> And things unknown proposed as things forgot."

Yet, it was pointed out that there is a contrary doctrine, based on long experience, that one should tell learners what he is going to tell them, then tell them, and finally tell them what they have been told. The conferees decided there is really no way to choose between these two precepts except in terms of who and what one is trying to teach, and under what conditions. In one situation, with one set of goals, it must be better to teach indirectly; in another, to teach directly and repetitively.

Wilbur Schramm, Director of the Institute for Communication Research at Stanford, who has studied instructional broadcasting in many parts of the world, reviewed the research on content elements of ITV as they seem to be related to effectiveness. He could report very few findings of broad generality. So much, he reported and the other researchers echoed, depends on conditions and particulars. "Only two straightforward guidelines of general importance stand out from the research we have reviewed," he said. "One of these is simplicity of presentation. The other is active participation by the students in the learning experience. . . . Simple television; active students."

On matters like these there was little disagreement, merely the usual difference in approach. For all their concern with creativity and professional standards, the broadcasters agreed with the researchers that on the whole we have placed rather too much reliance on the tactics of presentation, too little on the strategies of teaching. Both sides tended to agree that "fanciness" of production seldom helps; even embellishments like color are aids to learning only in special circumstances. Yet the circumstance may be determinant. A child accustomed to color in television may be more receptive to learning from color ITV. An instructional program placed deliberately in competition (like Sesame Street and The Electric Company) with commercial programs can hardly afford to be Plain Jane. One of the European broadcasters gasped when he saw The Electric Company and said he would never dare produce a teaching program moving at such a swift pace. Yet he agreed with Edward Palmer, who was at the meeting as research director of the Children's Television Workshop, that the speed and splashiness of that program were called for by the conditions in which it was to be viewed.

Anyone brought up in the belief that viewing television is a passive experience would have been surprised by the unanimity with which both broadcasters and scholars rejected that idea. Practice, participation, response were in everyone's formulation of the characteristics of an effective teaching program. So also was the idea that the best programs lead students to carry on their learning activities, past the program and beyond the classroom, to practice and problem-solving in the nonacademic world. Indeed, it was said that one index of how effectively we teach on television may be how fast we put ourselves out of business, for our purpose should be to wean students away from dependence on teachers and programs and prescribed regimens of learning, and help them grow toward the maturity of seeking their own learning sources, finding their own problems and their own ways of study.

The broadcasters approached this sort of common ground, hesitantly, from the basis of insight and observation; the scholars, just as hesitantly, from the research results. Both sides said that much depends on circumstances and situation. The broadcasters readily admitted that their evidence was impressionistic. The scholars were exceedingly modest about the order of evidence they could contribute. Their position might be summed up like this:

(1) We know a great deal more than we knew 20 years ago about

the science of instruction, but there is still a great deal more we need to know.

(2) Theory tends by nature to be general rather than specific. Thus, whereas research has demonstrated a number of important things such as the need of an optimum amount of repetition, of an appropriate rate of development, of motivation, of student activity in learning, and the like, there is still a need for detailed knowledge of conditions and the exercise of judgment and creativity before these findings can be applied in practice.

(3) Therefore, one of the principal uses of scientific research in instructional technology is not to form rules of great specificity, but rather to provide a way of looking at the acts of teaching and learning, and consequently at the problems of making effective programs. In a sense, research findings are most useful in challenging practice -- getting practitioners to ask more questions about the uses they are making or failing to make of the findings and the principles that have emerged from research, and to perceive deeper meanings and broader consequences in what they are doing.

(4) Because application of both research guidelines and creative skills depends so much on the conditions of application, research can and should be an ongoing tool of program making. Conditions must be studied, and proposed solutions must be tested. Therefore, although basic research leading toward general theory continues to be important, <u>formative</u> research designed to test programs and practices before they are widely used is of more immediate usefulness.

The two following papers represent the viewpoint of the scholars at the meeting. The first paper is a brief review of the literature on content elements as related to effectiveness, with some suggestions as to where to read more deeply into the subject. The second paper is a thoughtful consideration of the use and usefulness of research in making instruction effective.

WHAT THE RESEARCH SAYS

By Wilbur Schramm, Director, Institute for Communication Research, Stanford University

This is about the message, rather than the medium, of instructional television. It is concerned not with how television compares with other instructional media, but rather with the way subject matter is presented and instructional strategies are employed in ITV: what the teacher and the producer can do within the program to help their viewers learn whatever it is they are expected to learn.

This paper is intended for broadcasters and for educators concerned with the use of television for instruction. It is not really for scholars. There are some first-rate reviews of instructional media research, notable among them Lumsdaine's in the Handbook of Research on Teaching (edited by Gage, 1963). Scholars should read Lumsdaine and some of the other reviews and summary volumes listed below, together with as many of the original research reports as they can find.

The paper is a radar sweep rather than an exhaustive search for documents. There was insufficient time for that, particularly because a considerable part of this research literature exists only in mimeographed documents that are extremely hard to lay hands on. I went back to the reviews mentioned above: Lumsdaine's in the Handbook (1963); Allen's in the Encyclopedia of Educational Research (1960); May and Lumsdaine on Learning from Film (1958); Travers, et al., on Research and Theory Related to Audio-visual Information Transmission (1964, 1966). Then I went through the chief abstract volumes and some of the other summary publications: Reid and MacLennan, Research in Instructional Television and Film: Summary of Studies (1967); Duke and Nishimoto on audio-visual research in Asia (1963); Ely on educational media research in Latin America (1963); the Council of Europe book on audio-visual research in Europe (edited by Harrison, 1966); Hoban and Van Ormer, Instructional Film Research, 1918-1950 (1950, reprinted 1970); Chu and Schramm, Learning from Television: What the Research Says (1967); Briggs, et al., Instructional Media: A Procedure for the Design of Multi-Media Instruction, A Critical Review of Research, and Suggestions for Future Research (1967). For later titles I looked at Psychological Abstracts and the monthly ERIC listings in Research in Education. For research, listed in these volumes, with which I was unfamiliar, I went -- when possible -- to the original documents.

I found rather less than I expected. In contrast to the hundreds of experimental comparisons of ITV with "conventional" classroom teaching reported in the literature, there are at most a few score of studies specifically on the content and strategies of ITV. Fortunately, a considerable amount of research on instructional films seems to be applicable to television. But only by including these film experiments and a few studies from other media has it been possible to report here on just under 120 titles, representing fewer than 150 experiments.

It is worth noting that young pupils, and adults and professionals out of school, are very lightly represented among the subjects of studies of content variables, whereas college students and military personnel are very heavily represented -- indicating, as always, that experimental research is done where populations are readily available that can be studied under experimental controls. Here are the proportions:

Grades 1 - 4	3 per cent
5 - 8	17
9 - 12	19
College students	31
Military personnel	28
Adults, professionals	2

For some of the same reasons, science and military skills are heavily represented in the subject matter studied:

Science	26 per cent
Military skills	16
Applied or practical science (automobile repairing, slide rules, micrometer use, etc.)	12
Psychological and social sciences, including history	11
Professional and semi-professional skills (dental techniques, nursing care, education, etc.)	8

Language and literature	9
Motor skills (tying knots, physical education, etc.)	7
Miscellaneous (ranging from phonetic alphabet to photography)	11

The scholars who have done the experiments are, for the most part, psychologists or educational psychologists working in universities or in the training branches of military services. There seems to have been relatively little participation in the research by broadcasters.

In the following pages I am going to assemble some of the findings and try to suggest their implication for broadcasters and educators. They will be distributed under the following headings, which might be thought of as moving from (mostly) broadcaster variables to (mostly) teacher variables:

The Picture
The Sound
Picture-sound Relationships
Simplicity and Complexity of Treatment
The Teacher
Teaching Strategies

Research on the Picture

Guba's eye-camera studies at Ohio State produced enough unexpected results to show us how little we really know of how learners look at ITV.

His apparatus was so designed that anything the subject looked at was marked by a tiny spot of light which was photographed and appeared on a kinescope showing the original program with a white dot registering every eye position. The experimenters found great differences in the viewing patterns of low and high IQ students. In some programs when a teacher was shown with laboratory materials, slow learners focused their eyes for a long time on the talking mouth, never changing their gaze even when the instructor was using the apparatus and directing viewers' attention to it. Fast learners, on the other hand, seldom looked at the teacher's mouth. They swept rapidly over his face, hair, clothing, the objects surrounding, finally around the room in which the picture was being shown. When apparatus came into the instructional program, they scanned it, looked back to the instructor, then often away from the screen entirely. In other words, the visual component of the teaching was being used quite differently by the fast and the slow learners.

If Guba's results are generally true, then a great deal of what we think we know about fixations and sweeps in reading and viewing may be open to serious question. And these matters must be better understood if we hope to make long steps forward in understanding the visual components of ITV.

However, some conclusions, at least of a tentative nature, emerge from the studies:

Quality of picture. There is nothing in the literature to contradict the common-sense conclusion of classroom observers that a fuzzy picture is likely to produce less learning than a sharp picture. Poor picture quality becomes more damaging as it approaches the point where viewers cannot clearly see things they are expected to learn, and at times when motivation to learn from the picture is low. But fairly poor picture quality can be compensated for, in a great many situations, by other elements of content. For example, Duva and Lumsdaine (1956) found that a fuzzy kinescope did indeed produce less learning than a sharp film print of the same program; but they were able to make the kinescope practically as effective as the sharp print by introducing student participation questions (about which we shall have more to say later).

Color pictures. The research findings are consistent: color, *per se*, has no learning advantage over monochrome. For example, Fullerton (1956) found that eleventh- and twelfth-grade students learned *more* from a guidance film in monochrome than the same film in color. Hudson (1958) found that teaching work skills to South Africans was no more effective via color films than monochrome. Kanner and Rosenstein (1960) found that 10 out of 11 comparisons of efforts to teach electronics and photography skills to military trainees by monochrome or color films resulted in no significant differences. In the eleventh case the low-ability group got more help, the high-ability group less help, from color. Rosenstein and Kanner (1961) found no significant difference in color vs. monochrome films used for teaching military personnel the guidance and repair of missile systems. VanderMeer (1952) found n. s. d. in teaching science by color or monochrome to high school students, and reported the same result in 1954. Zuckerman (1954) found n. s. d. in factual learning from a black and white *filmstrip* and a color sound film in training Air Force pilots.

These findings should give pause to educators who are inclined to invest in expensive color equipment or programming.

However, we have been talking about color _per se._ There is at least one situation in which color is essential: when color is a necessary element of what is to be taught. For example, if one is teaching medical technicians to recognize the color of cells in a certain pathology, it is very difficult to do that with monochrome. If color coding is an effective way to teach certain necessary discriminations, then monochrome may not do it as well. Furthermore, by concentrating on learning rather than liking, we run the risk of paying too little attention to motivational elements in learning. For example, VanderMeer found that his high school subjects _preferred_ color, as most of us do in the case of non-instructional TV. The Rosenstein-Kanner experiments suggests that with low-ability students, and consequently low-interest and low-motivation, color may indeed attract more attention and contribute more to motivation than monochrome. But for general purposes, monochrome seems not to be at any great disadvantage over color in facilitating learning.

Subjective camera angle. If the camera is so placed as to record what the viewer would see if he himself were performing the skill he is supposed to learn, there is good reason to think he will find it easier to perform the skill when he tries it. This is exactly what Roshal (1959) found in studying different versions of films designed to teach Navy recruits to tie three different knots. One of the versions showed what the person tying the knot would see; the other, what he would see if he were watching someone else tie it. The "subjective" angle was more effective.

Gibson (1947) compared a film, an illustrated lecture, and an illustrated manual teaching aviation trainees to master position firing. This kind of cross-media design has obvious difficulties, but Gibson's analysis of his results was that the film was superior because it viewed the situation from the same angle as in actual combat.

These studies both dealt with manual skills. One can understand how such a skill as knot-tying might be more easily learned if it were not demonstrated with all movements reversed from right to left, as it is in the "objective" angle. But does the subjective camera angle make any contribution to the learning of more complex skills? One experiment casts some doubt on that. Grant and Merrill (1963) made two films of a conference on nursing care. The object was to teach the task performed by the group leader. One film version showed the conference from the angle of the team leader herself; the other, from the viewpoint of one of the conferees looking at the leader. In this case, the second version -- the "objective" angle -- proved to be more effective. It may well be, therefore, that the advantage of the subjective camera angle is limited mostly to simple motor skills, and more complex skills such as human relations may be learned as well or better by looking at them from the outside.

Eye contact. Does it make for more learning when the teacher looks directly into the camera and therefore seems to be looking the students right in the eye? Connolly (1962) and Westley and Mobius (1960), the former with a freshman English course, the latter with a course on computer applications, were unable to find that it made a difference. Possibly the result might not be the same if the purpose were persuasion.

Size of picture. Screen size seems to make no difference in learning if the viewer can see clearly what he is supposed to learn. Aylward (1960), Carpenter and Greenhill (1958), Diamond (1962), Greenhill, Rich, and Carpenter (1962), and Reede and Reede (1963) all found no significant differences between a regular screen and a very large screen, or magnified pictures. A number of these experiments was done at Penn State with a 24-inch television set compared to a very large Eidiphor screen. Diamond found some evidence that the large screen helped students of lower ability, and Reede and Reede found some evidence that on problem-solving the students who viewed the large screen did less well. On the other hand, VanderMeer (no date, a, b, and c) found that attention to the size and visual placement of elements within the picture made more difference than the size of picture. For example, increasing the size of labels, making printed matter on the screen read directly from left to right rather than scattering it "artistically," putting captions at the bottom rather than the top of a picture, and presenting tabular matter as diagrams rather than tables all contributed to learning.

Special pictorial treatments. One experiment with stereoscopic sound motion pictures (viewed through special optical glasses) showed no special advantage over ordinary two-dimensional pictures in teaching a motor skill (Cogswell, 1952). McGuire (1955) found that slow-motion did better than films taken at ordinary speed in helping viewers comprehend a mechanical process. LaJeunesse and Rossi (1960) compared a science film in which most of the shots were close-ups with a second version in which they were mostly at long-range, and a third version in which they were distributed among close-ups and long-distance views. This experiment is a bit hard to interpret, but in general seemed to find that the students who saw the close-ups learned more than either of the other experimental groups.

Over and over again, this kind of finding appears: what makes the difference is usually not a pictorial quality per se, but rather how the pictorial treatment fits the learning goal. For a large proportion of all learning tasks, slow motion would not be an advantage, and might even be boresome. For some learning objectives, long shots might be advantageous over close-ups -- for example, learning football formations or weather patterns as seen from a satellite. And if holography does indeed make three-dimensional photography readily available, there will be many educational uses for it. But the focus of a teleteacher, a producer, or an educational program planner should be on the message question -- what is the learning goal and how to achieve it -- rather than the media questions -- color or monochrome, motion or still, slow motion or standard speed, and the like. That is what the research seems to say.

Research on the Sound Track

Speed. A research activity of interest to broadcasters took place in the 1950's when Fairbanks and his colleagues (see, for example, Fairbanks, Guttman, and Miron, 1957) began to experiment with compressed speech. By using an electronic technique that chopped tiny bits out of a sound tape at random, they were able to achieve any level of compression they desired and squeeze the recorded speech into shorter and shorter time periods. Some of their results were remarkable. For example, they found that it was possible for most listeners to comprehend ordinary text at a rate of 300 words a minute, which is about twice the rate of fast lecturing or telephone conversation. And when they calculated the most "efficient" rate, they found that the greatest amount of information per unit of time could be absorbed at a rate between 250 and 300 words per minute.

When this technique was applied to media instruction, however, it proved to be less useful than had been hoped. A student who received two successive presentations at double speed learned no more than a student who heard the presentation once at normal speed. Nor was there any advantage in using the time gained by double speed to insert more information on key points. Those points were learned better, but the others less well, so that overall there was no apparent advantage in using the compressed speech for teaching.

Most studies of the optimal rate of speech for audio-visual or auditory instruction have come out on the low side rather than the high range explored by Fairbanks and his speech compressor. For example, Zuckerman (1949) found that a rate of 111 to 141 words per minute made for more learning by military trainees than a "low" rate (70-102 wpm) or a "high" one (155-185). Jaspen (1950) compared four rates of speaking -- 45, 74, 97, and 142 wpm -- in the verbal commentary of a film designed to teach Naval trainees the parts of a gun. He found 97 significantly more effective than 45, but not significantly different from either 74 or 142. Diehl, White, and Bark (1959) experimented with rates between 125 and 200 wpm in recorded informational speaking for college students, and found the optimum near 160. Goldstein (1940) found that comprehension declined as rate of speaking was increased from 125 to 300 wpm.

"Difficulty" of spoken material. Obviously, the effective rate of speaking on ITV must have something to do with the abilities of the student, with what is happening on the sound track, and with the difficulty of the material being presented. "Difficulty" in this sense is not an easy concept to operationalize in an experiment. Ideally, it should be calculated with the insights of linguistic, logic, and learning studies, but the theoretical basis for doing this is not readily at hand. Consequently, most of the experiments on difficulty of spoken material in ITV or film instruction have used devices such as readability formulas, which were made for reading from print rather than listening to speech. Using this kind of measure, the experiments have tended, like the studies of rate, to come out on the low side.

Readability formulas are typically standardized against written materials which have been found to be comprehensible (at a given level of efficiency) by a reader at a certain educational level. May and Lumsdaine (1958) tried different readability levels in preparing film commentaries for seventh- and eighth-grade pupils, and found that material measured at fourth grade or lower level of readability was more effective than material at ninth- or tenth-grade level. Chall and Dial (1948) also discovered that an optimum level of readability for commentaries was at or a little below educational level. On the other hand, Nelson and VanderMeer (1955) found no significant gain in simplifying the sound track of a film designed to teach meteorology to military trainees, and Moldstad was unable to obtain significant differences by varying the readability of a sound track for teaching seventh-grade science. It is apparent that there is no magic in applying readability formulas to sound tracks, and that the optimum difficulty level, and density, depend on a number of other variables including those named above.

Background music. The use of background music has become common in high-cost films and commercial television and has tended to be accepted as a characteristic of high-quality ITV production. The few studies that exist do not lead to much confidence that musical backgrounds contribute to learning. Hovland, Lumsdaine, and

Sheffield (1949) found that a musical accompaniment was no aid to learning. When Lumsdaine and Gladstone repeated this experiment, in 1958, the musical version of a film was actually found to be less effective. Remember that here, as elsewhere, we are talking about learning rather than liking. But the implication of the 1958 experiment is that the music may actually have distracted the pupils from what they were expected to learn. One other experiment on music is worth mentioning. Freeman and Neidt (1959) studied the relative effect on learning of familiar vs. unfamiliar music used as a film background. The subjects were a sample of college students and one of military trainees. No significant differences were found.

Research on Picture-Sound Relationships

Instructional television broadcasters would like to know what, in any given situation, to put into their sound track and what into the picture track, and how to relate the two tracks most effectively. Unfortunately, the research is not going to give them much help with such problems. These are enormously complex questions, and the necessary theory seems not yet to exist.

Two channels vs. one. Most of the early experiments in this area (summarized by Day and Beach, 1950), although they left something to be desired in design and method, appeared to conclude that a combined audio-visual presentation produced more learning than either the audio or the visual channel alone. This finding has generally been accepted, and has encouraged the instructional switch from radio to television, from silents and filmstrips to sound films. Yet it rests on fragile ground.

Lumsdaine is quite justified in challenging the generality of these earlier experiments (1963). When McGuire (1958) compared a film on a motor skill, with and without spoken commentary — with somewhat better control over the content of the two channels than most of the earlier experiments -- he, too, found that a group exposed to the film plus descriptive narration learned more than a group who saw the film without narration. Later experiments, some of which we shall discuss, concluded that certain uses of a sound track would contribute to the amount of learning from a picture track. But most of these still leave the nagging doubt of what would have happened with different material in the two tracks. And we are not yet prepared to generalize upon that.

In the last decade, some scholars in audio-visual instruction have been much influenced by Broadbent's theory of perception, which has been adapted to audio-visual instruction and tested experimentally by Travers, et al. (1964, 1966). This theory says that only one main channel carries auditory and visual information from the sense organs to the higher centers of the brain. Therefore, the inputs from either auditory or visual receptors must take turns for it, and the inputs must be stored briefly in a short-term memory until the channel is free. Inputs that do not gain access within a certain time are lost. The implication of this, as Travers points out, is that "one would not expect multiple-channel input of redundant information to facilitate learning. The possible exception to this is the situation in which information is transmitted at such a low rate that the learner can switch from channel to channel and hence perhaps increase his learning by having what amounts to an additional trial.

Many of Travers' experiments were done with nonsense syllables, making it easier to control the variables but presenting some difficulties in application to real-life situations. Two experiments, reported by Travers in 1964, found the auditory mode less efficient than either the audio-visual or the visual but no significant interaction between the material and the mode of presentation, indicating that auditory presentation is not very effective for nonsense syllables. When the syllables were presented for a longer time, the audio-visual channel did relatively better, as would be predicted from the theory.

Chan, Travers, and Van Mondfrans (1965) tried to find out whether presenting the nonsense syllables in color would make any difference in the amount of learning from different channels. They found it did. The pictures in color apparently competed more effectively than black and white pictures with the auditory inputs for the available channel capacity, and thus proportionately more was learned from the visual than the auditory track. But the <u>total</u> amount learned from the two channels was the same, regardless of color or monochrome pictures -- supporting the idea of a limited channel capacity.

So far we have been talking about experiments on nonsense syllables. Travers did an experiment on concept learning (1966) requiring his subjects to solve problems that required information (a) from the audio or the visual channel, but only <u>one</u> of them, (b) from <u>both</u> the audio and the visual channels, the information being non-redundant, (c) from <u>either</u> audio or visual channels, the information in the channels being redundant. This is a very interesting design, and I am loath to try to interpret the results without seeing the research report as a whole, which I have not been able to do. Travers, however, reports again finding no advantage of two channels over the visual channel alone.

Grosslight and McIntyre (1955) found that sound films interfered with or, at best, added nothing to learning from a single channel in the study of Russian vocabulary by college students. Ketcham and Heath (1963) found that college students learned more from a sound film on English literature than from the film sound track alone, even when the picture did not contribute directly to the knowledge tested.

Experiments like these that use meaningful material show what a vast area we have not yet covered in channel comparison studies. How realistic is it, for example, to compare the sound track of a film with _both_ tracks of the film? Would the sound track be precisely the kind of spoken commentary one would prepare to accomplish maximum learning effect if it were _not_ accompanied by a film?

The Broadbent-Travers line of research, however, seems to support these generalizations: (a) as long as information is presented to a student at a rate _equal to or greater than_ his ability to process information, then there is no apparent advantage in using _two_ channels carrying redundant information, over using a single channel; (b) if the rate of presentation is _less_ than the capacity of the student to process it, then there may be some advantage in using two modalities; (c) as the complexity of the learning task increases, the advantage of using the visual mode increases.

Use of sound track for labeling. The amount of information to be presented, and how fast, is thus a beginning point for thinking about how to use the two channels. The research literature offers a slight but practical guideline, through a number of experiments on labeling (Thomson, 1944; Jaspen, 1949; Wulff, 1955; Saltz and Newman, 1960; Maccoby and Sheffield, 1961, among others). This is too complicated a matter to discuss in a short space, and it relates to active student participation which we shall discuss later. But under suitable conditions it appears to be possible to increase the learning of objects, or parts of a task or a machine, by verbalizing -- naming -- the objects on the sound track as they are presented on the picture track. This verbalization has to be relevant (as May pointed out, 1958). It should take some account of the individual ways that people symbolize objects for themselves (Cook, 1960), and therefore, technical names of objects may not necessarily be the best ones to verbalize. But here at least we have a beginning of the kind of practical guidance an instructional broadcaster needs: how to use his two tracks so that a student can learn from them more than from either one alone.

Research on Simplicity and Complexity

The general conclusion that emerges from the studies of simple vs. complex treatments of material in the audio-visual media is one that should gladden the heart of a budget officer or an executive producer: More often than not, there is no learning advantage to be gained by a fancier, more complex treatment.

We have already spoken about the limited advantages of color, big screens, and three-dimensional projection -- none of which could conscientiously be recommended, on the basis of the research evidence, to a school system where money comes hard. Now let us add some more general evidence on embellishment.

Embellishments. Some of the findings concerning "embellished" audio-visual instruction may astonish broadcasters and present problems to educators. For example:

A "fancied-up" version? VanderMeer (1953) compared a straight lecture film with a version of the same film described as "jazzed up. . . with folk music in elaborate Hollywood style." Result: the two versions were about equally effective.

Elaborate visuals? Carpenter and Greenhill (1958) found that using a blackboard on television was more effective than fancier visuals in teaching air science to college students, not significantly different in teaching psychology.

"Professional" production techniques? Ellery (1959) tested the learning effect of "amateur" vs. "professional" production techniques -- dollying vs. cutting, production errors vs. none, flat lighting vs. key lighting, etc. Result: n. s. d. Mercer (1952) tested special optical effects such as dissolves, wipes, fades, in films designed to teach science to military trainees. Result: n. s. d.

Humor? Lumsdaine and Gladstone (1958), teaching the phonetic alphabet to military trainees, found that a plain version worked better than a consciously humorous one. McIntyre (1954) also found that a plain version of a military training film was more effective than a humorous one.

Animation? Vestal (1952) and Fordham (1953) found that animation made for no greater learning in teaching, respectively, naval science in college and electronics in high school. However, Lumsdaine, Sulzer, and Kopstein (1953) did find some advantage in using animation for teaching military trainees.

The other studies on program embellishments are consistent with these. As we suggested, they cause some troubles both for broadcasters and teachers. Broadcasters have great difficulty in believing that superior production techniques are not also superior for teaching purposes and that the higher budgets required for embellished programs are not reflected in the learning results. Teachers have a hard time reconciling their confidence in motivation with the apparent lack of effect of adding humor, entertainment, and attention-getting devices to programs.

The experiments on animation suggest a possible explanation for some of the seeming contradictions. Lumsdaine, Sulzer, and Kopstein employed animation to teach use of the micrometer, where it could effectively focus attention on the essentials to be taught rather than allowing attention to be diffused over the instrument, the hands, and the movements. In that situation it was helpful. Vestal and Fordham, on the other hand, apparently used animation in a more general way. Similarly, Neu (1951) reported that attention-getting devices in visual treatments add nothing to learning <u>unless they introduce additional information</u>; perhaps attention was already high enough. VanderMeer found that one kind of embellishment frequently contributes to learning: attention-<u>directing</u> arrows focusing on the material to be learned. And the Penn State Instructional Film Research Program (1954) found live films of actual riots were more effective than canned film clips in teaching riot control to military police. Apparently they contributed to a sense of realism and timeliness and motivation to attend closely.

The implication of these studies just named is becoming almost a theme song for this paper. There is little advantage in an embellishment used <u>per se</u>; but in a situation where animation is really needed to simplify a process, or where a pictorial device will direct attention to the essential items to be learned, or where the embellishments themselves contribute additional information -- in that kind of situation there is good educational reason to use an appropriate form of embellishment.

Of course, there may be other reasons, too. What can we say about the contributions of more "professional" production, humor, music, fancier treatments, and the like, to general interest and motivation?

There is an interesting conclusion in an experiment by Twyford (1951) who found a negative correlation between how much students reported liking a film and how much they learned from it. This has led Cook (1960) to suggest that "interest in a film is not the same as interest in the subject matter of a film; the amount of interest in the film does not predict the amount that will be learned from it, and as a rule technical slickness does not increase the amount learned from a film." This is probably the best guideline we can derive from the literature at the moment. If the goal is learning, then the content elements of an ITV program must be selected and used so as to contribute to the specifically desired learning. Greater embellishment, fancier treatments and production, although they are likely to be applauded by one's professional colleagues, are not necessarily advantageous to the student -- even though they make him like the program better -- if they do not make him more anxious to learn the subject matter.

Research on the Teacher

There is surprisingly little research on the qualities of a teacher that contribute to his effectiveness in television or film. A great deal has been written, of course, about effective classroom teaching, and much of that must apply to teaching on camera. And yet, we know that the qualities of an effective ITV teacher are not necessarily identical with those of an effective classroom teacher. At the moment, empirical tryout and the practical wisdom of educators remain better guides than any studies of teachers in the experimental literature.

A number of communication research studies deal with the prestige of the source of a communication. Prestige seems to divide into credibility and trustworthiness, and these do not always contribute equally to the effect of a message, although if a source is perceived as both credible and trustworthy, he is more likely to be persuasive than if he is not so perceived.

Research on <u>teachers</u> as sources of communication is not very extensive. Kishler (1951) found that a teacher perceived as having high prestige seemed to be able to get his students to learn more than one perceived as having low prestige. Scollon (1956) found no significant difference in learning clearly related to prestige vs. anonymity of the central teaching figure, but considerable difference when this figure seemed to identify with his audience (and probably they with him). Skinner found no significant difference in learning when the same actor, teaching the same subject matter, was introduced in terms intended to give him high or low prestige. Asher and Evans (1959) found that an audio-visual presentation brought about no more attitude change when it was identified as coming from a national network than when it was described as coming from a local origin. Skinner (1963) reported more learning resulted from a film in which the narrators were described as "good" speakers than from one in which they were described as "poor" speakers. Myers (1961) found that teachers classified as "experienced" managed to make a college class learn more from a film than teachers who were classified as "inexperienced."

This last finding, in a sense, typifies the unsatisfying quality of most of the research on television and film teachers. Whether the teacher is "experienced" is a secondary matter. We need to know <u>how he taught</u> in order to bring about the results he did. We need to know what qualities of his teaching or his personality, as they were perceived from the film, set off what learning processes. In other words, in the present state of research there is less to be learned from the studies of film or television teachers than from the studies of film and television <u>teaching</u>. Let us turn now to these.

<u>Research on Teaching Strategies</u>

Within the area that Edling and Paulson (1970) called "the nature and sequence of events in the learning experience," the most fully researched subfield has been student participation in the teaching-learning process. Studies in that field provide probably the most definite and most practically useful guidelines in all the research we are describing.

<u>Student participation</u>. A classic in this field is <u>Student Response in Programmed Instruction</u>, edited by Lumsdaine (1961). We are going to cite some of the papers in that volume, but scholars will want to turn to the book itself.

Student participation may take many forms. It may consist of repeating a response designed to be learned from the instructional material, answering a question, carrying out some activity described in the material, asking a question about the material, or any of a number of other things. It may be overt or covert, and it may or may not be accompanied by information as to whether the response was a correct one. Whatever the form, it constitutes an interactive process between student and teacher, and it concentrates on the student's own learning, rather than his being taught.

The striking thing about this research is the consistency of results. In many forms, with many kinds of subject matter, active student participation has almost invariably been found to contribute a substantial amount to learning. For example, Michael and Maccoby (1953) used active responding in only half of a film. The only significant learning gains they found were on material taught in the half to which the responses had been made. Repeating the experiment in 1961, Michael, Maccoby, and Levine found small gains in the part of the film not actively responded to, but much greater gains in the other half. This kind of finding has been reported over and over again. Hardly any other instructional element can be introduced into television or film teaching with as much confidence that it will be helpful.

Of course, like any other element of instruction, active student participation is more effective when used in some ways than in others, and for some purposes rather than others. These are coming to be understood, however, and it may be useful to spell out some of them.

How much active participation? A pioneering study by Gates (1917) found that learning steadily increased in a classroom situation as the proportion of time spent in active recitation or practice was increased from zero to 80 per cent. Kimble and Wulff concluded from their experiment reported in 1961 that the optimum time allocation to active student responses was probably between 50 and 75 per cent of total instructional time. Lumsdaine and Gladstone (1958) in repeating the Hovland-Lumsdaine-Sheffield experiment on learning the phonetic alphabet (1949) found that they could increase the performance of military trainees to near perfect by increasing the amount of active practice (which consisted in that case of saying the names of the phonetic letters as they appeared on the screen). Furthermore, the contribution to learning was greatest where it was most needed -- by the slower, less-interested student.

In other words, a very large proportion of the instructional time built around ITV can profitably be devoted to student participation. This presents something of a practical problem because individual practice may not be the best way to use high-cost television that is designed to fit general rather than individual needs. Yet, there are arguments for making as much use as possible of student participation during an ITV program, and still more reason to build the television into a larger instructional time unit which will include a great deal of active student practice and application growing out of the televised lesson.

Time required by student participation. Active student participation takes time. What is the trade-off between increasing the instructional time to accommodate active participation, and the increases in learning that result? We have a little evidence on that. Lumsdaine, May, and Hadsell (1958) added four-and-one-half minutes of student participation questions to a film on the human circulatory system that already ran eight-and-one-half minutes. (Lumsdaine points out that this is a cheap and easy way to revise films or video tape, in order to increase student participation, without changing the basic material of the program at all.) From the resulting 13-minute film, students learned more than from seeing the original film twice, which required 17 minutes. Michael and Maccoby (1953) achieved substantial gains by adding three minutes of student participation questions to a 14-minute film on defense against atomic attack.

Overt vs. covert. It is not necessary in all cases for students to respond orally or by other external action. For example, May (1947) found that inserting questions in a high school science film produced more learning than the same film without questions, even though no overt responses were called for. There is in the literature a rather bemusing experiment on mental practice of athletic skills. Harby (1952) tried to find out whether a student could improve his shooting of free throws with a basketball by merely rehearsing the act in his mind. At a later time, after some students had practiced mentally and some physically, performance was actually tested on the basketball court. The results are not completely consistent, and Harby would not contend that intensive mental practice of basketball is as helpful as intensive physical practice. Yet, under some conditions in his experiment, mental practice did significantly improve later physical performance.

Michael and Maccoby (1953) found no significant difference between the effectiveness of overt and covert practice in their experiment, and Kanner and Sulzer (1961) reported the same result. McGuire (1955) found that covert responses were more efficient at a faster rate of presentation. Rate and difficulty clearly are related to the choice of overt or covert response modes. For example, Ash and Jaspen (1953) had military trainees, who were learning to assemble a gun, hold the gun in their hands and follow along the steps of assembling it as described in a film. With a slow film, there was interference and confusion. Briggs (1962), Goldbeck (1960), Goldbeck and Campbell (1962), and others have produced evidence that the effectiveness of overt vs. covert responding varies with the level of difficulty of the learning task, as well as the rate. They found in general that easy items are often learned best by covert participation, more difficult items, by overt.

Most of the differing results on overt vs. covert responding seem to be interpretable on the basis of the kind of material being taught and the rate of presentation. Thus, for example, Stake and Sjogren (1954), who obtained more learning by requiring responses to be written rather than spoken or made covertly; Grosslight and McIntyre (1955), who found that pronouncing Russian words as they were spelled was no more effective in teaching their spelling than watching in silence; and Lumsdaine (1961), who brought about a great deal of learning by stopping a lecture to let the classroom audience finish what the lecturer was saying -- were operating under different time constraints and with different learning tasks.

Knowledge of results. Does it increase the amount of learning if a student is informed whether he has made the right response? In general, the answer seems to be yes, although the answer becomes more complicated when schedules of reinforcement are considered. There is a great body of evidence that it helps to practice correct responses. Much of this evidence is in the research on programmed instruction, less in the research on film and television. However, Michael and Maccoby found that active responding to a film was more effective when a student was told the correct response so that he would not continue to practice an incorrect one. The experimenters increased learning simply by requiring an active response, but increased it still further by giving knowledge of results. Gibson (1954) found that telling a student whether his response was correct helped him learn to identify aircraft. Kirsch (1952) obtained better results by presenting the correct answer than by simply saying "right" or "wrong." And Angell (1949) reported that knowledge of results contributed more to learning when given immediately than when postponed for a while -- for example, by not requiring a student to wait until a paper could be read and graded.

Practice or motivation. Is a rhetorical question (presented before the student has received the information with which to answer it) as effective a tool of active participation as a practice question (presented after the student has received the necessary information)? This is somewhat the same as asking how much of the effect of active participation comes from motivation rather than practice. The rhetorical question would supposedly motivate the student to listen for the right answer; the practice question would enable him to learn the desired response. In general, the research indicates that after questions are more effective than before questions (Maccoby, Michael, Levine, 1961; Lumsdaine, May, and Hadsell, 1958; and Michael and Maccoby, 1953). The most effective procedure seems to be to require a response, overt or covert, as soon as possible after the student has been given the information necessary to make the correct response.

Surrogate response. Two experiments have successfully used panels in the studio to respond actively, apparently as a surrogate for a response in the classroom and an easy way to provide knowledge of results. These studies were by Hayman (1962) and Muntone (1963).

Participation through "talkback." Carpenter and Greenhill (1958) tried out a "talkback" system, permitting students to respond actively from their classrooms by transmitting questions or comments to the studio. The students liked the talkback, but learned no more when it was available than when it was not.

Now let us turn from student participation to the variety of questions that might be included under organization and sequencing of materials.

Organization in general. Organization of instructional material is a complicated variable to study, and an ITV teacher or broadcaster can probably derive more guidance from what has been written on classroom teaching and lesson plans than from the research in the area we are talking about. One thing about which the research leaves little doubt, however, is that learning increases when the organization of a teaching film or television program is made very clear -- by the sequencing of ideas, by titles and subheads and directional cues, and the like (for example, see Northrop, 1952). Grosslight and McIntyre (1955) found that learning Russian words in some meaningful serial order was easier than learning them in a random order. Leboutet (1956) found that French schoolchildren under 12 had difficulty identifying the functional structure of a teaching film; older children profited by a logically structured organization, younger ones from a chronological organization. So the organization of ITV programs makes a difference.

The spacing of practice. It is almost impossible, as Smith and Smith say in their 1966 book, to make any generally valid statements about massed vs. distributed practice. Their relative effectiveness depends partly upon the rate of presentation, more importantly upon the organization of the particular subject matter being learned.

For example, no significant differences between the results of massed and spaced practice were obtained by Ash (1950) and by Miller and Klier (1961). Miller and Levine (1961) found that massed review in a particular film on high school science produced more learning than spaced review or no review at all. However, Maccoby and Sheffield (1958) found that it was more effective to practice just one segment of the task they were teaching and then pass on to the next one, rather than massing all the practice together. Theirs was a sequential task, in which one step had to be mastered before the next one could be accomplished. Similarly, McGuire (1961) found that he could bring about more learning by pausing, for review, three times during the presentation of nine slides than by showing the slides without a pause and then reviewing at the end. This was true, however, only when he showed the slides rapidly; if he showed them slowly, practice at the end was just as effective. Ash and Jaspen (1953) reported that it actually took less time to reach a criterion of learning, in a military task, when a film was presented in nine short steps, with a pause for practice after each step, than when the whole film was run through and followed by practice.

Repetition. Cook (1960) came to the conclusion that most audio-visual audiences could profit from more repetition than they get. There is undoubtedly a saturation point beyond which it is inefficient to add more repetitions, but where this point stands depends on the subject matter, the treatment, and the audience, and it is usually higher than one expects. Lumsdaine, Sulzer, and Kopstein (1961), as we have said, experimented with films designed to teach the reading of micrometers. When they varied the number of examples upward, they found that six examples were much better than three; ten, somewhat better than six. The effect of adding only three additional examples was so strong that it produced about twice as much gain as the use of an elaborate overlay animation technique in the original film. Kendler, Cook, and Kendler (1956) found that learning increased with one, two, or three repetitions of a review passage, although the gains were less with each added repetition. Ash and Jaspen (1953) found that the number of useful repetitions of a film depended upon the rate at which the film presented its content. With a fast film, two repetitions were better than one, and three better than two. With a slow film, two showings were better than one, but there was no advantage in a third one.

Rest breaks. There is evidence that learning can be increased, even in relatively short films or television programs, by programming pauses occasionally during the presentation. For example, Faison, Rose, and Podell (1955) were able to increase the learning from a 20-minute film by inserting three half-minute rest periods during the 20 minutes. They believed that the rest periods increased audience attentiveness, and tested this by using infrared photography to observe the audience during the picture. Without rest breaks, the audience seemed to become steadily less attentive during the 20-minute showing. After each break, however, they seemed to be refreshed and interested anew. Pockrass (1961) studied different uses of a one-minute rest break in the middle of a 30-minute ITV program. He found that when silence was maintained during that minute (supposedly giving the viewers a chance to think about the content of the first half of the program), the overall learning was greater than when the pause was used for supposedly relaxing music or for a nonrelated announcement (as broadcasters so often use it). If the objective is learning, therefore, there are some times when the announcer should be silent.

Methods of treatment. Unfortunately, no very general principles come out of experiments in this area. Blain (1956) found that an expository form of presentation, in teaching eighth-grade students about the Monarch butterfly, was more effective than a story form; with fifth-graders, n. s. d. VanderMeer (1953) obtained no significant difference from using a factual lecture form and a story form to instruct military trainees in hygiene. Kazem (1961) found significantly more learning resulted from an informational expository presentation of high school science than from a historical dramatic one. Brandon (1956) found n. s. d. in comparing the effect of a televised lecture vs. interview vs. panel in teaching college students, although the students found the interview and panel more interesting than the lecture. Kaplan (1963) found a problem-solving approach more effective in teaching college freshmen to solve problems, but not for general factual learning. Ishikawa (1959) found that a problem-solving introduction made fourth-grade Japanese students learn more from a film than an introduction that told them what points to look for. And May and Jenkinson (1953) had no success in getting students to check a book out of the library when they presented a filmed version of the entire story; but when they presented films of incomplete story units from the books -- "teasers" -- then a number of students did check out the book to find how the story came out.

One can hardly build general guidelines on information like that. What kind of story form? What kind of lecture? What kind of problem-solving? What kind of expository treatment? The content itself must be analyzed in a more generalizable way before there is much hope of arriving at general principles.

Summary and Conclusions

This is too short a paper to need a summary, and in any case, readers will want to look in it for whatever is of chief interest to them.

However, it must be clear, by this time, that the research on content variables comes down very strongly on two points which offer useful guidelines to anyone concerned with programming instructional television or film. One of these is simplicity of presentation; the other, active participation by the students in the learning experience.

Recall some of the details in which complexity, fanciness, costliness of programming have been shown not necessarily to contribute to learning:

-- Color seems not to increase learning unless color is what is to be learned or unless it is the best means available to code some discriminations that are to be learned.

-- A big screen seems to be of no advantage to learning if the ordinary television screen can be seen clearly enough to pick out the details that are to be learned.

-- Students like a "talkback" system, but seem to learn no more with it than without it.

-- Visual embellishments do not usually help learning unless (like directional arrows) they can help organize content that is not inherently well organized or (like animation) help a viewer to understand a process or concept that is very hard to understand without such simplification. In other words, visual embellishments *per se* are not especially useful in instructional material.

-- No advantage has been demonstrated for existing three-dimensional projection.

-- No learning advantage has been demonstrated for "professional" or "artistic" production techniques such as dollying rather than cutting, key rather than flat lighting, dissolves, wipes, fades, etc.

-- Eye contact seems not to contribute to learning, although it may contribute to persuasion.

-- There is very little evidence that narrative presentation ordinarily has any learning advantage over expository or that adding humor adds to learning effect.

Remember that we are talking about learning, not liking. Some of these complexities may cause a student to *like* a program better, and in special cases any of the special treatments we have mentioned may contribute also to learning. But for the most part, the research encourages us toward a simple rather than a complex or fancy style.

Another part of the literature also has implications for simplicity and economy. This is the group of experiments that casts doubt on the greater effectiveness of two channels over one in presenting essentially redundant material. This research suggests that the auditory channel may be more effective with simple than with complex material, whereas the visual is likely to be more effective than the auditory with complex material; and that there seems to be little learning advantage for an audio-visual treatment over a visual one as long as the program is carrying as much information as the student can process and as long as the two channels are basically carrying the same information.

These latter experiments deserve the consideration of educators and instructional broadcasters. They challenge us to analyze more carefully the uses of ITV that do promise a reliable advantage over a single channel, and the most effective ways we can go about presenting non-redundant information on the two channels. Furthermore, they challenge us to reconsider the tasks for which we can efficiently use the less expensive single-channel media -- radio, slides, filmstrips, sound tape, or even (pardon the word!) print -- in place of more expensive sound films and television, which in many cases may have less advantage than we had thought.

The chief positive guideline that emerges from the research is the usefulness of active student participation. Concerning that we have been able to report impressively consistent results. Participation may be overt or covert; spoken or written or done through practice with a model or a device; button pushing or asking or answering questions, or finishing what the instructor has begun to say. Different forms are more effective in different situations. Whatever the way in which students are encouraged to practice the desired responses, in most cases this activity is more effective if the students are given immediate knowledge of results -- that is, told whether their responses are correct.

There are a number of minor points in the literature that will be of interest to practitioners: when subjective camera angle is of aid to learning, the useful number of repetitions, and the usefulness of rest breaks are three that occur to me at the moment. It is unfortunate that research has not found out more in a general way about some of the big questions, like the organization of instructional television programs and the qualities of an effective ITV teacher. In general the literature is not at a very high level of generality. Findings must always be applied in terms of the nature of the instructional task, the situation, and the learners. And we are still at a stage when it pays richly to try out pilot programs and test the effectiveness at least of a sample of ongoing programs against the criterion they are expected to reach.

But at least two straightforward guidelines stand out from the research papers we have reviewed. Effective television can be kept as simple as possible, except where some complexity is clearly required for one task or another; students will learn more if they are kept actively participating in the teaching-learning process. Simple television: active students.

REFERENCES

Allen, W. H. Audio-visual communication research. In C. W. Harris (ed.), Encyclopedia of educational research. (3rd ed.) New York: Macmillan, 1960. 115-137.

Allen, W. H. Readability of instructional film commentary. Journal of Applied Psychology, 1952, 36, 164-168.

Allen, W. H. Research on film use: Student participation. Audio-Visual Communication Review, 1957, 5, 423-450.

Allen, W. H., and Cooney, S. M. A study of the non-linearity variable in filmic presentation. Los Angeles: Research Division, Department of Cinema, University of Southern California, May, 1963.

Angell, G. W. Effect of immediate knowledge of quiz results on final examination scores in freshman chemistry. Journal of Educational Research, 1949, 42, 391-394.

Ash, P. The relative effectiveness of massed versus spaced film presentation. Journal of Educational Psychology, 1950, 14, 19-30.

Ash, P., and Jaspen, N. The effects and interactions of rate of development, repetition, participation, and room illumination on learning from a rear projected film. (Technical Report SFD 269-7-39.) Instructional Film Research Reports. Port Washington, Long Island, N.Y.: U.S. Naval Special Devices Center, 1953.

Asher, J. J., and Evans, R. I. An investigation of some aspects of the social psychological impact of an educational television program. Journal of Applied Psychology, 1959, 43, 166-169.

Aylward, T. L., Jr. A study of the effects of production technique on a televised lecture. Dissertation Abstracts, 1960, 21, 1660-1661.

Blain, B. B. Effects of film narration type and of listenability level on learning of factual information. Audio-Visual Communication Review, 1956, 4, 163-164.

Blancheri, R. L., and Merrill, I. R. The step presentation of dental technic instruction. In Television in Health Sciences Education, USOE Project 064. San Francisco: University of California, San Francisco Medical Center, Sept. 30, 1963. 34-37.

Brandon, J. R. The relative effectiveness of lecture, interview, and discussion methods of presenting factual information by television. Speech Monographs, 1956, 23, 118.

Briggs, L. J., Campeau, P. O., Gagné, R. M., and May, M. A. Instructional media: A procedure for the design of multi-media instruction, a critical view of research, and suggestions for future research. A final report to the U. S. Office of Education, Pittsburgh: American Institutes for Research, 1967.

Carpenter, C. R., and Greenhill, L. P. Instructional television research. Report No. 2. University Park, Pennsylvania: Pennsylvania State University, 1958.

Chall, J. S., and Dial, H. E. Predicting listener understanding and interest in newscasts. Educational Research Bulletin, 1948, 27, 141-153.

Chan, A., Travers, R. M. W., and Van Mondfrans, A. P. in Audio-Visual Communication Review, 1965, 13, 159-164.

Chu, G., and Schramm, W. Learning from television: What the research says. Washington: National Association of Educational Broadcasters, 1967.

Cogswell, J. F. Effects of a stereoscopic sound motion picture on the learning of a perceptual motor task. (Technical Report, SDC 269-7-32.) Port Washington, N.Y.: U.S. Naval Special Devices Center, 1952.

Connolly, C. P., Jr. An experimental investigation of eye-contact on television. M.A. thesis, Ohio University, Athens, Ohio, 1962.

Cook, J. O. Research in audio-visual communication. In J. Ball and F. C. Byrnes (eds.), Research, principles, and practices in visual communication. East Lansing: Michigan State University, National Project in Agricultural Communications, 1960, 91-106.

Craig, G. A comparison between sound and silent films in teaching. British Journal of Educational Psychology, 1956, 26, 202-206.

Day, W. F., and Beach, B. R. A survey of the research literature comparing the visual and auditory presentation of information. Charlottesville, Virginia: University of Virginia, November, 1950.

Diamond, R. M. The effect of closed circuit resource television upon achievement in the laboratory phase of a functional anatomy course: A comprehensive investigation of television as a magnification device during laboratory demonstrations. Dissertation Abstracts, 1962, 23, 884.

Diehl, C. F., White, R. C., and Burk, K. W. Rate and communication. Speech Monographs, 1959, 26, 229-232.

Dietmeyer, H. J., Sheehan, A. C., and Decker, M. An investigation of concept development in elementary school science teaching by television. NDEA Title VII Project No. 527. Boston: Boston University, 1963.

Duke, B., and Nishimoto, M. Survey of educational media research and programs in Asia. Report to U. S. Office of Education, Washington: U. S. Office of Education, 1963.

Duva, J. S., and Lumsdaine, A. A. The influence of image quality on the teaching effectiveness of the kinescope. U. S. Air Force Human Factors Operations Research Laboratories. Unpublished HFORL report. March, 1956. Summarized in Lumsdaine, 1963.

Ellery, J. B. A pilot study of the nature of aesthetic experiences associated with television and its place in education. Detroit: Wayne State University, Jan. 15, 1959.

Ely, D. P. Survey of educational media research and programs in Latin America. Report to the U. S. Office of Education. Washington: U. S. Office of Education, 1963.

Faison, E. W. J., Rose, N., and Podell, J. E. A. A technique for measuring observable audience reactions to training films. Air Force Personnel and Training Research Center, Training Aids Research Laboratory. Note TARL-LN-55-45. Summary in Lumsdaine, 1961 and 1963.

Fordham University. Training by television: The comparative effectiveness of instruction by television, television recordings, and conventional classroom procedures. (Technical Report SDC

476-02-2.) Port Washington, New York: U.S. Naval Special Devices Center, 1953.

Freeman, J., and Neidt, C. O. Effect of familiar background music upon film learning. Journal of Educational Research, 1959, 53, 91-96.

Frey, Christer. The effect of colour on learning by television. Stockholm: Sveriges Radio, N.D. (1970?)

Fullerton, B. J. The comparative effect of color and black and white guidance films employed with and without "anticipatory" remarks upon acquisition and retention of factual information. Dissertation Abstracts, 1956, 16, 1413.

Gagné, R. M., and Gropper, G. L. The use of visual examples in review. Pittsburgh: American Institutes for Research, 1954.

Gibson, J. J. (ed.) Motion picture testing and research. (Army Air Force Aviation Psychological Program Research Report No. 7.) Washington: Government Printing Office, 1947.

Gibson, J. J. A theory of pictorial perception. Audio-Visual Communication Review, 1954, 2, 3-23.

Goldstein, H. Reading and listening comprehension at various controlled rates. Teachers College Contributions to Education, No. 821. New York: Bureau of Publications, Teachers College, Columbia University, 1940.

Grant, T. S., and Merrill, I. R. Camera placement for recognition of complex behaviors. In Television and Health Science Education, NDEA Title VII Project No. 064. Washington: U.S. Office of Education, 1963, 38-44.

Greenhill, L. P., Rich, O. S., and Carpenter, C. R. The educational effectiveness, acceptability, and feasibility of the Eidophor large-screen television projector. University Park, Pa.: Division of Academic Research and Sciences, Pennsylvania State University, 1962.

Gropper, G. L., and Lumsdaine, A. A. An experimental comparison of a conventional TV lesson with a programmed lesson requiring active student response. Studies in Televised Instruction, No. 2. USOE Project No. 336. Pittsburgh: Metropolitan Pittsburgh

Educational Television Stations WQED-WQEX and American Institutes for Research, March, 1961.

Gropper, G. L., and Lumsdaine, A. A. An experimental evaluation of the contribution of sequencing, pretesting, and active student responses to the effectiveness of "programmed" TV instruction. Studies in Televised Instruction, No. 3, USOE Project No. 336. Pittsburgh: Metropolitan Pittsburgh Educational Television Stations WQED-WQEX and American Institutes for Research, April, 1961.

Grosslight, J. H., and McIntyre, C. J. Exploratory studies in the use of pictures and sound in teaching foreign language vocabulary. (Technical Report SDC 269-7-53.) Instructional Film Research Reports. Port Washington, N.Y.: U.S. Naval Special Devices Center, 1955.

Harby, S. F. Evaluation of a procedure for using daylight film loops in teaching skills. (Technical Report SDC 279-7-25.) Port Washington, N.Y.: U.S. Naval Special Devices Center, 1952.

Harrison, J. A. (ed.) European research in audio-visual aids. London/Strasbourg: Council for Cultural Cooperation of the Council of Europe, 1966.

Hayman, J. L., Jr. A comparison of three presentational methods in educational television. Dissertation Abstracts, 1962, 22, 3678-3679.

Hirsch, R. S. The effect of knowledge of test results on learning of meaningful material. (Technical Report SDC 269-7-19.) Port Washington, N.Y.: U.S. Naval Special Devices Center, 1950.

Hoban, C. F., Jr., and Van Ormer, E. B. Instructional film research, 1918-1950. (Technical Report SDC 269-7-19.) Port Washington: N.Y.: U.S. Naval Special Devices Center, 1950.

Hovland, C. I., Lumsdaine, A. A., and Sheffield, F. D. Experiments on mass communication. Princeton, N.J.: Princeton University Press, 1949.

Hudson, W. Color vs. monochrome in a demonstration film used to administer performance tests for the classification of African workers. Journal of National Institute of Personnel Research (Johannesburg), 1958, 7, 128.

Instructional Film Research Program. Evaluation of the film: Military police support in emergencies (riot control) TF 19-1701. (Technical Report SDC 269-7-52.) Port Washington, N.Y.: U.S. Naval Special Devices Center, 1954.

Ishikawa, K. A study of teaching methods with educational films. Maebashi City, Japan: Prefectural Educational Research Institute, 1959.

Jaspen, N. Effects on training of experimental film variables, audience participation. (Technical Report SDC 269-7-11.) Port Washington, N.Y.: U.S. Naval Special Devices Center, March, 1950.

Kanner, J. H., and Rosenstein, A. J. Television in army training: Color vs. black and white. Audio-Visual Communication Review, 1960, 8, 243-252.

Kantor, B. R. Effectiveness of inserted questions in instructional films. Audio-Visual Communication Review, 1960, 8, 104-108.

Kaplan, R. Teaching problem-solving with television to college freshmen in health education. Dissertation Abstracts, 1963, 23, 3224-3225.

Kazem, A. K. M. An experimental study of the contribution of certain instructional films to the understanding of the elements of scientific method by tenth-grade high school biology students. Dissertation Abstracts, 1961, 21, 3019.

Kendler, T. S., Cook, J. O., and Kendler, H. H. An investigation of the interacting effects of repetition and audience participation on learning from training films. American Psychologist, 1953, 8, 378-379.

Ketcham, C. H., and Heath, R. W. The effectiveness of an educational film without direct visual presentation of content. Audio-Visual Communication Review, 1963, 11, 114-123.

Kimble, G. A., and Wulff, J. J. The effects of response "guidance" on the value of audience participation in training film instruction. Human Factors Operations Research Laboratories, USAF. (Report No. 35.) Audio-Visual Communication Review, 1953, 1, 292-293.

Kishler, J. P. The differential prediction of learning from a motion picture by means of indices of identification potential derived from attitudes toward the main character. Abstracts of Doctoral Dissertations, The Pennsylvania State College, 13. State College, Pa.: The Pennsylvania State College, 1951. 407-413.

LaJeunesse, L., and Rossi, R. Influence de certains modifications de la structure des films sur l'intégration des contenus cinématographiques par des enfants d'age scolaire. Revue Internationale de Filmologie, 1960, 10, 90-100.

Laner, S. Some factors influencing the effectiveness of an educational film. British Journal of Psychology, 1955, 46, 280-292.

Leboutet, L. Recherches sur les émissions de télévision scolaire (1ère series). (a) L'influence de la présentation des objects. Rapport de recherche du Centre Audio-Visuel, Normale Supérieure de Saint-Cloud, 1956.

Lumsdaine, A. A. Student response in programmed instruction. Washington: National Academy of Sciences, National Research Council, 1961.

Lumsdaine, A. A., May, M. A., and Hadsell, R. S. Questions spliced into a film for motivation and pupil participation. In M. A. May and A. A. Lumsdaine, Learning from film. New Haven, Conn.: Yale University Press, 1958. 72-83.

Lumsdaine, A. A., and Gladstone, A. I. Overt practice and audio-visual embellishments. In May and Lumsdaine, Learning from film, 58-71. q.v.

Lumsdaine, A. A., Sulzer, R. L., and Kopstein, F. F. The influence of simple animation techniques on the value of a training film. Human Resources Research Laboratories (Report No. 24), April, 1951. Audio-Visual Communication Review, 1953, 1, 140-141.

Maccoby, N., and Sheffield, F. D. Combining practice with demonstration in teaching complex sequences: Summary and interpretation. In Lumsdaine, 1961, q.v. Ch. 5.

May, M.A. Enhancements and simplifications of motivational and stimulus variables in audiovisual instructional materials (A working paper). Washington: U.S. Office of Education, 1965.

May, M. A. Word-picture relationships in audiovisual presentations (A working paper). Washington: U. S. Office of Education, 1965.

May, M. A. Do "motivation" and "participation" questions increase learning? Educational Screen, 1947, 26, 256-283.

May, M. A., and Jenkinson, N. L. Developing interest in reading with film. Audio-Visual Communication Review, 1953, 1, 159-166.

May, M. A., and Lumsdaine, A. A. Learning from Films. New Haven, Conn.: Yale University Press, 1958.

McGuire, W. J. Audience participation and audio-visual instruction: Overt-covert responding and rate of presentation. In Lumsdaine, Student response in programmed instruction, q.v., 417-426.

McGuire, W. J. Some factors influencing the effectiveness of demonstrational films: Repetition of instructions, slow motion, distribution of showings, and explanatory narration. In Lumsdaine, 1961, q.v., Ch. 13.

McIntyre, C. J. Training film evaluation: FB 254 - Cold weather uniforms. (Technical Report SDC 269-7-51.) Port Washington, N.Y.: U.S. Naval Special Devices Center, 1954.

McNiven, M. Effects on learning of the perceived usefulness of the material to be learned. (Technical Report SDC 269-7-54.) Port Washington, N.Y.: U.S. Naval Special Devices Center, 1955.

Mercer, J. The relationship of optical effects and film literacy to learning from instructional films. (Technical Report SDC 269-7-34.) Port Washington, N.Y.: U.S. Naval Special Devices Center, 1952.

Mialaret, G., and Melies, M. G. Expérience sur la comprehension du language cinématrographique par l'enfant. Revue International de Filmologie, 1954, 5, 221-228.

Michael, D. N., and Maccoby, N. Factors influencing verbal learning from films under varying conditions of audience participation. Journal of Experimental Psychology, 1953, 46, 411-418.

Miller, J., and Klier, S. The effect on active-rehearsal types of review of massed and spaced-review techniques. Presented at Symposium on Programmed Instruction, 1961, and see Lumsdaine (ed.), Student response in programmed instruction.

Miller, J., and Levine, S. A study of the effects of different types of review and of "structuring" subtitles on the amount from a training film. HRRL Memo (Report No. 17), 1952. And see Lumsdaine, op. cit.

Moldstad, J. Readability formulas and film grade-placement. Audio-Visual Communication Review, 1955, 3, 99-108.

Muntone, J. C. The effects of variables in instructional television on acquisition of information and attitudes. Dissertation Abstracts, 1963, 23, 4264-4265.

Murnin, J. A., Moll, K. R., and Jaspen, N. Comparison of training media: Trainee manipulation and observation of functioning electrical systems vs. trainee drawing of schematic electrical systems. (Technical Report SDC 269-7-101.) Port Washington, N.Y.: U.S. Naval Special Devices Center, 1954.

Myers, L., Jr. An experimental study of the influence of the experienced teacher on television. Syracuse, N.Y.: Syracuse University, 1961.

Nelson, H. E., and Moll, K. R. Comparison of the audio and video elements of instructional films. (Technical Report SDC 269-7-18.) Port Washington, N.Y.: U.S. Naval Special Devices Center, 1950.

Nelson, H. E., and VanderMeer, A. W. The relative effectiveness of differing commentaries in an animated film on elementary meteorology. (Technical Report SDC 269-7-43.) Port Washington, N.Y.: U.S. Naval Special Devices Center, 1955.

Neu, D. M. The effects of attention-getting devices on film-mediated learning. Abstracts of Doctor Dissertations, The Pennsylvania State College, 13. State College, Pa.: Pennsylvania State College, 1951. 404-417.

Northrop, D. S. Effects on learning of the prominence of organizational outlines in the instructional film. (Technical Report SDC 269-7-33.) Port Washington, N.Y.: U.S. Naval Special Devices Center, 1952.

Pockrass, R. M. Effects on learning of continuous and interrupted exhibition of educational television programs. Dissertation Abstracts, 1961, 21, 870.

Reede, A. H., and Reede, R. K. Televising instruction in elementary economics. Industrial Research Bulletin No. 5. University Park, Pa.: College of Business Administration, Pennsylvania State University, 1963.

Reid, C., and MacLennan, D. W. Instructional television and film: Summary of studies. Washington: U.S. Office of Education, 1967.

Rimland, B. Effectiveness of several methods of repetition of films. (Technical Report SDC 269-7-45.) Port Washington, N.Y.: U.S. Naval Special Devices Center, 1955.

Rosenstein, A. J., and Kanner, J. J. Television in army training: Color vs. black and white. Audio-Visual Communication Review, 1961, 9, 44-49.

Roshal, S. M. Effects of learner representation in film-mediated perceptual-motor learning. (Technical Report No. 279-705) Pennsylvania State University Instructional Research Program. Port Washington, N.Y.: U.S. Naval Special Devices Center, 1949.

Scollon, R. W., Jr. Relative effectiveness of several film variables in modifying attitudes: A study of the application of films for influencing the acceptability of foods. (Technical Report SDC 269-7-60.) Port Washington, N.Y.: U.S. Naval Special Devices Center, 1956.

Skinner, T. D. An experimental study of the effects of prestige and delivery skill in educational television. Abstracts of Doctoral Dissertations, University of Michigan, Ann Arbor, 1963.

Slattery, M. J. An appraisal of the effectiveness of selected instructional sound motion pictures and silent filmstrips in elementary school instruction. Washington: The Catholic University of America Press, 1953.

Smith, K. U., and Smith, M. F. Cybernetic principles of learning and educational design. New York: Holt, Rinehart, and Winston, 1966.

Stake, R. E., and Sjogren, D. D. Activity level and learning effectiveness. NDEA Title VII Project No. 753. Lincoln: University of Nebraska, 1954.

Travers, R. M. W., et al. Research and theory related to audiovisual information transmission. Office of Education Contract No. 3-20-003. Salt Lake City: University of Utah, Bureau of Educational Research, 1964, 1966.

Twelker, P. A. Rules, answers, and feedback in learning, retention, and transfer of concepts. (Paper for the AERA meeting, February, 1965.) Monmouth, Ore.: Teaching Research Division, Oregon State System of Higher Education, 1965.

Twyford, L. Film profiles. Pennsylvania State University Instructional Film Research Program. (Technical Report SDC 269-7-23.) Port Washington, N.Y.: U.S. Naval Special Devices Center, 1951.

VanderMeer, A. W., and Thorne, H. E. An investigation of the improvement of informational filmstrips and the derivation of principles relating to the effectiveness of these media. Study No. 1. University Park: College of Education, Pennsylvania State University, n.d.

VanderMeer, A. W. An investigation of the improvement of informational filmstrips and the derivation of principles relating to the effectiveness of these media. Study No. 2. University Park: College of Education, Pennsylvania State University, n.d.

VanderMeer, A. W., and Montgomery, R. An investigation of the improvement of informational filmstrips and the derivation of principles relating to the effectiveness of these media. Study No. 3. University Park: College of Education, Pennsylvania State University, n.d.

VanderMeer, A. W. Relative effectiveness of color and black and white in instructional films. (Technical Report SDC 269-7-28.) Port Washington, N.Y.: U.S. Naval Special Devices Center, 1952.

VanderMeer, A. W. Color vs. black and white in instructional films. Audio-Visual Communication Review, 1954, 2, 131-134.

VanderMeer, A. W. Training film evaluation: Comparison between two films on personal hygiene: TF8-155 and TF8-1665. (Technical

Report SDC 269-7-50.) Port Washington, N.Y.: U.S. Naval Special Devices Center, 1953.

VanderMeer, A. W., Morrison, J., and Smith, P. An investigation of the improvement of educational motion pictures and a derivation of principles relating to the effectiveness of these media. University Park: College of Education, Pennsylvania State University, 1965.

Vestal, D. A. The relative effectiveness in the teaching of high school physics of two photographic techniques utilized by the sound motion picture. Abstracts of Doctoral Dissertations, University of Nebraska, 13. Lincoln: University of Nebraska, 1952.

Vuke, G. J. Effects of inserted questions in films on developing an understanding of controlled experimentation. Dissertation Abstracts, 1963, 23, 2453.

Westley, B. H., and Mobius, J. B. The effects of "eye-contact" in televised instruction. Research Bulletin No. 14. Madison: University of Wisconsin Television Laboratory, Dec. 15, 1960.

Zuckerman, J. V. Music in motion pictures: Review of literature with implications for instructional films. (Technical Report SDC 269-7-2.) Port Washington, N.Y.: U.S. Naval Special Devices Center, 1949.

Zuckerman, J. V. Predicting film learning by pre-release testing. Audio-Visual Communication Review, 1954, 2, 49-56.

Zuckerman, J. V. Commentary variations: Level of verbalization, personal reference, and phase relations in instructional films on perceptual-motor tasks. (Technical Report SDC 269-7-4.) Pennsylvania State University Instructional Film Research Program. Port Washington, N.Y.: U.S. Naval Special Devices Center, 1955.

"CONTENT" AND THE OUTCOMES OF EDUCATIONAL PROGRAMS*

By Arthur A. Lumsdaine, Professor of Psychology and Education, University of Washington

The topic of this symposium has been identified as the content of ETV (and/or, more narrowly, ITV). However, most of what I want to consider concerning educational "content" actually relates almost equally to programs of instruction of all forms, such as those presented, for example, in individual tutoring or "programmed learning" modes, as well as those presented by television and other mass media of instruction.

Two Faces of Content

Most of the time educators seem to feel they know what they mean by "content." But the term "content" is actually a rather confusing one in reference to educational materials or programs. It becomes apparent that there are two overlapping but quite distinguishable things being referred to. First ("Content One"), what is presented (or, as an alternative emphasis, the objectives or intended outcomes of the program); and second ("Content Two"), how it is presented.

It is, of course, impossible to separate completely questions of content effectiveness (outcomes actually achieved) from questions of content aims (outcomes sought).** Nevertheless, we may, if we wish

---

*Elizabeth J. Hilton contributed substantially to the preparation of this paper. Its content derives primarily from the author's work on problems of program evaluation sponsored by the Ford Foundation and the U.S. Office of Education.

**A perhaps minor difficulty here is the purely semantic one that the single word "content" is frequently used (as in planning this symposium) to mean sometimes what is to be taught and other times to mean how (or how effectively) it is presented -- the pedagogical aspects of content and teaching. Since there is simply no way to legislate out or exclude by fiat this dual meaning of "content," we might -- if we

largely by-pass questions of "how" (and "how effective") when we wish to concentrate on *what* is to be taught, or on what *outcomes* are sought through instruction. Likewise, we can suspend, pro tem, our questioning of what educational aims or goals it is most important to seek when we are considering the research evidence on which presentation-content variables influence program effectiveness in achieving any specified instructional outcome.

In any case, as we consider ETV or ITV content, it is important to keep in mind this distinction between curricular content and pedagogical effectiveness or style, as it will continually be entering, implicitly or explicitly, into the dialogue.

With respect to the primacy of curricular content and effectiveness, Eugene Galanter (1959) once dichotomized each of these two major variables to form a fourfold table. In it, the vertical line divided the "right," or good, content on the right from the "wrong," or poor, content on the left; and the crossing horizontal line divided effective teaching or presentation, above the horizontal line, from ineffective presentation below. With so stark and confident a differentiation of the appropriateness of curricular content, it is further easy to agree, as Galanter pointed out, that we want both effectiveness *and* the right curricular content (or curricular goals) -- i.e., we want to teach the right thing, and also want to do it effectively. Thus, the best cell of the four obviously is the upper-right cell: positive on content, plus on effectiveness.

	Content		
		bad	good
Effectiveness	+	-+	++
	-	--	+-

---

dislike the subscript notation -- try to avoid the term altogether, in favor of speaking, first, of curricular *goals*, or *outcomes* sought, or educational *aims*, etc., for *that* aspect of content; and, speaking in terms of educational *effectiveness* (or style, or clout, etc.) when referring to the effectiveness aspect of how well we teach, how good a job we do of teaching whatever it is we are attempting to teach.

But is the worst cell the lower-left one -- i.e., wrong content, poorly presented? No, said Galanter, rather it's one of the two other cells (upper-left or lower-right) that presents the most melancholy picture.

The point is that if you teach the wrong thing, you'd better do it ineffectively (lower-left cell) -- rather than (upper-left cell) being efficient in teaching the wrong things! Also, if you are going to teach something ineffectively, probably it's better to turn students off on the unimportant curricular goals (lower-left cell) than to do so on important, desirable ones (lower-right cell) to which they might later be attracted. Thus, we'd better make sure our goals are the right ones before we go too far in our concern with the efficiency of our programs. Or, as Mager (1962) put it, as the moral of his prefatory fable, "If you're not sure where you're going, you're liable to end up someplace else."

How Much Wisdom from Research?

Research on "how" vs. "what" in program content

By far the largest proportion of experimental research on instructional programs has been concerned with aspects of presentation tactics ("Content Two"). That is, most of the research -- such as that discussed in this volume by Carpenter and by Schramm -- has dealt with pedagogic factors influencing the effectiveness of illustrative programs, rather than with the choice of basic subject matter. Subject-matter selection, or choice of educational goals ("Content One") certainly has not usually been the primary focus of research effort. This has been true of my own research, as well as more generally. But there has been a growing feeling (which I, among others, have been stressing in recent years -- e.g., Lumsdaine, 1961) that too little of the research and analysis has been on the more difficult question of what to teach as contrasted with that of how to teach.

In the present symposium, we have recognized that questions of choice of technique to maximize program effectiveness (e.g., expository vs. dramatic format; or utilization of student response in various ways, etc.) are properly of great interest in ITV. It is clear, also, that this "Content Two" domain is one on which there is much more prior research experience of which to speak than on "Content One" — the suitability of educational aims, etc. Nevertheless, I shall try, after discussing some implications of a few selected aspects of the "how" research, to deal a bit also with some thornier questions of the appropriateness of content -- that is, with instructional goals, with what it is intended to teach or communicate by means of ITV (or other kinds of programs)*.

Principles and guidelines

The things we have learned from research are of two general sorts. The first we might call substantive things. These are putative principles, or findings, that give us (largely in relation to the "how" question, not the "what" question), some guidelines as to what has seemed to work more effectively. Not just what has been guessed, or hypothesized, or pronounced to be better -- but what some hard data have really shown to work better -- at least in terms of some criteria and at least in terms of some situations.

Then, in addition to more substantive results, we also have some sorts of interpretive or heuristic things that we've learned. One of these we have had to learn is that, just as we know different experts will often have different interpretations, different experiments likewise come up with somewhat conflicting findings, too. Thus, the fact that one experiment in one context has come out to show that something called an "active student response" or "ample use of prompting" works better doesn't necessarily mean that the next experiment will come out just that way; and, indeed, the facts do bear out our skepticism. So we have to learn to brook disappointment, and learn to have reversals and inconsistencies in findings.

---

*"Content" is not the only two-faceted word that needs to be clarified. The terms "taught" and "communicated" each have two meanings also, and it is important to distinguish these in the present context. Sometimes the emphasis of "teach" (or "communicate" is on what is presented (or "transmitted"); at other times it is on what is learned or "received" (or what "gets through"). The student's actually learning what is presented clearly transcends the alternative connotation of a teacher's merely presenting it ("teaching" it in the sense that "I have to teach a class next hour" -- i.e., I at least have to meet the class). Likewise, "we've already covered that" seems to mean that, ergo, we needn't "cover" it again; though, of course, merely having "covered" (presented) it doesn't necessarily mean that all (or even any) of the students actually learned it -- much less that they will remember and apply it later. No doubt we should stick to a verb like "presented" when all we honestly can claim is "presented" -- that is, in the usual case where we lack any hard data that what was presented or "covered" was in fact more or less fully learned.

I think it is important to have the kind of skepticism alluded to above (but not complete skepticism). Perhaps it is more important to have this balanced kind of sophistication about the nature of research findings than an inventory of specific results about what methods are reported to work best, or a catalog of "how to do it" techniques. However, it is also important to become familiar, for example, with some substantive findings, such as the kinds of reported results which have been very ably summarized by Schramm in his background paper and in related summaries by Carpenter and others.*

In looking at those reported findings, I think we have to ask: What is their nature? How much can we count on them? And do we seek data and do studies like these to supplement our preconceived notions of knowledge, or to discover newer and better guidelines than we could derive from our previous theories? I think a good part of the answer is that why we do such research, even though it often comes up with somewhat inconsistent findings, involves two things: (1) If you think there is disagreement among the conclusions that different individuals have drawn from some research findings, you will find even more disagreement among people who argue as to what methods are best without the data before them. (2) The other reason is almost the opposite of that. Out of disagreement and inconsistency we find paths to further knowledge. For example, consider such research findings as those about the use of color, as compared to black-and-white presentations, or about the use of how much prompting you should give (how easy you should make it for the student vs. how much you should stretch the mind and challenge the student by making it tough for him), and so on, and so on, through the catalog of variables. You will find inconsistencies in the results on virtually every variable. That makes you start asking more questions, and pretty soon you ask a better, sharper question than you had formulated earlier. In short, I think part of what we have learned from research is that we have to keep revising the questions that we ask of research. We aren't asking the same questions any more, by and large, that we were asking 20 or even 10 years ago. So it should not be a surprise to find that considerable parts of the review of research that I published in 1963 aren't too apposite anymore (though there can be found a few points that one still might want to refer to in it).

But if much of what we have found out is merely to learn how to ask better research questions, we also must ask: What can we do

---

*For another survey of research, the reader may want to consult the 1965 review by Lumsdaine and May. See also Lumsdaine, 1963.

better now in ITV production and use, with what we have learned thus far? (This relates also to the question of research vs. development, discussed later.) What we can do now is two different things. First, we can take the leads, the guidelines, the suggestions that we have from research, and also from other sources, and we can keep those in mind as some kind of a verbal check list, or, maybe better, we should even use a written check list that we trot out occasionally at key decision points when we're approaching "points of no return" in program development -- points where the decisions that we are about to make are ones that we're going to have to live with for quite a while. At these points, we might well get out our schema of key issues and key points and ask ourselves -- have I taken this into consideration? Have I taken that into consideration? Research suggests possibilities of gains through individualization of instruction: Have I considered them adequately? Am I taking into account the cost factor? Have I considered the alternative of using something other than television, instead of it, or along with it? If we are at the program-planning stage or the lesson-planning stage, are there opportunities to make the students more active and enthusiastic participants that we have overlooked? Or, if we are at the stage of planning and evaluation, are there ways of getting hard data on important outcomes of this program that we have not anticipated and might overlook? If we want data on the effects of a program in engendering interest, what ways have been used for observing interested activity instead of relying just on whether people say they're interested, whether they seem to be enjoying the program as they look at it? What evidence can we get as to how much it really stimulates them to go out and do something in consequence?*

Putative content "rules"

There are various kinds of rules that one could state concerning content. I notice, with interest, that looking back at some of the criteria for the Japan Prize, a key question seems to be whether the program satisfies the educational needs of the country or region. This is really the question of what the content aims of education should be ("content") and clearly relates to the needs of national development.

---

*I will not deal here with any of the more technical, or detailed, questions of methodology arising in assessing the effectiveness of educational programs. The reader interested in these matters is referred to such other papers as those by Lumsdaine (1963, 1965) and Campbell (1969). These are relevant to more general discussions of evaluation as well as to specific context of educational TV program content.

Another question is whether the aims of the program are "clear." We have talked quite a bit about clarity in various ways -- mostly meaning, operationally, whether aims are fully attained. This gets us to the question of how one can best evaluate this, or what kind of data we need to know whether, in fact, they have been attained. One can, of course, predict outcomes judgmentally, a priori, by looking at the program -- e.g., viewing a video tape. But this only postpones the question of how to get hard data so that one can document the extent to which intended aims are attained in actuality. And the same is true for the related question of whether a program stimulates interest. This is clearly a primary concern (though usually given insufficient effort in the planning and conduct of studies) since as educators we must be interested not only in the immediate effects but also in how a program stimulates learners to go on to further learning.

I find much to concur in (at least as the best educated guesses I can make from the still sparse evidence available) in the prescriptive points that Rolf Lundgren has given us and (in the same sense) in a number of the implications Schramm has drawn from the research literature. Having said that, however, I feel an obligation to stress the limitations of the knowledge we have now (and of what we are likely to have for the immediate future -- say, for the coming decade or so) in view of the far from clear-cut nature of many experimental results and the still severe shortage of sufficiently precise and unambiguously interpretable hard data.

Thus, though questions of "how" have been extensively researched, relatively speaking, we still have an enormous amount yet to learn about them. For one thing we have some good intuitions that haven't really been subjected to any adequate experimental tests. If we go through Lundgren's paper, I see a dozen reasonable sounding propositions with most of which I am tempted strongly to agree. Yet, when I look at them, either there is no real evidence from the experimental literature to support or refute them, or else the evidence there is is too thin and too particularized. Research to amass the amount we need to know if we are really going to have a science of instruction thus still seems to lie pretty much in the future.

Alternative rules: take your choice

One can also think of reasonable alternatives, not ruled out by existing data, to some of the propositions presented by Lundgren, Carpenter, and Schramm. Also, there are instances where, it seems to me, whether the proposition is true or false, useful or not, depends so much on the conditions as to be of dubious usefulness. To take Lundgren's point that television "is at its best when it does not instruct," -- well, of course, there's a semantic problem here to begin with. If a program's purpose is to instruct, then that proposition becomes a little odd on the face of it; but even if we interpret "instruct" in a special way, I think the truth of the proposition is not self-evident. Perhaps it may be true or false depending on what you want to teach. Consider two classical pieces of contradictory advice: Alexander Pope said: "Men must be taught as if you taught them not, and things unknown proposed as things forgot." That seems in line with Lundgren's advice. But another widely cited and venerable proposition of pedagogy says you should first tell your students what you're going to tell them; then you should tell them; and finally, tell them what you've told them. Now which of those are you going to believe? Either? Neither?

Maybe both, to some extent, depending on the circumstances. Undoubtedly, there are instructional situations in which it is indeed important for the teacher to tell students just what he proposes to teach them -- or better, just exactly what they are to learn. Perhaps the best example of this would be in basic skill training. Mager's experience in teaching engineers also seems like a good instance of carrying this to a successful extreme. But there are other situations, or other kinds of educational goals, for which it may be counter-productive to announce in advance what it is one is trying to teach. Thus, if one's aim is that of persuasion, of winning acceptance for a new idea, perhaps Pope's advice applies; i.e., one should not call his shots so explicitly. If so, then which advice to follow depends on the situation, or as in Louis Untermeyer's parody of relativism: "The things that we knew are not always true; we must change them to suit the conditions."

The uses of guidelines

I think this is a good example of the truth status of most of the prescriptions or, better, perhaps let us say, hypotheses that come from educational-media prediction as guidelines on how to make programs effective. Even those propositions that derive from experience in careful empirical research on production variables may not always be such a clear guide. For one thing, sometimes it is hard to know from research summaries what is only hypothesis, unverified if plausible, and what has actually been rather well buttressed by the evidence of hard data. Second, it is often hard to know just how to apply the propositions effectively even if they are well grounded in data.

But still, they are useful to think about. That may seem like a weak claim to usefulness. But just thinking about the pertinent things and asking some of the right questions, even without a firm guiding rule, can give the producer some helpful structuring. And trying to decide whether a given rule applies in a given case may help provide a basis for decisions on what to do. Even if it turns out later that the rule is quite wrong, it may be better to pay some attention to it than not having any notion at all about what to attend to. Perhaps it is mainly in this sense that prescriptive rules are most likely to be useful. It is probably less important that one might disagree with one or two of them specifically than to ask the question of how each may be applicable. For example, one rule seems to say, in effect, that we want to have clarity. On the face of it, that's a little bit like being for "motherhood" (in an era before everyone was worrying about the population explosion, that is). One of the problems is how to decide just what it is you ought to clarify. A kindred problem is how to determine whether you have in fact really clarified it. Well, probably you can clearly tell whether some things are clear, such as the purely sensory-perceptual aspects of a film or TV picture. Either the picture is in focus or it isn't. That's pretty clear (i.e., the clarity or lack of it is itself pretty clear).

But it's another matter when we ask questions about the conceptual aspects of clarity. Then one must face the question of whether his judgment as to clarity is a very good guide. I think the answer is that in most cases it is not a very good guide, and the question of how one can determine clarity becomes the crux of the matter. The basic key to the answer that we always have to keep coming back to is hard data on the instruction's actual effects. That is, in some way, to keep asking the audience (students) that we are instructing. We have to keep asking them questions to find out what they have really understood. We must decide whether the message is clear not by whether it seems clear to us, the teacher-communicator-producers, but rather by whether the students give clear evidence of its being clear to them, in terms of how they can respond. And we should start doing that as early in the game as possible, so as not to get way down the road on the wrong track before we are aware of it.

Simplicity and complexity

A further point about these rules or principles is that they are simple statements dealing with very complex things. One must, of course, simplify. That's good, but one doesn't want to oversimplify too much. Consider, for example, the general principle of active student response. There are probably more experiments (and also more fairly good experiments, I believe) in the field of active student participation than on any other single class of instructional variables. Yet, even in this field, the surface has hardly been scratched; and some studies find that overt responding to questions helps, while others find that it doesn't seem to help, or that the help, if any, is quite slight.

Results here, as elsewhere, involve the conceptual mire of the "nonsignificant difference" (on which I want to make a brief comment later). And still other studies find that sometimes at least having students overtly respond or participate is positively harmful, instead of beneficial or ineffective. Now, how can this be? The reason that this can be (and probably is bound to be) is because the human being is a very complex organism and the circumstances of learning are likewise extremely complex. So if we are going to have dependable guidelines that go beyond the level of "here is a thing to look at" -- a sort of check list of questions to ask oneself -- then I submit we are going to have to have rather more complex rules than statements like "always do thus and so." Rather, we need rules more like: "Given Condition A, then you do X; whereas, given Condition B, then you don't do X." Some illustrations of proposed contingent rules of that kind are given in the formulation that Mark May and I offered in our 1965 review on the rule of active student response.

In trying to resolve the question why a number of experiments came out finding that overt responding helped while other experiments came out finding that it didn't help, we asked: _Under what conditions_ will it help? Our guesses were something like this -- that first, overt responding would be especially important where _response_ learning is required; that is, where you have to learn _what_ to do, e.g., to learn how to spell or pronounce a word, not just to hook it up to its referent, or learn what goes with what. Where you have to learn to formulate a new response, and not just to connect an already learned response to a new stimulus, then active practicing seems to be rather essential. Second, that overt responding, as such, is probably less important when you are dealing with meaningful material than when you are dealing with relatively rote or simple skill-type material. (This is, by the way, a result first obtained by Arthur Gates, back in 1917, in a different context; so there seems to be _some_ stability in the universe!) Third, that an important function of overt responding is simply to insure that the learners "stay on the ball." It's a way of insuring that they're awake, and of keeping them alert. Often what is important is the insuring that some appropriate internal responses (through which much learning takes place) are likely to be occurring -- rather than just the overt responding itself. One more hypothesis (and this one has some fairly decent data to support it, at least in some contexts) is that the advantage of overt responding is likely to be more with young children, with difficult material, and under conditions that are inimical to learning -- such as distraction, high temperature, boredom, etc. By contrast, overt responding is likely to help less under more favorable learning circumstances. A final hypothesis is that overt responding will help most when it leads to something differential -- when there are immediately different consequences depending on what response occurs. That is, in contrast with programs that go right on no matter what, the overt response made by the learner (or group of learners) is used somehow to modify the sequence of learning or has other real "here-and-now" consequences.

A note on individualization

This suggests that one thing that can improve the effectiveness of education is to try, to the extent that we can, to individualize instruction. At least we can look for ways to arrange things so that a student's responses have consequences, such that the way he responds makes some difference in what happens next. Let me try also to relate the questions of student response and individualization to some questions of economics. Max Egly says in his paper, "It's not possible to discuss here the merits of individualization." This suggests that only the rich countries have the means to try such experiments and, by implication, the poor countries do not. If we are talking only about something like all-out computer-assisted instruction, this may be true, maybe for a decade, maybe for longer. But I think we need also to recognize that the advantages of individualization of instruction can be realized in various ways, some less costly than others. Learners do differ enormously in native ability and background, even within a fairly homogeneous setting. Thus, to put everybody through a fixed-pace lock step can be enormously wasteful. We are stuck with it sometimes, but maybe we can figure out a way to get a more efficient approach within the cost constraints, if we work at it. At least we should try. And this means, I think, two things: (1) new approaches to individualization, and (2) using mass media combined with some kind of individualized instruction to meet the needs of the individual student or individual small group of students. For example, we might look at the follow-up activities a teacher undertakes or that the students themselves undertake. Here is a place where there is room for variation even with a constant ITV program (and with the economies of the big denominator of many students against whom cost can be prorated).

The ways that such individualization might work out are many.*

*Mager (1961) tried, with what he reports were excellent results (unbuttressed by very detailed evidence, however), an ad lib procedure in lieu of a standard lecture course. After objectives were very fully spelled out, and resources identified, students were turned loose to learn at their own pace and in their own style.

One very economical way that worked out quite well with teaching elementary reading to first-graders in the United States with a wide variety of socioeconomic backgrounds is a system developed by Douglas Ellson of Indiana University. Ellson calls his system "programmed tutoring." It has been successful in improving the reading of children with a wide range of kinds of reading difficulties, as a 15-minute a day "additive" to their basic reading instruction, which wasn't (but might have been) presented by television.

Essentially what is done is to take inexperienced teacher-aides (e.g., housewives) and provide them with a sort of contingent, branching-decision tree. An aide starts by reading something to the child and then asking the child a question. The aide has a script, but it is a branching script, such that if the child responds one way, the next question asked is question A, but if he responds a different way, the next question asked is question B, and so on. This system has been very carefully worked out and "engineered" so that it can be used effectively by even a completely inexperienced teacher-aide. The aide need only be able to do two things: (1) read out loud passably well from a printed page and follow simple printed instructions -- e.g., point to a particular picture or word; and (2) the aide must have some reasonable discrimination of the adequacy of the response, so as to be able, using a check list, to categorize the response and thus know what question to ask next. In effect, this is an inexpensive form of "computer-assisted instruction" without a computer.

Another related kind of system that a good many people have worked with (but generally without pushing it very far) is to use children to tutor each other. I'd like to suggest that rather more work be done in adapting mass media to flexible individual participation, by providing exercises in which children are given sets of questions and a supervised tutoring routine is used for them to help each other.

There are two forms of this. One is to use peers; that is, children at the same level, each alternately taking turns asking the other a set of questions and checking his partner's answers. These might be questions that are based on, or even posed by, a television program. Each student alternately serves as a monitor to guide his partner's responses. Another pattern is to have, instead of alternating peer tutors, an arrangement in which the eighth-grader helps the child in the seventh grade or sixth grade, or in which students who have started earlier or gotten along faster can serve as tutors to individualize the instruction for their more junior (or more backward) classmates. This also has been the subject of considerable experimentation of an informal sort. It seems to work well, but it takes a lot of doing to make it work. Such ways of adapting the mass media, to take account of the special capacities and problems of the individual, is something on which we could well do a great deal more development and experimentation.

Research and Development

The question of research versus development comes up frequently in such discussions as ours. The "versus" doesn't mean to imply that they are necessarily antithetical; on the contrary, they are complementary, though they may compete in terms of allocation of resources as well as in terms of philosophy and point of view. (By "development" here, I mean development in the sense of product and program development and not, as such, national development; though, of course, that, too, is prominent as a context.)

Along with the question of research versus development, there is also a question of so-called "basic" (or fundamental) research -- oriented toward principles, rules, and hypotheses -- versus "applied" (or specific, product-oriented) research. The relative priority of these is necessarily a concern in view of limited research resources, and the problem of how best to allocate future effort between them may be more important than any specific findings, as such, which may have been obtained in the past.

Empirical data in program development

Check lists, or sets of guidelines and suggestions based on past research (based both on the *problems* that have been attacked and the *results* that have been obtained) do not provide us very definitive recipes. They do provide us, though, guidelines and suggestions and maybe a basis for making better educated guesses than we would without them. But in addition to the suggestions as to how to proceed, there is another thing we can do, which has nothing to do with general principles or general findings, but rather with procedures. And that is applying our research procedures, rather than our research findings, for the assessment of particular programs. The thing that I would most urge is something that several people at this meeting have talked about -- Palmer, for example -- that is, to use data, both informally and formally, as a basis for revising each program. (I don't just mean numerical data, but all sorts of data and observations.) Though there are economic constraints about this, and also temporal constraints, I believe that wherever we can, we ought at least to *try* first to make a pilot, trial version of every program that we produce. We ought always to be experimenting with what we are doing. This is not just my opinion; I think the available data bear it out.

Program revision

Where programs have been tried out in preliminary form, and where their revision has been based on empirical data thus obtained rather than on a priori wisdom and insight and inspiration -- those programs have turned out to be more effective than the preliminary versions and also more effective than revisions not based on data. Sometimes those differences have been pretty impressive, particularly where the programs have been revised several times (each revision based on the previously obtained data (see Allendoerfer, 1969, and Markle, 1967).

A further step -- before the final stage of a program -- is an iterative process of trying out the program several times with successive revision after each tryout. Such procedures can lead to revision not only of presentation aspects of content (to improve program clarity based on data as to what is getting across and what isn't getting across), but also to some extent, of the program objectives. Data from a series of studies -- not all of them in the field of television (Allendoerfer, Markle, Gropper, Gropper and Lumsdaine) show pretty consistently that where such a process has been tried, a better program is the result.

The applicability to TV of such findings from other media is another thing I think we have to accept. Learning is learning, and while there are some very special things about television, research results from other forms of instruction can help us a great deal in television and in other forms of mass media instruction.

Payoff from "principles" versus "product" research

If one looks at most of the variables that have been manipulated on the "how" side of instruction -- things like prompting, repetition, color, and so on -- the differences, even where they are somewhat consistent and where they are statistically reliable, tend to be rather small. An increase in efficiency (where we have the kind of scores that permit us to speak of that meaningfully) of as much as 10 or 15 per cent is quite a rate. But for the use of empirical data to improve programs, it may be possible (e.g., Markle, 1967) to improve the effectiveness of the program by 100 or 200 per cent. So this use of empirical data as a sort of applied research ("educational engineering") can be a massive factor compared with the results of manipulating most content variables.

However, such empirical, atheoretical research is not the kind of research that is very popular among researchers. Maybe this is because it doesn't quite fit the prevailing academic standards for what constitutes a good Ph. D. dissertation. But, in terms of practical realities, I feel (and at least some of my colleagues agree with me) that more attention should be given, both in developed and developing countries, to product development research than to fundamental theoretical questions about basic principles of learning and instruction.

Economic factors

In terms of economy in program development, there is an enormous amount of room for innovation in sharing programs among different regions. I mean not only making existing resources available, but joint planning. There are many values to be obtained from this, both direct and indirect. The most direct one is that if we can make one program or even one program format (one set of background, subject-matter, research) do for 10 countries, or 20 states or 100 schools, instead of each one working out its own, then obviously we are far ahead economically.

I know there are many obstacles to this. There are "States' rights"; people want to "do their own thing"; sometimes they don't want to use anyone else's program. But I think that there is a great deal more we can do here if we have some faith that these obstacles can be overcome. That brings us to an indirect benefit of cooperative programming: If we think that the most urgent single human goal is to keep the world from blowing itself up by one means or another, then the most important educational goal of all is to learn to cooperate and get along with each other well enough so that we can at least buy time to do some of the other things that we need to do. Learning that we can work together is a product of joint efforts, whether they're joint endeavors of the Soviet Union and the United States in space exploration or between two schools or any two groups of people in producing a common educational product that both of them will use. (This doesn't necessarily mean close collaboration on producing each lesson; it may involve a common set of materials in which it is agreed that you do lesson one and I do lesson two, and so forth; in any case, we share our resources instead of both having to do the whole thing.) Through such efforts we both achieve better economy and also learn how to cooperate.

Change, planning and sharing

The problems of rapid change are so many and they are so often expounded these days that we tend to become a little blasé about them. But in relation to research, we do have to keep reminding ourselves that things are going to be so different 20 or 30 years from now that we can hardly conceive of them because change continues to accelerate. Great as are the differences between the media which we have now, as compared to what we had 50 years ago, they are probably much less than the differences between what we now have and what we shall have by the end of this century. So, in terms of planning our research and our development, we dare not think only about is it feasible now? We need to be looking ahead to what might be feasible, in terms of both hardware systems and the psychology of cooperation and pedagogy, 30 years from now. In terms of basic research as well as development, we really need to look far ahead. The only sensible way to do basic research, I believe, is to have it satisfy two conditions. First, that it looks ahead and tries to ask what problems should we be trying to answer that will confront us some years hence, not what problems confront us right now. Doing good research takes time; by the time we get it done, the immediate occasion for it may have passed. The other characteristic of basic research (i.e., research on fundamental variables) is that it not only takes a long time, but also is risky. It has a low rate of payoff, a high rate of mortality. So if we're going to devote resources to it, we must be prepared for disappointment and for revision (and that, again, increases the time). So that kind of research ought to be done cooperatively; we need here more than anywhere else to share our resources, to pool our efforts.

When basic research studies are done, I also think they should almost always, if not always, be done in the context of an ongoing development project. In that case, if the data turn out not to verify your beautiful hypothesis, and perhaps to be quite inconclusive, you have at least worked on that in a context of a here-and-now product to which it may be of some use even though the scientific aims may have failed.

Future Needs

What other things could help us get where we want to be five or ten years from now? One answer is that we need to practice the kinds of things we are doing here and share a lot more experience data. We need not only to share research results, but to share approaches and insights that come from producers and researchers talking to each other and looking at each other's products.

Better indices of outcomes

I think we need to pay more attention than we have to certain kinds of outcomes. Let me mention two of those. One of those kinds of outcome is what you saw on the faces of the children that were working with Egly's programs -- indubitable enthusiasm. At that immediate level, it is pretty unmistakable. But there is also the question of interest stimulated by a program in terms of later follow-up activities, including the kinds of follow-up exercises that Lundgren told us about -- the children's activities subsequent to the broadcast.* And there is a question of how we can get better and sharper and more convincing measures of this.

We need to make a real effort to supplement, on the one hand, the spontaneous impression that one can get from just looking at children as they watch a film or perform an activity, and, on the other hand, the more routine kinds of verbal test data or questionnaire responses ("Yes, the program was very interesting," etc.) with the kinds of quantitative measures of the degree of spontaneous activities that it in fact aroused, both immediately and later on. We haven't done enough of that.

Both in evaluating our products and in testing our principles, we need to try to look for ingenuity in measuring interested or enthusiastic behavior -- kinds of behavior that will lead to generating new learning as well as reflecting what has been learned. Another way in which we need to improve our measures of outcomes is the kind of thing that is suggested by the earlier mentioned relationship between education and economics. Here what we need is technical development and research on measurement that would lead us not only to the better formulation of aims (both in broad terms and in specific terms), but also to the translation of those aims or outcomes of our efforts into economic terms. This is salutary per se, and also makes possible comparison of effectiveness across content areas.

It also helps us to get a better solution to the kinds of problems that we all face, some of us more acutely than others. Obviously, many budgets for education are inadequate in relation to the needs. In addition to merely complaining about that, perhaps one can do something about it, one way being persuasion, wailing, and other ways of influence. But in the long run, the thing that will perhaps be most persuasive, in getting us the tools to do what we need, is to be able to present research data on program outcomes -- a description of results that clearly have undeniable economic value -- so that one

---

*See May and Lumsdaine, 1958, chapters 13 and 14. For other examples used as measures in multi-group experimental comparisons at WQED, Pittsburgh, see Gropper, Lumsdaine, et. al. (1961).

can directly show the worth of programs in terms consonant with the resources put into them. There may be ways that we could make the results of research and evaluation contribute honestly, but effectively, to increasing our ITV budget, perhaps by setting up measures of outcome in such a way that they are more directly translatable into dollar or economic payoff terms. For example, "time saved" by instruction as a measure of its effectiveness isn't exactly an economic measure, but it is a lot easier to translate that into economic terms than it is to translate the difference between a score of 140 and a score of 120. Yet, it is in the latter terms that almost all of our research results are expressed. That is one of the deficiencies, I think, of the research today, and one of the limitations I think we need to try and improve as we go on into the future.

A comment on "creativity"

Probably there is no educational goal more important than to be able to develop and assess creativity. How to create it? The only honest answer to that question is, "I don't know," and then to try to go on from there. But let me add diffidently a couple of thoughts. For one thing, creativity results from giving yourself a lot of possibilities to choose from. But creativity, in terms of being merely prolific, is not, of course, synonymous with being effective. In teaching, one may proliferate examples all over the place; but the various examples that one comes up with may be ineffective, or may obfuscate rather than clarify. Therefore, one has to think of effective creativity. Thus, we must come back again to the thing that everyone has said a number of times -- keep going to the students, from the beginning to the end, to find out whether the creativity, in terms of imaginative presentation, was effective or not.

As an aside, I would like to take this occasion to say that a place where creativity is really needed is in interpreting research findings. You can't take the "findings" as recipes, for various reasons that have been stated. But there are ways to use imaginatively the results of research. Findings (or even alleged findings) of research can be very useful as stimuli to creativity. If research conclusions say do thus and so, and you do so and it doesn't work, try to see what changes, perhaps slight ones, might make it work. For example, if I've tried to introduce more active participation by students into a program and it didn't seem to be working, what other ways might help elicit more appropriate student responses?

Creativity is needed in thinking of ways to get better measures, better observations, more rapid and reliable measures of how well we're hitting the target. It is needed not just in creating the program, but also in the whole strategy of instruction, including particularly research and evaluation.

"Significance" and import

Both in more "basic" studies and in applied product-improvement experimentation, we often are handicapped by not having sensitive enough (as well as not penetrating enough) measuring instruments or techniques. One can always do an experiment that yields nonsignificant differences because of too small a sample, not having made enough observations.

The logic of significant and nonsignificant differences is a rather peculiar and in a sense asymmetric one. As some of you know, the logic really doesn't allow you to say that the factor that you are investigating didn't make any difference or was unimportant. It only allows us to say that you haven't shown that it made a difference. So many of the nonsignificant differences reported do not necessarily mean that the factors investigated were of no importance. They only mean that we haven't the evidence yet to say whether they're important or not.

There is also an opposite side to this which is that many of the so-called "significant" differences that have been reported showed up as significant only because somebody did a very extensive, very expensive experiment, which succeeded in showing that some small, relatively unimportant factor made a reliable difference, even though that difference was so small as to be of very little practical import. This deficiency in the application of experimental rationale is another problem that we have to try to overcome to do a more useful job of research.

Educational Goals as Content Problems

In conclusion, I want to summarize briefly several issues that I feel should be dealt with more fully in subsequent discussions of educational content in the sense of goals ("Content One").

(1) I would continue to argue for emphasis on outcomes or objectives as supraordinate to and logically prior to "content" and to urge the more specific as well as the broader characterization of the outcomes in behavioral terms. This seems, for one thing, necessary in order to specify what indices of successful outcome we should develop for evaluation. Also, I believe that doing so is probably

(though putatively) likely to yield more effective instruction by focusing instructional effort.

(2) We need to concern ourselves seriously with educational objectives which are not provided for in traditional curricular subjects. These stem from identifiable needs for the survival, freedom, and welfare of the individual, culture, or species, yet often are educational needs which, as such, don't fit into traditional academic subject-matter categories. Among these are such things as the ability to think independently, intelligent skepticism and intellectual curiosity, the ability to estimate, a sense of proportion, tolerance and adaptability, and various other traits of character or intellect.

It seems to be assumed that such desirable traits will somehow get inculcated somewhere along the line; and of course they may, indeed, in some cases be achieved or at least contributed to by formal education -- even though they are not explicitly tested for and are not really stated as curricular goals, certainly not as goals tied to specific course content. In any case, the need for reanalysis of such objectives is a most important consideration, particularly when one considers the probable gross discrepancy between what is included in most curriculums and what would be identified by independent analysis as the most crucial current educational needs of a particular country (either a developing country or a developed one).

(3) Although it is important to allow for diversity, various considerations also point to the need for a greater showing of commonly agreed-on educational objectives. Both rapid advances in knowledge and the increased mobility of students make it increasingly important that sequences of courses be defined in terms of describable, observable outcomes for particular courses (or programs) -- especially those that are prerequisite to other courses -- so that succeeding courses can be planned on the basis of a more secure knowledge of what prior knowledge or skill an entering student can be counted on actually to possess.

(4) Further, there are two economic aspects of current educational history which suggest a need for improving the extent to which common course objectives can be agreed on. The first of these is the increased use of educational hardware technology, via use of the mass media and programmed materials. These are very costly to prepare, and can be economical only if they reach very large audiences. One could hardly have, for example, programs broadcast over a wide area from an educational satellite unless one can agree on a considerable share of the content and objectives of the program to be broadcast. A special aspect of cost is that the reaching of such large audiences both

justifies and demands very careful testing and revision of programs. This involves extensive development and testing costs, both prior to and during the production of programs. For this to be economically feasible, we have to have program content and objectives common to a sufficiently large group of school (or nonschool) audiences to warrant the investment and to get payoff from the inherent mass character of the media.

Even where the most compelling constraints are not imposed -- e.g., in the production of low-budget modular films or self-instructional programs (for which selection and tailoring through selection of particular local program options is possible) -- a fair proportion of basic curricular objectives and content still have to be agreed upon for a rather large number of people in order to provide a large enough denominator to prorate the development costs of well-designed and tested programs. This is likely to mean some reduction in the viable number of independent competitors as compared with the number of individual firms that currently produce many textbooks all on the same subject. One could well argue (even for textbooks) for some degree of "cartelizing," such that a smaller group of publishers would produce a textbook on a given subject matter with less total expenditure of resources, or with the same total resource expenditure, but with more development costs going into the improvement of a smaller number of different texts.

(5) The problem of agreeing on educational goals and course objectives has been of considerable interest to some of my colleagues at the University of Washington and elsewhere. At the university level, the concern is with basing long-range goals, priorities, policies, and plans of the university on the articulated views of faculty and students. One of the consequences of such concern is the need not only to examine curricular goals in terms of specific kinds of outcomes, but also to examine underlying assumptions upon which formulation of goals and priorities seem to be predicated. These assumptions are in some instances fairly fundamental ones about the nature of current world society -- economically, culturally, etc. -- and about future situations for which it should be the task of education to prepare.

Deliberations of planning and policy committees concerned with trying to articulate goals and priorities, even where the committees are in some sense representative of student and faculty constituents, make it clear that in order really to base policy formulation on actual knowledge of the range of views of faculty and students, considerable work is needed surveying adequate cross-section samples of opinion. Such surveys to determine felt priorities with respect to course and program objectives are needed, together with development of "Delphi-like" techniques and related ways of achieving consensus, and determining the degree of achievable consensus with respect to underlying values and educational aims.

REFERENCES

Allendoerfer, C. B. An experiment in the evaluation and revision of text materials. Seattle: University of Washington, 1969.

Campbell, D. T. Reforms as experiments. American Psychologist, 1969, 24, 409-429.

Galanter, E. H. (ed.) Automatic teaching: The state of the art. New York: Wiley, 1959.

Gates, A. I. Recitation as a factor in memorizing. Archives of Psychology, 1971, 7, 40.

Gropper, G. L., and Lumsdaine, A. A. The use of student response to improve televised instruction: An overview. Report No. 7, Studies in Televised Instruction. Pittsburgh: American Institutes for Research, Rept. No. AIR-C13-61-FR-245, USOE No. 7-36-047, 1961. Abstract in Audio-Visual Communication Review, USOE Installment, 1961, 2, 56.

Gropper, G. L., Lumsdaine, A. A., Willis, Y., and Willis, R. H. An evaluation of television procedures designed to stimulate extra-curricular science activities. Report No. 6, Studies in Televised Instruction. Pittsburgh: Metropolitan Pittsburgh Educational Television Stations WQED-WQEX and American Institutes for Research, 1961. Abstract in Audio-Visual Communication Review, USOE Installment, 1961, 2, 54-55.

Lumsdaine, A. A. Improving the quality of instruction. Report of the twenty-sixth educational conference (Traxler, A. E., ed.). New York: Educational Records Bureau and American Council on Education, 1962.

Lumsdaine, A. A. Instruments and media of instruction. In Gage, N. L. (ed.) Handbook of research on teaching. Chicago: Rand-McNally, 1963, 583-682.

Lumsdaine, A. A. Assessing the effectiveness of instructional programs. In Glaser, R. (ed.) Teaching machines and programmed learning, II: Data and directions. Washington, D.C.: Department of Audiovisual Instruction, National Education Association, 1965, 267-320.

Lumsdaine, A. A., and May, M. A. Mass communication and educational media. Annual Review of Psychology, 1965, 16, 475-533.

Mager, R. F. Preparing objectives for programmed instruction. San Francisco: Fearon Publishers, 1962.

Markle, D. G. The development of the Bell System first aid and personal safety course: An exercise in the application of empirical methods to instructional system design. Palo Alto: American Institutes for Research, 1967.

May, M. A. and Lumsdaine, A. A. Learning from films. New Haven: Yale University Press, 1958.

III

PROBLEMS OF COMBINING PRODUCTION AND RESEARCH

Thus there was relatively little trouble in finding common ground and common language with which to talk about it. There was general agreement that we know less than some people think we do about what makes for effective television, but nevertheless more than we typically use. And the conference turned to the problems of how to put it into use, in particular how to combine the insights and abilities of both producers and researchers to make better programs.

The conferees had before them the remarkable case of the Children's Television Workshop, of New York, which has done perhaps more than any other producer of instructional programs to use research creatively and to guide creativity with research, and in the course of so doing has produced the all-time hit series of children's television, Sesame Street, and a second program series, The Electric Company, which promises to challenge the record of Sesame Street.

The two papers which follow are documents of historical importance because they set forward more fully than has been explained up to this time how the Children's Television Workshop went about doing what it did.

The first paper is by Gerald S. Lesser, Professor of Psychology at Harvard, specialist in the study of Child Development, and Chairman of the Advisory Board of the Workshop. The second is by Edward Palmer, who is a psychologist also, and Research Director of the Workshop.

They make clear that the process followed by the Children's Television Workshop was nothing so simple as making programs and then testing them. Rather, as Lesser describes it, a set of guidelines, examples, and objectives were prepared, drawing on the best available information from the literature of learning, child development, and instruction. The scholars tried to tell the writers and producers what to expect of their child audiences and what their audiences expected of them; what they might hope to accomplish; and what methods they might employ. These were translated into program objectives, and by the magic of creativity into characters and scenes and action. Then the researchers put their skills to work, and tested parts or all of the programs on the kinds of audience they were supposed to reach.

Somewhat to the surprise of many onlookers, the process actually worked. The writers could use the guidelines from previous scholarship and experience. The researchers could tell the writers, by testing, some things about their programs they would not have known by insight alone. The artists did accept the help from science, and did use it to improve their programs.

Some persons think of research as illuminating the past. And some of the Children's Television Workshop research did have that result; the summative research, conducted by the Educational Testing Service, was able to report what children had viewed Sesame Street and what they had learned from it. But the greater part of the research, as research should in this field, was intended to contribute to the future. As results came in from field tests, they were reflected not only in the programs that were tested and altered, but also in a better understanding of how children learn, and what they enjoy, and how to use television for such an audience. Consequently, the ultimate result was a slow but certain increment in understanding that will help any teacher, any broadcaster, whether in the Children's Television Workshop or elsewhere, provide more usable learning opportunities for children.

The two papers that follow are of such importance because they sketch out this broadening knowledge resulting from the work on Sesame Street and The Electric Company, and the process by which it was obtained and utilized.

Yet, two caveats are in order. To combine the strengths of research and creativity, as Sesame Street did, requires (a) determination to do so, extending from project leadership down through all the scientific and artistic personnel, and (b) sufficient money to pay for high-quality research personnel as well as high-quality production talent, and to pay for field study and remaking programs on the basis of research findings. Few programs, especially in ITV, are budgeted that way. Sesame Street had $500,000 for research, which seems large but actually represented only 6 per cent of the budget. The size of the non-research elements in the budget are as significant as the size of the research allocation.

In the second place, the conclusion of Lesser's paper is instructive regarding the state of knowledge in this field. He recalls that his paper has discussed some informal principles of learning and teaching, and some production and writing methods used experimentally in television for children. Concerning both of these, he says, we have "only vague, beginning glimpses," and our "understanding of the relationships between them is entirely tenuous and uncertain." Principles like those developed for Sesame Street "do not dictate directly the proposed production and writing strategies: all [they] accomplish is to suggest conditions of learning and teaching that, at least, should not be violated in televised presentation for children." The experience of developing television materials for children and observing children's responses to them "has been full of surprises and mysteries both for the producers and for the researchers using the visual medium to learn about how children learn."

For examples of some of these "surprises and mysteries," the reader need only note what Lesser has written about the function for children of music in television in contrast to its apparent function for adult viewers of television, and what Palmer has written about the unexplored dimensions of television as a stimulant to children's learning.

ASSUMPTIONS BEHIND THE PRODUCTION AND WRITING METHODS IN SESAME STREET

By Gerald S. Lesser, Professor of Psychology, Harvard University, and Chairman of the Advisory Committee, Children's Television Workshop

Between the statement of educational goals for Sesame Street and the designing of production methods lay several intermediate steps. To facilitate the production staff's understanding and use of the statement of educational goals, the research unit of the Children's Television Workshop prepared (1) descriptions of "behavioral objectives" and illustrative teaching strategies, (2) estimates of the initial competence of children in the different skills to be taught, and (3) suggestions of situations familiar to young children in which the various skills could be displayed.

From Goals to Production

"Behavioral objectives" and teaching strategies

First, the exact intent and meaning of the goal had to be fully clarified; one way to make the goal statements clear and concrete is by stating them as "behavioral objectives" for the child. That is, what would a child actually be able to do, what behavior would an observer see, if the child had mastered the particular skill? For example, one of the limited number of selected social goals was the ability to take another person's point of view -- to understand that another person may see and feel things differently from the way you do, and then to be able to put yourself in that person's place imaginally. Although some estimates in the psychological literature suggest that taking another person's physical or social perspective is an advanced skill that cannot be acquired before roughly age seven, we decided to experiment with it for several reasons: It seemed especially suitable to treatment through a visual medium, its importance for school preparation could be defended, and it appeared to be a general skill that could help a child to acquire a wider variety of other specific skills and information.

The first effort to translate this goal into behavioral terms was as follows:

Social interactions

1. Differences in perspective
   The child recognizes that a single event may be seen and interpreted differently by different individuals. Ex. given a picture showing one boy in a bathing suit and another boy in a snowsuit, the child can express the feelings of both boys in the event of snow.

To further clarify the meaning of this goal for the producers and writers, some general teaching strategies also were proposed:

> (1) Start with the child's point of view and then present the opposing point of view in juxtaposition with his, (2) Have the child pretend he is someone whose point of view is obviously different from the child's, (3) Start with a two-person situation where one person is totally oblivious to another's point of view and develop a need for communication, (4) Keep the situation constant and have several characters enter, in turn, and react differently in the same situation. (Reeves, 1970, p. 4)

Estimates of initial competence

Even with these clarifications supplied by the behavioral objectives and illustrative teaching strategies, the goal statement still only told production in which directions it should be headed but did not specify at which levels it should begin. The producers and writers obviously needed some indication of the initial level of competence of their potential audience and how high these children might be expected to reach. Occasional normative data are scattered throughout the educational and psychological literature, but estimates of initial competence in most of our goal areas were not available, particularly for urban disadvantaged children, and therefore had to be collected by the Children's Television Workshop's research staff (Reeves, 1970). These data gave the producers rough estimates of the levels of skills they should aim to present.

The Writer's Manual

The research staff made another resource available to the producers and writers, the Writer's Manual. For each goal this manual suggests an array of situations familiar to young children in which the goal could be played out, along with specific teaching strategies that might be used in those situations. Without expecting that all or even many of the ideas in the Manual eventually would be used by the producers, the researchers prepared it to serve as another bridge between the goals statement and script development.

Script writing then was tied to each of these ingredients, the statement of goals and priorities, the translations of these goals into behavioral terms, the data on competence levels in different goal areas, and the suggestions for familiar situations and teaching strategies contained in the Writer's Manual. Within each script, writers were asked to distribute material across the full range of curriculum objectives, representing each of these major topics in each show.

I. Symbolic Representation

   A. Letters
   B. Numbers
   C. Geometric Forms

II. Cognitive Processes

   A. Perceptual Discrimination
   B. Relational Concepts
   C. Classification
   D. Ordering

III. Reasoning and Problem-Solving

   A. Problem Sensitivity
   B. Inferences and Causality
   C. Generating and Evaluating Explanations and Solutions

IV. The Child and His World

   A. Self
   B. Social Units
   C. Social Interaction
   D. Man-made Environment
   E. Natural Environment

No effort is made to sequence material from show to show, but within each one-hour program, time is allocated for each goal area. To be certain that some balance is retained among goal areas across the full broadcast year, writers' assignment sheets are prepared in advance of each show, informing the writer of roughly how much time to allocate in that show to each topic.

Collaboration between production and research

What production and writing methods could be designed to convey these educational goals through television? The creative staff was experienced in developing programs for children and brought highly developed intuitions about what makes for good entertainment for preschoolers. These intuitions were combined with a continuous flow of information about the viewing habits of children from the research staff of the Workshop.

A fundamental decision was made to try to meld production and research into a single force directed toward continuous program improvement. There always is lots of talk about educational program developers and researchers working together, combining their efforts instead of cancelling each other out. But despite the pious hopes of collaboration, research almost always is used to police the educational program, to evaluate its effectiveness but not to contribute directly to improving the quality of the program as it grows.

Surely there is nothing wrong with research telling you how well you have done, even after you have done it. This judging of overall program effectiveness is the function of what is called "summative evaluation," which is designed to supply information on whether or not the program has met its goals. Ordinarily, such program evaluation is done independently by researchers who do not have a direct stake in the program's success and whose observations will not be biased by their enthusiasm for the program. In the case of Sesame Street, this outside summative assessment was conducted by the Educational Testing Service of Princeton, New Jersey.

This type of assessment, however, does not give the necessary information for producers and writers to know, early in program development, if they are on the right track, or how to get on it if they have lost their way. To serve this purpose, a contrasting form of measurement, called "formative evaluation" is used to guide the program while it is being planned and conducted. It acknowledges that the program will not be perfect from the start and that knowledge of what appeals to children and teaches them effectively will help to improve the series as it goes along. Perhaps even more useful is the information on what approaches fail to attract and teach children, suggestions for modifications to strengthen them, or recommendations to abandon hopeless approaches while there still is time. Several sources of information can serve the formative purpose of continuous program improvement, including the reactions of educators, parents, critics and reviewers, and experts in child development. However, the most valuable source of information is, of course, the children themselves, and the research staff of the Children's Television Workshop has devised several techniques for providing producers with a direct link to the preschool-age audience. Going out to watch children watching television does not sound complicated, but it indeed is if you are trying to learn what appeals to children and teaches them and if you intend to put this information into specific recommendations for program changes.

As production and research began to search for ways to collaborate, writers and producers expressed some doubt that it could be done; perhaps there were some very good reasons why it had never been done before. David D. Connell, Vice President of the Children's Television Workshop and its Executive Producer, described his early skepticism:

> My background was in commercial television where we felt we had developed a pretty good set of instincts about what kind of show would appeal to children of any given age. I frankly was skeptical about the idea of researching every moment of a television show, and certainly of being told how to design it. There was the risk of intellectualizing the material to death and ending up with a program most notable for its monumental boredom. It would be like trying to analyze the elements of a joke, only to find that when we had isolated all the pieces, there was nothing learned and nothing to laugh about. But if Sesame Street was an experiment -- and it very definitely continues to be one -- this notion of broadcaster/researcher cooperation was the most bold experiment within it. I kept thinking of the biologists who cross-bred a crocodile with an abalone in hopes of getting an abadile. Only something went wrong and they ended up with a crocoblone. Nothing quite like this had ever been attempted before. (Connell and Palmer, 1970, p. 3)

But as the project progressed, both the researchers and producers have learned a great deal about how to be useful to each other. The researchers not only have learned to make useful observations about what works or does not work with children, but to convey this information in a usable form to the producers. The producers have learned how to absorb and use this information and how to ask reasonable questions of the research staff. The following observations about production and writing methods are the joint products of the creative staff's experience and intuitions and of the research staff's observations, along with their instincts based on these observations.

Production and writing methods often remain unrecorded, the exclusive preserve of the creative professionals who ordinarily have no strong reason to describe and analyze carefully what they do and why they do it. The following descriptions of methods inevitably will not reflect accurately what really goes on when a television series is produced; lists of techniques obviously do not generate television programs. But we had better try to begin some sort of explicit record if we are to build on what has gone before.

Some principles to guide production

The instincts of the creative staff and the early observations of children by the researchers suggested some guiding principles and some possible writing and production methods to begin experimenting with. These are separated here, for purposes of analysis, with each idea being considered singly in turn. No piece of television material, however, grows from a single idea, and all appear in varied combinations in actual television production.

Assumptions about Children's Learning

Viewing styles

Styles of television viewing differ so much among children that no single program should be expected to reach all children with equal impact. We probably never will get an exact understanding of what goes on in the mind of a young child when he watches television, but variations in overt viewing styles began to appear early in the researchers' observations. These different overt styles, however, do not seem to relate closely to how much a child will learn; each style can be effective or ineffective depending upon how the child uses it. The research staff described observing these variations:

> Some children can view television for hours with their eyes rarely leaving the set. We were so struck by this viewing style when we first began doing research on appeal that we

> coined the term "zombie viewer" to refer to the child that sat seemingly hypnotized, in front of the set. Other children constantly keep a check on all outside activities in the room while they view. We found these styles to be no guarantee of how much the child was absorbing from the program. (Reeves, 1970, p. 11)

This last viewing pattern, in which a child seems able to watch television while simultaneously keeping track of other interesting events around him, has been described as "dual attention" in other psychological research (e.g., Maccoby, 1967, 1969; Maccoby and Konrad, 1967; White, Watts, et al., 1972) and seems to characterize competent young children. What overtly may appear as distractibility may be a constant alertness and monitoring of many events surrounding the child. Of course, in other children what appears to be distractibility is just that. Similarly, "zombie viewing" may reflect either intense concentration or stupor.

In addition to "zombie" and "dual attention" patterns, another common viewing style displays overt, active physical and verbal participation in the televised action. Certain children sing or talk along with (or even talk at) the televised characters, reply to questions directed toward the children on the set or toward the viewing audience, yelp or tremble in mock fright at monsters or cliff-hanging sequences, offer delighted or disdainful comments on what they see -- and generally respond with a high level of both physical and verbal activity. Although active participation is encouraged through numerous programming devices, we again do not yet know how it facilitates or inhibits learning. It does insure the child's orientation to the set, interrupts periods of physical passivity, and reflects active rehearsal by the child. On the other hand, participation can become so compelling or engrossing in itself that some children seem carried away by their own activity, losing contact with the material that initiated their participation in the first place. How this viewing style relates to the effectiveness of learning also remains to be established.

Motivation

There probably are some people in the world who work hard at odious tasks because they have acquired an exotic taste for doing so. A heavy and persistent dose of the Puritan ethic may do that to you. But most children probably learn best what they want to learn, whether we think that it is good for them or not. And here is where television's nonpunitiveness comes in. The child has nothing to fear when tuning in, no threat of humiliation, no possibility of disappointing others' expectations for him. If he does find television threatening or simply uninteresting, he can reduce it to personal oblivion. This principle of personal initiative in television viewing, allowing a child full control over directing his own attention, seems crucial to children's learning but is in sharp contrast to our hardy belief that children never do what is good for them unless they are forced to through some form of compulsion. Since we always have seen entertainment (which is all right as a momentary relaxant after you have earned it by prior diligent work, but is not really good for you) as competing with education (which really is good for you, but is earnest and hard), we have little experience in combining them to reinforce each other. In discussing writing methods we shall return to the idea that entertainment and education need not be "either-or" alternatives.

Practice

Not only do children learn what interests them, but they also learn what they have the opportunity to practice. For many years, psychologists observed that children in cultures that lacked certain forms of environmental stimulation never do learn to perform important mental skills. For example, children who do not live in modern "carpentered" environments (Segall, Campbell, Herskovits, 1966) and who consequently are not as familiar with squares, rectangles, and other regular geometric forms, differ from other children in their visual perception. But they can learn these skills very quickly when given opportunities to practice them (e.g., Cole, et al, 1971) despite the absence of supporting environmental conditions. They learn what they are given to practice.

The importance of opportunities to practice was a major theme of early psychological research, with studies ranging from archery and ball tossing to switchboard operation and telegraphy (Woodworth, 1938). In learning from films and television specifically, the value of practice is an early and well-established finding (e.g., Hovland, Lumsdaine, and Sheffield, 1949). Whether the practiced responses are overt or covert, physical or mental, practice is crucial. This principle relates to several writing and production techniques discussed later, including the use of repetition, anticipation, participation, and the value of involving the young child's parents and siblings in sharing his viewing experience.

Learning from format as well as content

Every communication medium has its conventions. Starting with the simple understanding that books written in English are read left to right, with lines read in descending order, many more subtle conventions affect the ways in which books are written and read. Television's conventions seem to have evolved without deliberate design, but operate strongly to expedite a viewer's understanding. Certain conventions have become so conventional that their triteness no longer expedites but instead intrudes upon the viewer's attention; swelling music, dramatic pauses, fade-outs and zoom-ins and freeze-frames now elicit groans from adolescents who have grown up on television and regard these conventions as unimaginative and archaic.

But format cues can provide important prompts to facilitate learning. For example, in Sesame Street's first year, speech balloons were introduced in ten-second segments to teach letter names; soon viewers learned that the appearance of the balloon itself was a signal to the learning of letters. During Sesame Street's second year, we decided to expand the reasoning and problem-solving curriculum to teach the child that his mind can perform several essential functions for him, including pretesting alternative solutions to problems imaginally before acting, planning a sequence of steps to solve a problem, guessing intelligently from progressively revealed clues, etc. We adopted another convention to signify the mind at work, in which the televised thoughts appeared above the character's head, signaling the viewer that the character was thinking and working through a problem in his mind before acting. One further example: In teaching a variety of classification skills, a particular song ("One of These Things Is Not Like the Others") and associated visual formats were used to provide a consistent conceptual bridge, permitting the viewer to associate all instances of instruction on classification and to relate them to each other. In beginning to teach classification, a particular visual format was used along with the song. We then were able to introduce variations of this visual format as long as the song remained consistent. The song thus served as a signature, cueing the child to the nature of the problem and to what was expected of him.

In contrast to these positive cases, format clues, including music, can be distracting and interfere with learning. For example, a child may concentrate on the music or on the quality of a voice and miss what the speaker is saying. In evaluating the appeal of stories read on television, Lauren Bacall's voice "sounded funny" to many children and they concentrated on this voice quality instead of the story itself. These children may have been engaging in significant incidental learning about variations in vocal patterns but their attention had been diverted from the intended focus.

Visual and auditory formats can provide valuable vehicles to facilitate the learning of content, and, once again, the "either-or" form of argument should be avoided. We do not ask if a child learns more effectively from format or content; instead, we seek to discover how format and content can be melded into the most effective combination.

Modeling

In defining television's potential for teaching young children, we concluded that, although we presently do not understand the exact mechanisms by which modeling effects occur, simply watching others without any direct reinforcement for learning can teach a child a variety of both socially desirable and undesirable behaviors. One serious drawback to techniques that depend on direct reinforcement is that the behavior must appear before it can be reinforced. In contrast, modeling through television permits inducing or initiating a pattern which normally might never be manifest in the child's behavior so that it can be reinforced. This should not suggest that modeling and reinforcement are separate processes, with modeling being superior. Indeed, the tendency of children to model ordinarily will depend upon their prior histories of reinforcement from significant figures who resemble the models. But television's capabilities can elicit new behaviors from children who never would display them in the model's absence.

Our early observations of children watching television contained innumerable instances of specific modeling. It became obvious that physical imitation was heaviest among children when a televised character performed with his body. When *Sesame Street* cast members count on their fingers or use their fingers or other parts of the body to shape letters or forms, many children copy them. In particular, one device used on *Sesame Street* has evoked a remarkable amount of physical imitation: All the viewer sees on the screen is a hand trying in various ways to make a noise. As the hand tries snapping its fingers and other movements, children often imitate these actions. When the hand delightedly discovers that, with the cooperation of the other hand, it can make a gratifying clapping sound, the hands of young viewers tend to share in this gratifying response. Also evoking considerable imitation are giggling, washing, scratching, hopping, rubbing, and various comical actions. If a character on television does something absurd, such as stepping in a bucket, children will get up and pretend to walk around with a bucket on their foot, too.

Modeling, of course, extends far beyond simple physical imitation. Modeling of effective verbal communication has been a guiding principle behind many writing and production methods. Whenever possible in the production of the show, attempts are made to demonstrate models of constructive communication among the live characters, both adult and children. For example, televised children are shown asking questions as a way of acquiring information, talking through to a solution of a problem, or simply enjoying the feel and the sound of words. Since modeling effects are strengthened through the child's identification with the character he is watching, we decided to introduce varieties of speech forms on the program, including some spoken dialect and a considerable amount of informal "street" language, in order to enhance the viewer's identification, to contribute to his self-concept by implicity insuring him that his speech pattern is recognized and accepted, and to promote acceptance of speech forms different from the child's own. For similar reasons, several forms of presentation of Spanish speech and culture also are displayed.

Observational learning does not demand direct teaching to be effective. Simply displaying activities that convey an implicit or underlying attitude also can produce effective modeling. In this way, altruism, kindness, courage, and tolerance can be communicated indirectly through the actions of the televised characters, without explicit labeling. The discovery of writing and production methods that will convey these attitudes effectively to young children only had just begun, but the principle of modeling provides another powerful base for writing and production efforts. It is conveyed succinctly by the young Black child who exclaimed while watching <u>Sesame Street,</u> "Look! He's Black like me and he knows the right answers!"

<u>Narrow-focusing</u>

In communicating a message to a young child, the less "noise" masking the message, the better (Reeves, 1970). In many learning situations, preschool children will have difficulty in discriminating what is essential or relevant from what is incidental or irrelevant to the specified goal, and this certainly is true when they respond to film or television. Young children are readily distracted from the central content of a program by responding to peripheral details. As a child gets older, he becomes more capable of attending selectively to those features that have the greatest potential utility (Collins, 1970; Stevenson, 1971). Knowing that young children have difficulty in making such discriminations and in attending selectively, special care must be given to make salient what the child is expected to learn. For young children, television's special capacity (Deutschmann, Barrow, and McMillan, 1961) to isolate and highlight the central concept must be exploited, and this became an important principle behind many writing and production techniques.

Television can be designed to screen out irrelevancies, reducing the extraneous material, either visual or auditory, that confuses the child and causes him to lose interest. One example that reflects this simplicity is the story of the hand that wants to make a noise, with only the hands appearing on the screen. Another piece that is stripped of irrelevant features is the "dot bridge," designed to teach rhythm and the anticipation of elements in a sequence. A series of these consists of dots marching onto the screen, one at a time, to a musical background. The dots form a pattern but a single dot goes away to spoil the pattern. The children readily understand the problem, find it amusing, and express relief when the pattern finally is formed correctly in the last episode of the series. As a last example, "The Triangle and the Square" presents these two animated geometric forms against a solid background. To a musical accompaniment, they each demonstrate what they can do and how they differ from each other. Again, the episode is bare of irrelevant or peripheral detail.

Total stripping of irrelevance from the material to be learned must be handled judiciously, because several risks are involved. At times, children seem to learn most from what are considered irrelevancies by adults. One man's irrelevancy may be another's primary source of learning, and this especially may be true when an adult decides what will be trivial to a child. Second, total stripping may render the material so bare and unembellished as to be simply uninteresting. When a televised episode is repeated, children will seek new aspects and meanings and sufficient embellishment is necessary to supply these new meanings. Third, if an entertaining way cannot be invented to teach the central content, and a nonessential but amusing feature can be added to hold the child's attention, the risk of adding this peripheral element may be worth taking. Then the writing and production problem is to tie this nonessential feature to the central content, or at worst, to keep the peripheral content from totally distracting the child from the content to be learned. Whatever the risks, however, television can provide for the young child a narrow, precise focus on central content, carefully eliminating irrelevancies and distractions. This provides another useful principle for children's television production.

Cross-modal reinforcement

Another of the perennial "either-or" arguments in which researchers have entangled themselves is "Which works better, words or pictures?" They have not solved this one either (Lumsdaine, 1963; Yamamoto, 1969). Inducement to continue this search, however, comes from theories that human information-processing is characterized by low capacity and a single-channel transmission system (e.g., Broadbent, 1968, Travers, 1964), suggesting that there is no advantage to supplying redundant information through more than one sensory modality and thus flooding the learner with more information than he can handle. According to these views of information-processing, messages fed simultaneously through two modalities will tend to interfere with each other.

Even these pessimistic views, however, do allow that information-processing of messages fed through two modalities can be efficient if the two sources are well coordinated. Although there are rare occasions when television will present either pictures or sounds without the other, its special capacity is in their coordinated combination. Pictures coordinated with sound effects provide simple examples. For instance, Big Bird, an eight-foot-tall feathered puppet, is characterized by a tendency to become confused easily. In a segment designed to teach letter discrimination, Big Bird is shown painstakingly drawing an E and an F side-by-side on a blackboard. Viewing children attend to Big Bird's efforts until the letters are completed (they are alert to Big Bird's tendency to make mistakes which they enjoy correcting), then their interest fades. Soon, however, while Big Bird watches in befuddlement the bottom line of the E migrates mysteriously to the neighboring F, making an E out of the F and an F of the original E. As the bottom line of the E begins its magical move, a slide-whistle sound effect accompanies and matches the jerky progress of the line as it seeks its place. A sense of comical physical movement is conveyed by the sound of the slide-whistle because it is one of television's familiar conventions, being widely used in film and television slapstick comedy. The children who had begun to lose interest in the Big Bird sketch evidently recognize this synesthetic sound, associate it with comic fun and snap back to full attention. Once the attention of the viewing children has been brought back to the Big Bird segment, it continues to be held by the peregrinations of the magic line and the accompanying slide-whistle. Some children imitate the slide-whistle sound associated with the line. The sketch succeeds in making the letter element which distinguishes E from F the center of dramatic interest and does so through the use of arresting sound accompanying the visual change.

Another type of cross-modal reinforcement of sight and sound is illustrated by a puppet sequence in which Kermit the Frog describes the letter N as having "three lines." "Zap! Zap! Zap!" Even without accompanying gestures -- Kermit's manual capabilities are limited -- the words are curiously appropriate to the shape they describe.

This principle of synchronizing sight and sound to provide cross-modal reinforcement instead of interference is clear. Carrying the principle into actual writing and production requires that we begin to learn how one modality can be used to support another, instead of cancelling out or interfering with each other. Since most existing research asks how the different modalities compare when considered singly, much remains to be learned.

Displayable skills

The value of learning simple symbolic skills (letters, numbers, the names of common geometric forms, etc.) is questioned on several grounds. Those who believe that the choice of symbolic skills that schools traditionally teach is arbitrary and whimsical will believe, in turn, that any early preparation for learning those skills is equally mindless. Those who believe that learning information is useless when compared with "learning to learn" will note the futility of the early acquisition of simple symbolic skills. Still others are repulsed by the adult society prescribing in an authoritarian, dictatorial manner what the younger members of the society must learn. They believe that children will never learn to guide their own behavior if such choices are taken out of their hands and made for them, and also object in principle to the arrogance implied when small, often self-selected groups of adults insist that they know what is good for all young people in this society.

These good arguments are balanced against some equally good arguments in favor of the early learning of some elementary, displayable skills: the value of an older person recognizing and admiring the real accomplishments of a younger person. How a child develops a view of himself as competent and effective remains a profound mystery and surely the process does not proceed in a neat succession of discrete steps. Yet there must be important effects upon a child's self-concept when he acquires certain displayable skills, exhibits them in the presence of someone who cares about him, and receives attention and admiration. The child then knows that he is capable of learning something worth knowing, thus acquiring a sense of competence that motivates further learning. Psychologists continue to argue about the exact benefits and risks of direct, specific reinforcements in affecting a young child's learning, but reward in the more general sense of an older person taking visible pleasure in a younger person's accomplishments surely will go a long way toward making that child feel good about himself and what he is capable of learning.

Assumptions about Teaching

Assumptions about how children learn can make no sense in the absence of corresponding assumptions about effective teaching. Not everyone would agree with this assertion, contending that "effective teaching" is an undemocratic, dictatorial concept and that the teacher's role should not go beyond assisting the child to progress in his own natural directions. But looked at in another way, there probably is nothing offensive in an older person telling a younger person (or, even, a younger person telling an older one) -- in as interesting a way as he can contrive -- what he thinks he knows about the world and how people, ideas, and events interact in it. How can this version of teaching be done effectively on television?

Entertainment and education

We always have regarded entertainment and education as competing for a child's attention. We view entertainment as frivolous, an indulgence to be engaged in by the rich because they can get away with it and to be earned by the poor only after the prior, ennobling sacrifice of hard work; too much entertainment produces flabbiness and decadence. Education is seen as serious and earnest, but awfully good for you if you have the strength of character to persist in tedious, backbone-building hard work; not only does education teach but it builds character by forcing children to work at what is not, and should not be, much fun. Inserting doses of entertainment into such education can only contaminate it, robbing children of the opportunity to learn how to do things that they really do not want to do. And doing things that you do not want to do is what life is really about anyway, isn't it? How will a child learn, after all, to accept the confinement of a job and other responsibilities if we do not start early to teach him to accept tedium? In this view, making education exciting or entertaining is a true disservice to its higher purpose of producing disciplined character. To use entertainment in the service of education is tantamount to coddling.

Since we have been wallowing in this lunatic view for some time, it is not surprising that we do not understand how to combine entertainment and education to the mutual benefit of each. We have begun to recognize that they need not be incompatible but have not pursued or found ways to make them compatible. We perhaps acknowledge that entertainment need not be empty of educational value and that education need not be unentertaining. What we now need to discover is how to make entertainment instrumental to learning and how to frame a child's learning experiences so that they contain the excitement and joy that he only has experienced while not being "educated."

The familiar as bridge to the unfamiliar

Teachers always have known that new learning is expedited by starting from a base of objects and experiences that are familiar to the child and then building and extending into new and unfamiliar material. There may be occasions when a teacher will choose to confront a child with a totally novel and unfamiliar situation, removing the props provided by previous familiarity with any of the elements of the new situation. The child then is forced to generate entirely new solutions and to test the limits of his creativity. Under most circumstances, however, the child will learn new material most effectively if it builds upon something he already knows.

Several examples of using the familiar as a bridge to the unfamiliar are provided by our televised episodes on letter recognition in which similarities are illustrated visually between the letter forms and the shapes of familiar real objects. At the start of one animated film, two boys are invited by an unseen narrator to watch a story about the letter J. As a large, upper-case J descends between them, one of the boys remarks that the J looks like a fishhook. The voice of the narrator intones, "It's not a fishhook, it's a J." This is followed by a rhythmic sequence in which the letter is used as part of a short story filled with J sounds and with words beginning with J. At the end of the story, the second boy says, "So that's the letter J." The first boy replies, "It still looks like a fishhook to me." Similar analogies are developed between other letters and familiar shapes. Y, for example, has on different occasions been compared visually with a fork in a road and a branching trunk of a tree.

Other examples of using the familiar as a bridge to the unfamiliar involve the use of the parts of a child's body. Films that encourage and guide the child to use his fingers to form letter shapes provide him with a physical analogy always available to him and adds a kinesthetic dimension to letter learning. At various times, characters on *Sesame Street* have used their fingers to make U, V, and, by putting two V's together, to make a W. Given television's lack of control over the behavior of the viewing child, our inducement cannot guarantee that every child will imitate these movements physically. Observation of children watching these show segments, however, suggest that most children are drawn irresistibly to imitate the performers.

Another bridge from the familiar to the unfamiliar is the search for letter forms embedded in the child's real environment. In one *Sesame Street* segment, a puppet finds the letter E repeated in the structure of a door, and in another, T is discovered embedded in the railing around the basement windows of an apartment house. When such embedded letters are found, a cut-out letter is matched to the embedded letter to confirm the presence of the embedded form for the child who may not have seen it. This search for embedded letters not only teaches letter recognition but also provides practice in another essential cognitive skill, distinguishing between figure and ground by isolating relevant characteristics from noise. In all these instances, the child's familiarity with his real environment is used as a base upon which new and unfamiliar concepts are introduced.

Direct and indirect teaching

Only a small part of what children learn is taught to them directly with, so to speak, malice aforethought. The importance of informal learning opportunities in undirected play is beyond dispute. On television, direct teaching might be expressed by both telling and showing the child what you intend to teach him, then telling and showing it to him, and then after that telling him and showing him again what you have taught him. The intended message is made fully explicit and direct attention is focused, in pictures and in words, on exactly what the child is being taught. For example, on *Sesame Street* the teaching of basic numerical skills and the labels for common geometric forms often takes this direct form. Many of television's commercials also are of this direct sort: Here is the product, here is what it does better than any other product, buy it (please).

In contrast, most of television's messages are covert and indirect; the message is illustrated in action but not taught directly. On commercial television's family-situation comedies, father is bumbling and helpless, but lovable -- doubly so if he happens to be a professor. We are not told this in words but we watch him constantly bumble. On game shows, women are greedy, grasping, and orgiastically hysterical with gratitude when receiving a refrigerator or dishwasher for nothing. On soap operas only bad people have sexual impulses; good people's sex is apologetic and engaged in solely for purposes of reproduction (Efron, 1965). Good children are respectful and reverent, dogs are heroic and loyal, fish are clever (dolphins) or vicious (sharks). The stereotypes abound but are communicated indirectly through action.

Indirect teaching on television indeed can be extremely effective: Recall the long list of behaviors that children can learn by modeling the behavior of others without any direct reinforcement, deliberate teaching, or overt practice, ranging from self-sacrifice to aggression and back to altruism. *Sesame Street* uses direct methods to teach basic intellectual skills, but adopted indirect teaching methods to display certain social attitudes, such as people treating each other with kindness and courtesy, respect for racial differences, taking another person's point of view, modes of conflict resolution, and accepting rules of justice and fair play. Indeed, almost all the aspects of social development that Sesame Street experiments with are approached in this way. We decided to employ the full range of direct and indirect teaching methods on television, trying to discover how to fit the approach to what we were trying to teach.

Showing the world

Television's great power is its capacity to transport, to show the world to children -- to display people, events, and ideas that they have never encountered before and are unlikely ever to have the opportunity to meet in person. This awesome capacity coincides with the oldest of teaching ideas, the one we often lose sight of: An older person telling a younger one -- or better, showing him -- the world and what is of significance in it. Used properly, television displays interesting events and interesting things that happen to people along with how people respond to these events and to each other. These events, in sequence, can add up to stories, and these stories can contain and convey ideas. And with the stories and ideas we may once in a while connect with the child. We all know the power of television to succeed in that most uncommon accomplishment -- catching a child's imagination -- but so far television has used this power only in ways that seem trivial or unworthy. As we begin to use television to help us to understand what really moves a child and really excites him to want to know more about what he sees and hears, it also will help us to find the more worthy purposes for its power to show the child his world.

Granting this capacity to transport, difficult choices still remain. What parts of the world, and what events and experiences? If a child lives in a city ghetto, what do we gain in using television to depict its harsh realities? What does the child gain if, instead, we show the brighter and gentler, indeed, the sweeter side of how things are and what they could be? In our early planning of Sesame Street, we tried to keep the full range of options open on these questions, but as we went along, our drift toward the sweeter side of life emerged. We knew that if we persisted in this drift, we would be criticized for sugar-coating and distorting the unpleasant realities, and for abdicating the responsibility to show the conditions that children must learn to change rather than tolerate passively. But we somehow could not find the inner resources necessary to resolve that, in order to depict reality, Sesame Street should add more stridency and bitterness to the harshness already present in the child's environment. The drift continued toward showing the warmth and kindness that might exist. With all its raucousness and slapstick humor, Sesame Street became a sweet show and its staff will claim that there is nothing wrong in that.

The issue of showing the world as it is or as it might be centers on how to depict the difficulties of urban living, and here is one simple televised example. Sesame Street has taken children visually to an automobile assembly plant, a fishing ship, the back of a bakery, an African play area for children, a farm, a junkyard, several zoos, down a mail chute, and to several other places that he could not visit on his own. One such trip is a bus ride around town, showing what the driver does and how the passengers handle things. Now, we all know that a bus driver usually is not society's best example of someone who is honest, loyal, reverent, clean, and brave. But on Sesame Street's bus trip, the driver responds to his passengers' hellos and thank yous, tells a child who cannot locate his money, "That's all right, you can pay me tomorrow," and, when seeing a young woman running after his bus just as it has left the curb, actually stops to let her on. Why present to gullible little children such an outrageous misrepresentation of the realities of a city transportation system?

Here are two extreme options: (1) display how people can act with decency toward each other, and even sometimes do act in this way, or (2) display common uncivil and inconsiderate behaviors so that children will recognize these occasions and be prepared to cope with them more effectively. Although we did decide to include on Sesame Street some incidents of conflict among people in order to display possible forms of conflict resolution (the curriculum for Sesame Street, 1970-1971, contains a major section on "conflict resolution"), our basic position was to show the child what the world is like when people treat each other with decency and consideration. Our act of faith -- supported by some evidence on the modeling of kindness and altruism -- was that young children will learn such attitudes if we take the trouble to show them some examples, even if we stretch familiar reality a bit in order to do so. The harsh realities of a child's world surely are out there. We lose credibility to the child if we ignore them entirely and no effort to teach can afford this. But, even at the risk of sugar-coating these realities, perhaps we can suggest the vision that things can be better.

No preaching

Preaching at children often works. If adults are committed enough to their version of what is right and true, and if they have a strong enough hold over children to keep them captive long enough, the children cannot escape. What children should learn through being preached at has been slipping and sliding around a bit through the centuries, but the known virtues always share a fine, spiritually enriching phrasing. Starting with Aristotle's temperance and good temper, we have progressed historically through self-sacrifice and service, renunciation and self-control, loyalty and patriotism, honesty and responsibility and diligence, cleanliness and Godliness, and most recently respect for law and order. Without question, preaching to children -- hard enough and long enough -- succeeds.

We finally have developed some faint qualms about all of this. Many of us still believe we know what is right for others, but we are not quite so sure anymore and we have begun to wonder about the justice of preventing children from struggling through to reach their own conclusions about virtue and morality. Even without these general reservations about preaching, we know that preaching on television, in particular, simply does not work. Maybe preaching demands a captive audience and television's audience exercises free choice. Maybe the difference between preaching and what people have come to expect from television is too great. In designing Sesame Street, we never did consider preaching to children but we did give considerable thought to the various forms that preaching on television has taken in order to avoid slipping into them. Others before us had done so. Our assumption about teaching by television was that children abhor preaching and that our first inadvertent excursion into it would be the last time that many children would watch the program.

No trivializing

For some reason, when adults on television speak to children, their voices assume a strange, "talking to children" quality, rising a few tones, lisping a little, and sing-songing along. Perhaps this happens whenever adults speak to children they do not know as individuals. On television, this nonhuman quality of adult speech somehow seems especially chilling. Although we have no evidence of how children perceive the "voice talking down," its unctuousness seems inescapable and as belittling as any other continuous, undeserved punishment.

Equally unctuous is the common practice on children's television of trivializing or reducing a topic in the misguided effort to present it at the child's level of understanding. Simplifying material for children often is quite necessary, extracting the essence of the message and presenting it without distracting irrelevancies. But simplifying and trivializing are not synonymous and children probably know the difference when they see it.

Numerous commercial television programs display what seems to be, each time you see it, the ultimate patronizing condescension toward children. Take a locally syndicated Bozo the Clown's treatment of birthdays -- special occasions full of important personal meanings for most children. Here's the picture. A group of roughly 50 children is assembled and seated in a grandstand, each with a funny hat propped on his head, each having a worked-up, frenzied good time. Bozo is introduced by a ringmaster with a "funny" German accent who tells the children that Bozo is ". . . flown in at great expense, straight from the Klingenstein Pavilion." (The Pavilion is a hospital in New York City. One of the more vomitous habits of adults on children's shows is to needle and amuse each other, totally oblivious to the presence and understanding of the children in the studio or in the viewing audience. Children do not really count. They simply are props, and since no viewing adults are likely to be watching Bozo the Clown, the adult performers can get away with anything for their own pathetic amusement.)

What does Bozo now do? He gets the props in the grandstand to accompany him in a rendition of the Happy Birthday song, picking the name "Joanna Ruth" at random. There is no "Joanna Ruth" in the studio, the props have no idea to whom they are paying such homage -- indeed, the child exists only in Bozo's mind, but the props are singing away anyway. All this singing to an unknown child may seem like harmless fun, but can a child really be unaware of how he is being treated and how these adults must regard him? Such blatant abuse of children seems so heartless that one wonders how it is allowed to continue. The answer: No one cares.

Final example: We never have had a news program for young children on television. If one ever were created, the news would have to be presented in a simplified form and in language that a child could follow. But this simplification need not remove the meaning and importance to the child of knowing what is going on in the world. The simple observation that television has never even tried to achieve this gives eloquent notice of our image of children.

Writing methods and production techniques

Many of these ideas about learning and teaching are incorporated in the writing methods and production techniques used on Sesame Street. Several principles converge in pointing to the importance of catching, directing, and holding the child's attention and of providing extensive and varied opportunities for active mental rehearsal.

No topic is more fundamental to the understanding of children's learning than the development of attention. Teachers have been trying for generations to find ways to capture, focus, and sustain their children's attention; researchers have been picking away at the topic for decades. What do we know about how to promote and use the child's attention? Again -- and I know that it gets monotonous -- not very much.

The term "attention" has several meanings. In its ordinary use, it means being alert, or at least being awake. But often it means ". . . to pay attention to . . . , that is, to direct oneself toward a particular element in the environment, excluding other elements. . . ." (Day and Berlyne, 1971, pp. 308-309). This function of attention as a gating or filtering mechanism relates to the narrow-focusing capability of television discussed earlier. Still another meaning appears when teachers and parents complain that a child ". . . does not pay attention"; this usually describes the child whose attention drifts in and out and never is sustained for as long as the adult thinks that it ought to be. All these meanings of attention are important guides to television writing and production: (1) catching it, (2) directing it, and (3) sustaining it.

Catching Attention

> When a farmer purchased a mule from a neighbor, the mule was described as being especially responsive to kind treatment. Days later, the neighbor was shocked when he observed the farmer beating the mule over the head with a large club. The neighbor protested, reminding the farmer that the mule required kindness and not cruelty. "I know," said the farmer "and I'm going to treat him kindly . . . but first I want to get his attention."

We mostly have passed beyond our long history of regarding large clubs and other instruments of physical coercion as useful teaching tools for children as well as mules. We continue to be shocked periodically by stories of physical abuse of children as a means of school discipline, and we now prefer to exploit a child's natural curiosities as a means of eliciting his attention. To anyone who has tried to restrain an infant's nonstop efforts to explore his environment, these natural curiosities will seem to exist in a boundless surplus. Indeed, the early researchers on infant behavior (e.g., Moore, 1896) seemed to worry more about "quieting" and "inhibitory movements" than they did about getting a child interested in exploring.

Given this natural motivation to explore, finding ways to elicit a child's attention should be less difficult than finding ways to direct and sustain it. Given a child's apparently natural affinity to television viewing, attracting his attention to television would appear to be the easiest part of using the medium educationally. But when a child turns on the television set, he usually has many alternative programs from which to choose, some of them being unworthy of his attention. What does it take to get the child to watch an educational program in the first place?

An expensive appearance

Children are accustomed to watching television that is expensively produced, providing high quality in visual appearance and form if not in content. The primary exceptions are the inexpensive, locally produced children's shows (Bozo the Clown, Romper Room, and many others) and the "instructional television" programs that are created locally for in-school use. Neither example of inexpensive production seems to elicit much attention from children; the programs simply do not resemble the expensive look of the television that is most familiar to them. Indeed, much of the instructional television produced for school use (showing teachers lecturing in front of blackboards, and science instructors demonstrating experiments from behind laboratory tables) is really not regarded by many children as television at all.

No matter what we think of the merit of the commercial television programs that children are exposed to, one characteristic is clear: Lots of money is spent to produce them (Brown, 1971). In order to compete with these commercial television programs for the child's attention, a program that aims to educate as well as entertain must be of equally high production quality. It must look as good as commercial television programs look.

For example, commercial advertisements use expensive production techniques, including animation and appealing music and other sound effects, all designed to get the viewer's attention quickly and to hold it tightly for the commercial's short duration. The situation comedies that the child knows so well use skillful professional actors, settings that look good, and a variety of camera techniques to hold the child's attention. Science fiction shows are full of visual gimmicks, but the gimmicks often are slickly contrived and convincing in appearance. The young viewer's attention will not be diverted to an educational program by its good intentions. It must compete for his attention with shows that spend large amounts of money on professional, high-quality production.

Music and sound effects

Music in films and television often is referred to as "background," and perhaps for adults its primary function is to provide accompaniment to action and dialogue. But for children, music and sound effects play more essential roles. As we watch children watching television, music appears repeatedly to be crucial in attracting, directing, and sustaining attention. It perhaps has been our most consistent and reliable observation.

Traditional teaching of music to children, still called "music appreciation," concentrates on such matters as recognizing the names of composers and compositions, the difference between "largo" and "allegro," and the structure of symphonies. It is astonishing to see, however, how much implicit learning about music young children have absorbed long before they are exposed to its formal traditions. This implicit understanding provides equipment that can be exploited to convey or facilitate additional learning.

Music and sound effects serve a remarkably wide range of functions for children, functions that demonstrate the children's abilities to discriminate and give meaning to many different musical forms and styles.

Perhaps music's most obvious function on television is to regain a child's lost attention by signaling the entrance of a familiar, appealing character or episode. Nothing characterizes the television viewing of young children more than the drifting in-and-out of visual attention. As this happens, the "dual attention" abilities of most young children allow them to listen without quite listening, even when they are not actively watching. Auditory cues, usually in the form of music or sound effects, then signals them that an uninteresting sequence has ended and that a new character or episode, recognized by a consistent musical signature, has begun.

Equally obvious is music's function in providing mnemonic devices as an aid to memory in learning material in sequence. Almost any child can more easily sing the alphabet than recite it, and the learning of other sequenced materials, such as counting or recalling the order of the days of the week and months of the year, seems easier for young children when put in rhythmic and musical form.

Music and sound effects also provide a direct means of teaching basic skills. For example, our curriculum suggests teaching "auditory discrimination" skills, one subcategory being "Sound identification: the child can associate sounds with familiar objects or animals, e.g., car horn, wood saw, moo of a cow, etc." Here sound effects can provide one direct teaching device, as in the following episode. One puppet character, dressed in hat and overcoat, comes to the door of another puppet's house asking if he may use the telephone to call an auto repair shop for help. The puppet making the request looks and acts in a perfectly normal fashion and explains that when he stopped his car to wait for a train to go by, his car stalled and he was unable to get it started again. As he talks, however, he displays one unusual attribute -- most of his description is provided in words, but whenever he arrives in his narrative at a key phrase (e.g., car driving, train going by, car stalling) -- he speaks this part of his message in the sound effect representing what he is describing. His story then proceeds to involve a baby crying, a cow mooing, and other distinctive sounds, all of this delivered with accompanying sound effects as the other puppet listens in increasing amazement. When the other puppet then tries to repeat the message to see if he has heard it correctly, he finds to his own surprise that he also speaks in the same sound effects. This episode illustrates the direct teaching of the particular skill of auditory discrimination by use of sound effects, adding the incongruity of a normal-appearing character speaking through sound effects as the source of humor that appeals to young children and holds their interest.

A more subtle example of the use of sound effects in direct teaching is provided by an effort to communicate a basic reasoning and problem-solving skill to young children. As an alternative to acting upon the first problem solution that occurs to them, we show children that they can try out different possible solutions, pretesting them imaginally before choosing any one to act upon. In one such episode, sound effects are employed to play out imaginally the consequences of placing a large vase on different-sized shelves, only the largest shelf being sufficient to accommodate it. One puppet (Ernie) approaches another (Bert) to ask his advice on where to place a large vase. Bert, distracted from reading his newspaper, tells Ernie to "figure it out for yourself." Ernie then imagines what would happen if he were to place the vase on the small shelf. We see none of this action; all we indeed do see is Ernie's face as he thinks about these consequences. But as we watch Ernie thinking we hear in turn the vase falling (a slide-whistle sound effect), breaking (crashing sound effect), and Ernie's ejection from the house (Bert's angry voice, door slamming). Having pretested this option imaginally and rejected it, Ernie then projects the likely consequences of placing the vase on the shelf of correct size; sound effects again play out the placing of the vase, exaggerated congratulatory voices, a trumpet sound signaling success, all followed by a magnificent fanfare. Having imagined the consequences of this option, Ernie proceeds to act it out successfully in reality.

Beyond music's more obvious uses in signaling entrances and exits, providing mnemonics, and teaching directly through sound effects, a range of other functions operates including some mentioned earlier to illustrate the principles of learning and teaching behind our production and writing methods. In discussing the principle of cross-modal reinforcement, I mentioned the slide-whistle effects that contribute to a sense of comical physical movement as parts of letters move about and seem to lead lives of their own, all operating to Big Bird's befuddlement. In discussing the child's learning from format as well as content, I noted the use of songs as a consistent conceptual bridge, with a "classification" song and a "word family" song as examples. But the striking range of functions of music for young children is best displayed by the following list of musical forms, each readily discernible to most young children.

- magical occurrence music
- denouement music
- solemn music
- detective music
- emotional states music
  - joy
  - sadness
  - anger
  - fright
  - threat, etc. . . .
- racing music
- escape music
- chasing music
- colliding music
- near-miss music
- reverie music
- graceful movement music
- awkward movement music
- thinking music
- imagining music
- wishing music
- animal movement music
  - snakes slithering
  - kangaroos bounding
  - turtles strolling
  - penguins strutting
  - birds flying
  - elephants swaying
  - gorillas swinging, etc. . . .
- danger music
- trying-hard music
- sneaking-up music
- frustration music
- resolved frustration music
- mischief music

. making-a-mistake music
. fast-motion music
. slow-motion music

Each musical form singly can convey its meaning to young children, but when two or more forms are placed in contrast by means of musical shifts within an episode, their impact can be heightened. For example, within a single episode displaying the movements of several animals, the playful and whimsical music accompanying the activities of penguins and small monkeys changes abruptly to ominous and powerful music when gorillas are shown. The contrasting shift makes each form of music more salient than it would have been if presented singly.

One reason for music's great utility with young children as a facilitator of learning is its capacity to evoke physical participation in the viewers. Variations in musical style evoke different forms of participation. Simple melodies tend to induce rocking and swaying in young viewers. The bouncier the tune, the more intense the physical reactions. With some songs the child almost seems compelled to "get up and dance." The more the child knows the words to a song, however, the greater the verbal as well as physical response. Thus, a song with a bouncy melody might at first induce dancing; then, as the child becomes more familiar with it, he is more likely to rock back and forth in his chair while singing along. All such forms of participation provide important ways to catch and sustain a child's attention.

With all these values in the judicious use of music, one caveat remains: A child's attention will be lost if the music is associated with static visual material. To be effective, music and sound effects must be integrated carefully with the movement in the visual content. If the visual elements are static (e.g., a seated orchestra playing, a stationary folk singer accompanying himself on his guitar), the music -- no matter how appealing in itself -- will not attract or hold the child's attention. Static visuals apparently stymie physical participation and violate a child's expectation that televised visual action will accompany music. Whatever the reasons for the failure to respond to music unaccompanied by visual action, the principle of synchronizing sight and sound to provide cross-modal reinforcement once again is apparent.

Our experiments in the use of music with young children provide an excellent example of how researchers and producers have come together on practical matters of television production. Joe Raposo, one of our exceptionally talented composers, is responsible for much of the original music prepared for <u>Sesame Street.</u> During his discussions with the researchers about how children were responding to his music, Joe raised the question of whether it was more effective to time his syncopation to the primary instructional punch line or to time it to the absence of a musical note. Which would make the message more salient and memorable? Without a clear answer to this practical question, field testing began in order to determine whether the moment of syncopation or the offbeat is more effective for delivering the educational message. The raising of the question reflects how research oriented members of the production staff have become through the continuous researcher-producer collaboration.

Repetition

Repetition is indispensable to children's learning and no television program for young children will succeed without its planned use. It is impossible to produce television material that is always new and unfamiliar to all children, and our child-watching suggests that children would not like such material very much even if it could be produced. Repetition is very important to them for several reasons. One clear function is to elicit attention; the reappearance of a familiar character, episode, or format often will recapture a child whose attention has drifted away. Repetition also provides opportunities to practice tasks as they become increasingly familiar, teaches the television formats and conventions that facilitate learning, and provides the bridge from familiar to new and unfamiliar concepts.

What production and writing methods will extract these potential values of repetition? What pieces of material should be repeated and on what schedule? Segments can be repeated often or infrequently, with longer or shorter intervening intervals between repetitions, in their entirety or only in part, within a single program or across several programs, and exactly in their original form or with variations on that original form. We do not have detailed answers to these practical production decisions, but child-watching removes all doubt about the general importance of repetition in learning from television.

Certain pieces of televised material seem better liked after children have seen them several times. This seems especially true of short films or animation that build step-by-step to a humorous or incongruous outcome. This progression permits a child to anticipate each step in turn, while still holding the denouement in abeyance, saving the humorous outcome for the end but giving the child the safety of knowing that it indeed will occur after the child has followed the episode through the preceding steps.

Another key factor determining increasing appeal with repetition is the child's initial reaction to a televised segment. If this first viewing contains some surprise for him, and also contains more elements than he can grasp in a single viewing, repetition permits the child to confront the grounds for his surprise and to sort out some of the complexities. In general, repetition thus offers opportunities to introduce the relatively complex concepts or situations which a child cannot easily understand fully from a single exposure. Far from being simply a vehicle for simple, rote, or memorizable material (although it certainly accomplishes that purpose very well), the repeated segment can act as a "mind stretcher," permitting the child to return repeatedly to a subject incompletely explored during its first presentation. Even exact repetition of a segment being repeated without change is probably experienced differently each time, giving the child the opportunity to explore all of its facets.

As important as exact repetition, but serving a different purpose, is repetition that includes variation of either format or content. Such repetition with variation is designed to promote generalization of learning and to develop a literacy in the auditory and visual conventions of television. Variation appears in two general forms: (1) keeping the content constant and varying format, and (2) keeping the format constant and varying content.

On _Sesame Street_ the more common form of variation has been to keep the content constant and to vary the formats in which that content appears. For example, teaching recognition of the letter _W_ was the subject of three different animated films, four different segments video taped for repetition, and a number of incidents using the live characters on _Sesame Street_. In these various formats, the letter _W_ appears sometimes as a three-dimensional object, sometimes as a line drawing, sometimes as a cardboard cut-out, etc., but always retains its distinctive features as a letter despite its different surrounding format. Almost every curriculum objective is presented in several different formats so that the child learns to generalize what he has learned across several different forms of appearance.

Another form of variation in repeated segments is to keep the format constant while varying the content. For example, the format convention of the "speech balloon" is used in teaching recognition of all the letters of the alphabet except _Q_. In each of these 10-to-15 second animated films, called "balloon bits," the figure of a character, different for each letter, appears against a plain white background. This character pronounces the name of the letter, a word beginning with that letter, and the name of the letter again. As the letter name is spoken, a balloon emerges rapidly from the character's mouth and the letter in its lower-case form appears within the balloon. As the word is spoken, its remaining letters also appear in the balloon. The balloon then assumes a life independent of the character who produced it, who now is helpless to control the action that takes place within it. Within the balloon, the word forms into the object it names or dissolves into a scene illustrating the use of the word. A quick visual joke ensues, generally involving the original character, and the scene within the balloon then dissolves back to the letter as the character pronounces it the second time.

The word used to illustrate the use of the letter a, for example, is ape. The printed word dissolves into an animated ape, who strums a ukulele and sings in a high falsetto voice the first phrase of "Tiptoe through the Tulips." The ape disappears, a reappears, and the original character, who has been observing the spectacle, turns to the camera with a quizzical expression and says, "a"? Brief episodes of different content, but each following the same general format, are designed for other letters.

Repeated use of this "speech balloon" convention has several advantages. Recognition of the convention whose previous use has been amusing creates a pleasurable anticipation for its subsequent use. Also, if a previous use of the convention has contributed to the mastery of the content, similar success with the new material will be anticipated by the child. Finally, although 25 different letters and the same number of different words are presented through the use of this "speech balloon" convention, only letters and words are presented; thus, the format serves to group into a class the symbolic material it presents.

Another instance of repeating a constant format while varying the content demonstrates the consistent use of a convention that combines music with other consistent visual and auditory cues. Sorting and classification skills have been taught on Sesame Street by means of a game involving the viewer at home. A card divided into quadrants shows three identical drawings and a fourth drawing which is different. One of the show characters stands next to the card and sings a song that gives the rules of the game: "One of these things is not like the others/one of these things just doesn't belong. . . ." At the end of the chorus, the screen fills with a view of the entire card. Instrumental music continues while the viewing child attempts to select the drawing which should not be grouped with the other three. The correct choice then is indicated in a second chorus of the song, and at the end of the song the difference is carefully pointed out. Repeating the same song and the same visual context each time the game is played, but varying the content within the quadrants on the card, has, presumably, the same motivational advantages of those enjoyed by the convention of the speech balloon. In this instance, the concept of classification and the importance of fine discrimination to its successful exercise are the instructional freight carried by the convention.

As with most other production and writing methods, the use of repetition carries its own list of limitations and caveats, and it must be used judiciously. Although repetition enhances some television approaches and adds to their appeal over time, other material suffers badly when repeated. For example, interest in slowly paced segments tends to decline with repetition. The length of the segment also seems a factor in how well it stands up with repetition; longer segments generally do not maintain attention as well with repetition as shorter ones. Lastly, when a segment presents many facets or perspectives that can be explored over repeated viewings, its appeal with repetition will be maintained; but when the child has exhausted these different facets, and no new elements are injected into the segment, its hold upon repetition then is diminished sharply.

Directing Attention

We now have identified some of the elements of television production and writing methods that help to capture the child's attention or recapture it if it has drifted away. How do we exploit that attention to the television screen once we have captured it? Are there production and writing methods that will help the child to focus or direct his attention to the salient and distinctive features of the material to be learned?

If such methods as repetition, music, and sound effects work to elicit the child's attention, other production and writing methods must be used to exploit that attention by directing it, providing the narrow-focusing capability of television (to highlight relevant material and screen out or eliminate irrelevancies) that we identified as one important principle of learning applied to television. At least three related methods provide some leverage here: (1) the use of surprise and incongruity, (2) the value of animation and pixilation techniques as means of directing a child's attention, and (3) including the symbolic material to be learned within the televised dramatic action.

Incongruity

A child will direct his attention to what surprises him, to an image or event that violates his established expectations about the regular and natural order in his world. He focuses upon these deviations from his expectations because they pose a puzzle for him. When such violations occur, he is forced to confront them in order to reestablish his sense of order and regularity. The incongruity demands unraveling: Did he actually see the surprising event correctly? If he really did see it, how could it have happened? Few people can let such violations of expectation rest without working hard to resolve them, and this motivation is a powerful one for children, apparently operating as early as the first year of life (Day and Berlyne, 1971; Kagan 1970, 1971b; Piaget, 1952).

In response to discrepancy, what does a child do? Clearly, he attends closely to it, trying to unravel its meaning. But what he probably is doing by attending closely is to transform mentally the discrepancy to a form with which he is familiar, to develop a hypothesis about how the novel experience can be fitted to his previous experience and understanding of the world. Failure to assimilate the discrepant event causes discomfort (Kagan, 1970, 1971b), and most children will continue to work hard mentally until it is resolved.

Television provides several means of confronting children with such surprises and incongruities. Slow-motion and fast-action techniques show people and objects moving at unaccustomed speeds; one of the most appealing devices for children is the "pixilation" technique that produces the kind of speeded-up comic movements used so well by Buster Keaton and others in the days of silent movies. Also, stop-action technique is used, for example, to stop a horse's jump in mid-air, giving the child an opportunity to observe more closely the characteristics of the jumping horse, but also surprising the child through the novel experience of watching an animal in flight suddenly fixed in space. Running video tape backwards runs people and events backwards, providing other strange and unexpected visual experiences; for example, water flowing forward in a stream is suddenly stopped, and then magically flows backward into its source. Other camera and editing techniques permit appearances and disappearances to occur far more suddenly than they do in the child's normal experience. This abruptness catches and directs attention. Close-up shots show unexpected characteristics of common objects; looking really closely at the skin of an orange or the surface of an automobile tire or a manhole cover reveals unanticipated properties of these objects. Long shots, allowing views from unusually great distances, are another source of discrepancy. Who has not been stunned by the view of the earth from the astronaut's perch on the moon?

Sound effects and music bring their share of surprise to the viewing child. The puppet who speaks in sound effects while describing his recent misadventures brings an incongruity that captures attention through its novelty.

Other televised incongruities depend less on television's mechanical capabilities. Since adults often spend considerable time in the effort to convince children of adult infallibility, one of the most remarkable and pleasing novelties for children is to observe adults making errors that children easily identify as such. One series of segments on Sesame Street was designed to exploit the attentional pull for children of adults making obvious mistakes while trying to solve simple problems. "Buddy and Jim" are two adults who confront a series of such simple problems, but can never seem to get the obvious solution quite right. They attempt to place a picture on a wall by hammering the blunt end of the nail into the wall, fail to observe that the nail should be turned around, and then conclude that they must walk to the wall on the opposite side of the room in order to point the nail-head into the wall. In another segment, they conclude that making a peanut butter and jelly sandwich is an impossibly sloppy undertaking because both the peanut butter and jelly always seem to end up on the outside of their sandwich. Here the source of incongruity is the spectacle of adults failing to solve problems which most viewing children already understand easily. The important element of surprise is augmented by the special appeal to the child in knowing that he, for once, knows more than the adults seem to know. These ingredients have a long history in children's programs; "Laurel and Hardy" and "The Three Stooges" traded on the same combination of incongruity and the child's occasionally permitted thrill of finding that he knows more than an adult. Our effort was to use these elements of surprise for their instructional value in directing a child's attention.

We have experimented with other devices for surprising the child. Using the television screen as a magical drawing board allows us to induce the same source of surprise as showing an adult making a mistake, adding to it the opportunity for the viewer to observe children correcting these mistakes. For example, the viewing child sees the beginnings of a line drawing being formed on the set representing a familiar form of an animal such as an elephant or an object such as a house. A group of unseen children is heard giving instructions in how to draw the object. The artist is in effect the television set, since the lines appear as if of their own accord. As the line drawing is formed, however, certain lines are drawn incorrectly and the viewing child hears the spontaneous children's voices commenting on the composition and correcting the mistakes as they appear. That the television set itself can make mistakes and that children can correct them by instructing the set provide unanticipated experiences that seem to hold special appeal for young children.

Animation

A powerful production technique for creating incongruity is

animation. Decades of the chronic, distressing exploitation of televised cartoons give clear testimony of human avarice and also of animation's appeal to children. Since the primary theme of these animated cartoons is an endless cycle of annihilations and resurrections, animation is used only for one of its effects: reversibility. But its values extend far beyond this. It generates a wide variety of the illogical surprises that fascinate young children.

> In animation, anything can turn magically into anything else and children love it for the illogic that is a visual equivalent of their nursery rhymes and jingles and word games. (Pauline Kael, 1970, p. 229)

For example, on Sesame Street several forms of animation are used to achieve the one curriculum objective of letter recognition. The "speech balloon" format is one style. Another shows a ball thrown by a little girl as it bounces between ruled lines drawn across the screen, leaving a visible path in the form of the letter M. Also, the animation technique of "pixilation" is used in teaching letter recognition. This "pixilated" effect is achieved by placing the actors on the set, clocking off several frames of film, moving the actors minutely and clocking off several more frames, etc. When the film is run in speeded-up action, the actors are seen to move in the choppy, exaggerated, Buster Keaton style that children find unnatural and amusing. In one use of this technique, two live actors appear, each carrying a part of a huge three-dimensional letter. Through grotesquely inaccurate trial-and-error, accompanied by silent-movie chase music, they discover the correct fit. Suspenseful attention to the comically incorrect assemblies, and to when the correct arrangement finally is achieved, helps the viewer fix in mind the correct letter form.

Other animation techniques exert their magic by endowing abstract symbols, such as letters and numbers, with life and movement, permitting them to become part of the televised dramatic action. For example, in producing "clay animation," clay is molded in successive stages, each photographed on a single frame of motion picture film. When the film is projected, the clay appears to re-form itself into a succession of shapes. In a typical piece of clay animation produced for Sesame Street, a small blob separates itself from a larger narrator blob and forms into the letter E. Next, from the clay E are rapidly produced two G's, and the three letters are aligned to spell "EGG." A clay egg forms behind the word and hatches to produce a baby eagle. The word "EGG" changes to "EAGLE," and the eagle eats the word. More conventional graphic animation is used on Sesame Street to produce similar effects, but these omit the presentation of whole words in print. Instead, the letter featured in each film transforms into objects or actions whose names illustrate the sound of a letter. The letter constantly reappears only to transform again. The transformations succeed one another continuously to the accompaniment of music, while a voice recites a dreamily poetic narrative full of alliteration of the letter sound.

Animation thus animates letters and other symbols with a magical life of their own. Children direct their attention to visual action on television, ignoring everything that is not functionally related to that action. Giving life to abstract symbols allows their participation in the dramatic events. Through animation, the symbols to be learned (and even the concepts, if put in concrete visual form) can join in as actors, instead of being superimposed or appended to the action as stationary bystanders.

Action

Animation is only one way of directing attention to the material to be learned by means of making it a part of visual action. All forms of television production for children must find ways functionally to bind the educational content to the visual events. If the content remains superimposed or peripheral to the dramatic movement that children now expect from television, that content surely will be ignored. In directing a child's attention to relevant educational content, one accurate rule-of-thumb is that children will watch certain forms of dramatic activity but will ignore inaction totally.

The forms of televised inaction that children almost always ignore are familiar. Most common is the message monologue, where a single character appears on the screen, facing the camera from a more or less stationary position, telling the audience something. Most in-school instructional television is forced to take this form due to insufficient funds, and its failure to attract children's attention now is legendary.

Adding another stationary character to give the first stationary character someone to talk with does not help much. Such segments remain heavily loaded with verbal content that is not integrated into any form of visual action. Soap operas generally follow this format with, for example, two women seated on a living room sofa, sipping coffee (which often is the extent of the action) while discussing their misadventures or the unseen misadventures of their unseen acquaintances. Although these soap operas are not designed for children, and the tolerance of most adults for sheer, secondhand gossip far exceeds that of children, the static quality of their visual conventions is an excellent example of televised inaction that will not hold children's attention.

A similar form of inaction often appears on programs that are intended for children when the adult hosts, in such programs as Bozo the Clown, play to each other for their own amusement, ignoring both the viewing children and those in their studio audience. These verbal exchanges between adults exclude these children, who respond with appropriate inattention and disdaine. Still another example of inaction common in children's programs is the "verbal gag" which television writers often create to break the monotony of their work. These short verbal jokes or puns simply are added to the physical action but are not integrated into it and usually do not register with young children. Inaction in any of its many televised forms rarely holds a child's attention.

Action then is a key ingredient in children's television, and, as with inaction, it assumes many forms and styles. One of its most familiar forms is perhaps the most criticized: zany, slapstick comedy that often also displays one person harming another. Our premises regarding the use of slapstick comedy for children are that the elements of zaniness and harm are not inseparable and that forthright, absurd comedy, even when its elements of harm are extracted from it, still will retain its great appeal for children. Behind these premises is the speculation that slapstick's appeal lies mostly in its incongruity and surprise and not in its harmful outcomes. Thus, action on <u>Sesame Street</u> is, from time to time, as nonsensically slapstick as the real world is nonsensically slapstick, from time to time. Surely our larger aim on children's television should be for larger doses of wit, whimsy, and useful knowledge, but small doses of good, honest, forthright silliness can only make us more credible to our children who, after all, know as well as we do how absurd life at times can be.

Other examples of the importance of action are those in which the instructional content is engaged directly in the visual events instead of being imposed upon them superfluously. Some examples from <u>Sesame Street</u> already have illustrated how animation and pixilation techniques are used to integrate the educational content with the visual action. Other techniques to integrate action and content appear in the following examples: As Big Bird (the eight-foot tall puppet who is clumsy and not very bright but charming and lovable) enters <u>Sesame Street</u> from the right, a small letter <u>h</u> enters from the left. Big Bird greets the <u>h</u> amiably and then decides that, since he is tired, the <u>h</u> looks like a comfortable place to sit. As Big Bird tries to sit on the <u>h</u>, it moves away from him to off-screen, the accompanying sound effect communicating that the h considers Big Bird too large and heavy to sit on it. Jointly, Big Bird and the letter decide that, given their relative sizes, the h should sit on Big Bird instead of the reverse. Here, the h is an essential part of the action and inevitably draws the children's attention.

In a similar Sesame Street incident, Big Bird is left to guard a three-dimensional i. As soon as Big Bird is left alone with his charge, the dot of the i jumps down from its position. Alarmed that he will be accused of failing his responsibility if the dot escapes, Big Bird gives chase. The dot eludes him, eventually disappears over a fence, but then returns and Big Bird is redeemed. By endowing the dot on the i with a magical life of its own, the episode includes a distinctive feature of the letter in the visual action and makes it highly memorable.

In one script Kermit, the saturnine but gentlemanly puppet frog, involves the letter W in the action accompanying his lecture describing the letter's attributes. Indeed, in this instance, all of the action is initiated by the incongruously movable letter W itself, while Kermit becomes more and more perplexed by the letter's antics. In the first segment, the W progressively deteriorates into its component parts (W, to N, to V, etc.) as a consequence of the Cookie Monster's voracious appetite, with Kermit desperately trying to retain his composure in the face of these unexpected events and to keep up in his lecture. In the second segment, the W comes to life as Kermit names selected words beginning with W, and the W itself acts them out. After a series of more minor surprises produced by the W acting out such words as "walk," and "wander," the W engages Kermit in mock battle when Kermit continues with such words as "war," "weakening," and "woe is me!" Again, the action is salient and includes the educational content directly within it.

Puppets also appear in another example of making symbols the focus of dramatic action. Two puppets -- Bert and Ernie – become involved in a dispute over who has access to a cabinet containing cookies. Bert, in an effort to establish his exclusive right of access to the cabinet, has painted a B for Bert on the front doors of the cabinet. Ernie has noticed that the letter spans the division between the doors. In apparently innocent elaboration, Ernie establishes that the initial on the door designates the name of the person who is allowed to enter the cabinet for cookies, and Bert impatiently confirms the rule. Ernie then matter-of-factly opens wide the right-hand cabinet door, removing from sight the bumps on the B and leaving a skinny but discriminable E for Ernie, and helps himself to a snack.

Given the salience of action in directing children's attention, including the educational content as an inherent actor in the action seems certain to enhance the chance of it being observed closely and therefore learned. When the content is instrumentally involved in the movement of a segment, it cannot be ignored. To the extent that the segment is remembered, the content is remembered. When not integrated into the action, content as the intended signal is lost in the noise of the salient action.

Sustaining Attention

To teach effectively, the child's attention must not only be caught and focused, but it also must be sustained for periods of time that are sufficiently long to allow learning. It is this "attention-span" meaning that is contained in the common complaint of teachers and parents that "I just can't get him (her) to pay attention!" This usually is applied to the child whose attention may be caught momentarily, but who will not hold still long enough to persist in completing the task at hand. What production and writing techniques induce this necessary sustaining of attention over time?

Humor

Since we have regarded humor as a slightly disreputable diversion from the hard, serious work of education (and have regarded teachers who indulge in it as coddling or currying favor with their students), we know virtually nothing about how to make humor instrumental to learning. Forms of education that can rely upon the captivity of its students perhaps can continue to survive without such knowledge, but the televised teaching of children is so completely dependent upon the effective use of humor that some beginning understanding of it is demanded. Yet, in children, humor probably is as much a matter of individual taste as it is in adults and therefore it seems to defy neat generalization.

Can humor be analyzed? Recall David Connell's admonition, when he was worrying about overintellectualizing children's television, about the risks in analyzing the elements of a joke: Nothing is learned and nothing remains to be laughed at. But since there is no more important single ingredient in children's television than humor, it may be worthwhile to identify a few consistencies that do appear in what children seem to find funny.

Several of these sources of humor for young children contain the surprise and farcical incongruities that I described earlier as being so useful in directing a child's attention. Slapstick comedy indeed is a favorite with preschoolers and they find it more amusing than any other comedy form we have observed. They laugh when Ernie outsmarts Bert, when Bert retaliates, when the Cookie Monster foils one of Kermit's lectures, and when a chef falls down with his cakes and pies. The exaggerated physical action characteristic of slapstick seems related to its success with children. Although there are some forms of play with words that young children do find amusing, what seems funny to young children tends to be physically rather than verbally funny. Stand-up comedians attract little attention until they fall down, not necessarily because falling down is injurious but because of the unexpectedness of this action.

Trickery always has been an essential element in slapstick comedy, where one person, through guile, takes advantage of another. But today a more advanced level of morality seems to characterize the slapstick comedy that amuses young children: the "underdog-turns-the-tables" form of justice. Here the "worm turns," and the person who is attempting to take advantage of another through trickery ends up at a disadvantage himself -- being tricked through his own guile or cunning. For example on Sesame Street, a puppet Ernie (innocent and guileless in this episode) encounters a shifty Salesman puppet dressed in trench coat and slouch hat, who tries to sell Ernie a collection of cut-out number 8's. The Salesman's manner is insidious and fraudulent; he flatters Ernie, agrees with everything Ernie says through a soothing "Riiiight," and engages in other forms of swindling persuasion that clearly communicate his belief that Ernie is an easy mark. In the earlier days of slapstick comedy, the episode might have ended with the Salesman's successful sale. But today the episode has a more sophisticated outcome. Ernie gently frustrates the Salesman by having already acquired a large stock of cut-out numbers, although he has no 8's. Explaining that he has no money, Ernie offers to exchange his own number collection for the Salesman's 8's, depriving the Salesman of his opportunity to make a financial profit. The innocent Ernie has turned the tables and the would-be trickster instead becomes the victim. Justice is restored. Although Sesame Street's producers and writers had some early misgivings about how well young children would understand the intended salesman characterization and the justice represented in the worm-turning outcome, this and similar episodes, with repetition, were understood by and entertained young children.

Another example illustrates other sources of humor for young children: the incongruity of adults making obvious errors and the humor derived from idiosyncracies of character and exaggeration of style. A puppet named Professor Hastings, who verges on senility, gives comically confused lectures about such diverse matters as the shapes of letters and the benefits of physical exercise, interrupting each lecture at unpredictable occasions for short naps. Kermit the Frog acts as introducer and assistant to the Professor, doggedly unraveling the Professor's confusions and gently awakening him from his naps so that the lectures can continue. Amidst the Professor's rambling confusions, he is sporadically capable of remarkably clear insights, discovering in a sudden revelation that his assistant Kermit, whom the Professor has been perceiving and addressing as "young man," is really a frog: "Young man, do you realize that you are a frog?" Or, when failing to rise from a deep knee bend while lecturing on the benefits of physical exercise and consequently remaining bent over and observing the ground, the Professor remarks, "Young man, do you realize that you have webbed feet?" All of this illustrates several humorous uses of incongruity and surprise, but also reflects the use of character humor and the comic exaggeration of style as means of sustaining attention.

Another source of humor for children stems from the suspense attached to waiting for the incongruous to occur. The viewing child cannot predict the exact outcome, but he knows that a particular format will follow a predictable sequence in its early stages before proceeding to an unexpected conclusion. For example, a series of short animated films is designed to teach counting backwards from ten. In these films, an identical situation -- a countdown to a rocket blast-off -- results in a variety of comic endings. The launch director counts off the seconds in a solemn voice as a surrounding group of dignitaries waits expectantly. The numbers appear at the top of the screen as the countdown progresses. In every film but one, something catastrophic happens to embarrass the launch director: The rocket blasts off prematurely leaving the charred launch director sheepishly completing the countdown for his disgruntled audience; the rocket blasts off at the right moment but in the wrong direction and disappears into the ground; the launch director himself blasts off, his panic-stricken count of "Oooooone," fading in the distance, and so on. To the naturally suspenseful situation of the rocket countdown is added the additional suspense of waiting for a particular form of disastrous payoff, with the child's attention being drawn compellingly to the number sequence. The one exception to the otherwise consistently catastrophic launches is a successful launch which is greeted with cheers and waving of banners. This straight version itself becomes comic. The viewer has come to expect incongrous disaster, in what precise form he cannot anticipate; he now is further surprised by incongruous success.

Language can be another source of humor for children. Although play with words, divorced from action, must be used cautiously, most children do take pleasure in playing with language and certain emphases on verbal humor on Sesame Street are designed to promote this pleasure. Several catch phrases used repeatedly for comic effect have been widely recognized and repeated by viewing children as part of their spontaneous play away from the set: For example, "Cookie!" repeated in guttural tones by the voracious monster puppet who plagues Ernie and Kermit the Frog; or the insidiously soothing "Riiiiight!" uttered so persuasively by the mysterious salesman puppet who tries to sell Ernie everything from fresh air in a bottle to the number 8. In addition to being fun to repeat, such phrases call attention to the idiosyncratic nature of spoken language and the social purposes to which it can be put.

Alliteration and rhyming in language also can be used to produce comic effects. For example, the story of "Ira and Inez," and other segments like it, is a whimsical alliterative fable enacted by puppets, with interspersed narration read by one of the human characters on Sesame Street. In this fable, almost all the words used begin with the sound of the letter i, carrying alliteration to the point of comic exaggeration and focusing attention on the sound of the letter to be taught.

A related use of wordplay is contained in "The Story of Wanda the Witch," an animated film designed to teach recognition of the letter W and its associated sound. Included in this film is a brief section at both beginning and end in which the witch uses her wand to write the letter W as an off-camera voice announces: "This weird story of Wanda the Witch is brought to you courtesy of the letter W." The story includes 50 repetitions of the sound of the initial W in one minute and sixteen seconds. The female narrator employs a harsh, penetrating vocal quality, appropriate to a story about a witch, amusing to the children observed watching the film, and also effective in making salient the sound of the letter W. Here, alliteration is used for the fun of wordplay and for its usefulness in focusing on initial letter sounds. Similarly, rhyming can be used both for fun and as an exercise in auditory discrimination.

Wordplay also can capitalize upon children's enjoyment of certain large words and nonsense words that seem to hold a certain magic for children. "Bubble," "vigilante," "Monday," and "neighborhood" all seem to roll around on the tongue, and when children hear them, they tend to try to repeat them. Invented nonsense words also may possess this magic, and Sesame Street's writers constantly attempt to create new tongue-tickling words that acquire their own meaning on the show.

Again, a caution: Although young children seem to enjoy wordplay, they do not respond well to puns and other play on words. Puns inevitably depend upon the double meanings of words and phrases, and perhaps because young children do not possess such verbal sophistication or because puns generally are unattached to television's visual action, these verbal pyrotechnics do not seem to interest or amuse young children.

In addition to sustaining the attention of young viewers, humor serves another function on Sesame Street: attracting parents and older siblings to share the young children's viewing. In discussing television's potential for providing shared experiences within families, I noted both the importance and the infrequency of such sharing. To capture the interest of older family members, several forms of humor are used: verbal humor, spoofs on familiar television game shows and soap operas, the use of guest celebrities, etc. This principle of parent and sibling involvement, however, also had its upper limits. Although every effort was made to induce family involvement instead of using Sesame Street as the traditional baby-sitter, nothing was included in the program solely to attract this older audience and nothing was made to depend entirely upon their participation with the young child.

One final caveat: Granting the power of humor in sustaining children's attention, it must be used with care lest it compete with the intended instruction. Comedy has been most successfully used when the comic moment coincides perfectly with the critical learning opportunity. Otherwise, the child may learn the joke but not the lesson. Of course, even when the educational message is submerged by the humor, all may not be lost. Simply learning to laugh is not a useless lesson, all by itself.

Anticipation and participation

We call it the "James Earl Jones Effect."

The use of humor is one way to get parents and older siblings to watch with younger children. The appearance of well-known guest celebrities is another. Some celebrities, for example Batman and Robin, are enlisted because of their authority directly with four-year-olds. But others not so familiar to the preschooler, like Burt Lancaster, Carol Burnett, and Odetta, are used for their appeal to the older members of the family. James Earl Jones was one of the first celebrities to offer to help by appearing on Sesame Street, and his performance yielded some unexpected returns.

We asked Mr. Jones, a stage and motion picture actor of

imposing voice and appearance, to recite the alphabet in any manner he desired, so long as he paused long enough between letters to permit editing of the video tape. Mr. Jones' recitation of the alphabet takes a full minute and a half. He stares compellingly at the camera throughout. At this time, his head was shaved for his role of Jack Johnson in the "Great White Hope" and his bald head gleams in the close-up. His immense hollow voice booms the letter names ominously. His lip movements are so exaggerated that they can easily be read without the sound. The performance should be seen by every actor who ever complained about his lines.

As Mr. Jones recites the letters, they appear on alternate sides of his head. Each letter appears visually for a moment before it is named. Once named, the letter disappears, and another brief pause ensues before the next letter appears and is named. So powerful is Mr. Jones' presence that we were concerned that very young children might be frightened, but observation of viewing children established the contrary, and still further observation confirmed the presence of the James Earl Jones Effect.

The effect appears in stages. The first time a child sees the Jones' performance, he begins almost at once to respond to the implicit invitation to say the alphabet along with the performer. On somewhat later repetitions, the child begins to name the letter as soon as it appears, before Mr. Jones has named it; Mr. Jones' naming of the letter then confirms or corrects the child's identification of it. With still further repetition, the child begins to anticipate the printed symbol. As soon as the preceding letter disappears, the viewer names the next, saying the letter before Mr. Jones does. Even without the capability of two-way interaction between television and the viewer, the child progresses from following the instructional message to anticipating it. The pace of the presentation induces the child to shout out the next letter before it actually appears, its appearance then confirming or disconfirming the child's response.

The apparent value of anticipation in the James Earl Jones sequence led us to try to induce it deliberately. When Pat Paulsen volunteered to perform, he was asked to recite (the alphabet, the sequence of counting numbers, etc.) with several hesitations, as if he were unable to recall the correct sequence. The timing of the performance is roughly the same as Mr. Jones' performance: the letter appears, pause, letter is named, pause, letter disappears, pause, next letter appears, pause, etc., until Mr. Paulsen falters. At this point, the letter matted next to his head flashes several times as if to remind him (or induce him to think hard); Mr. Paulsen sneaks a quick look at the letter, names it in happy relief, and goes on. Again, the pace allows the child to anticipate, to respond overtly, and then to have his response checked against the letter's or number's actual appearance.

This anticipation effect, discovered by accident but apparently powerful in sustaining attention, now appears in other forms on Sesame Street. For example, to teach the contrasting meanings of the relational words "around," "through," and "over," five children appear in a three-minute, live-action film playing "Follow the Leader." The children shout out each of the words and then demonstrate its meaning by going "around" a clothesline in a backyard, "through" a large pipe in a junkyard, and then "over" a sawhorse in a lumberyard. Our Gang Comedy music accompanies their activity. One child fails to negotiate the going "around," "through," and "over" on his first try, but remains cheerfully willing to try again and is helped by the other children until he succeeds. At this point, the anticipation effect is introduced: After establishing the meaning of words by showing the children acting them out while labeling them verbally, the film is run in reverse action, with the children seen actually moving backward physically through each of the demonstrations although still moving "over," "through," and "around." This provides an opportunity to rehearse the meaning of these words. The children are seen jumping over the sawhorse backwards (a visually surprising spectacle as each child jumps high, but in a backward direction), then they shout the word "over." While watching the reversed action the viewer has had time to anticipate the label "over"; while watching the children demonstrate going "through" the pipe in reverse, the viewer can anticipate that label before the children supply it, and the film ends with a similar opportunity to anticipate and rehearse the word "around."

Incidentally, this segment illustrates the effort made on Sesame Street to build into each episode whatever surplus values can be introduced without distraction from its central message. Although the film is primarily designed to teach the contrasting meanings of "around, through, and over," note that the child who often fails on his first efforts to perform these activities maintains a cheerful, undefeated attitude in the face of his failure and persists until he succeeds. Note that the other children playing "Follow the Leader" do not deride or mock his failures, but take commiserating notice of them and then help him to succeed. Note also the magical incongruity and surprise inherent in the reverse physical movements during the rehearsal phase of the film, a valuable device for holding the viewer's attention.

These examples demonstrate the inducing of anticipation within a segment of the program. Several segments may be arranged sequentially to provide another inducement to anticipation. For example, a sequence on letter teaching will start with a human or puppet character on the street providing a preliminary lead-in to a film or animated segment on the same letter, which then is followed by another illustration of the letter's use in words, either by returning to the human or puppet character or through another film or animated sequence. The sequence of segments, all focused on the same content, is designed to induce a learning set or anticipation for each segment in turn.

Inducing anticipation is one means of inducing active participation. We assume that getting the child to respond verbally or physically promotes both entertainment and learning values, interrupts periods of physical passivity, and insures active rehearsal.

The ability to recite the alphabet is regarded by many as a relatively trivial skill. We had several reasons for including it on Sesame Street, however, and it illustrates our efforts to induce verbal and physical participation. We included alphabet recitation because (1) it can become a badge of competence for the very young child -- an important displayable skill, (2) it seemed important to include in each Sesame Street program all of the letters of the alphabet, lest any viewer be misled to believe that the few letters stressed in each show were the complete list, (3) by presenting the letters visually, as their names are rehearsed, alphabet recitation constitutes a review of letters already learned and a preview of those yet to be taught, (4) presentation of the full alphabet may provide an opportunity to discriminate between visually or orally confusable letters, and (5) reciting the alphabet is a natural occasion for the type of overt participation that we sought in response to the program.

The traditional alphabet song is sung by adults on Sesame Street on several occasions, usually with children on the set joining in. On these occasions, the child at home is asked to sing along. The same traditional song has been used with less success in an animated film. This film shows a little girl who walks out on a stage apparently for an audition. An off-camera voice, presumably that of her mother, tells her when to sing and corrects her delivery during the song. The letters appear on the screen as the child sings. The film seemed amusing to the Workshop staff, and initially it tested well for appeal with children. However when children were observed watching the program over a longer period of time, it was found that the film frustrated many of them. Children who had already learned the alphabet song and wanted to sing along found the interruptions confusing. The rhythm of the song was broken and the off-stage comments were distracting. Those who were still struggling to learn the song found the film difficult for the same reasons. Here is an instance where the intended humor of the mother's remarks and the child's reaction to them apparently interferes with the intended instructional message.

Children seem to like to have a chance to guess, and participate actively in the "Mystery Drawings" and "Skywriter" segments. The "Mystery Drawings" -- already mentioned as providing the humorous incongruity of the television set itself making mistakes that a child can correct -- shows the progressive formation of a line drawing of a familiar object or animal. Viewing children will shout out their guesses as to what object or animal is being formed and where the television set is going wrong in composing the drawing. "Skywriter" shows the progressive formation of a letter, apparently written by a plane in the sky, and again children actively guess its correct identity. Guessing games that are built around progressively revealed clues thus induce considerable overt participation.

Again, some caveats: Some educational conditions demand the child's participation, whether he willingly offers it or not. However, in response to televised invitations to react or participate, no matter how compelling the inducement may be, certain children will not display an active verbal or physical response. This is part of television's nonpunitiveness; the child may respond less energetically and enthusiastically than we hope, but each child is free to decline the invitation without fear of punishment or of attention of any kind.

Another caution: Since a television set cannot respond in turn to the child's participation, congratulating the unseen audience for its supposed correct reactions may confuse the child who has not found the solution or who has confidently chosen an incorrect solution. It also may confuse the child who had declined to participate at all. Indiscriminate mass reinforcement will diminish the credibility of its source.

Diversity of Characters, Content, Style, and Pace

Basic to sustaining the child's attention over time is the use of a diversity of program elements. Children lose interest when the program dwells too long on one subject or remains too long in one pace or style. This "feeling of sameness" (Reeves, 1971) appears in several guises, loses the child's attention in each instance, and clearly indicates the need for diversity in characters, content, style, and pace.

For example, in the early planning of *Sesame Street,* we assumed that if the action on the street itself were tied to a common theme within each program (a pet show, a birthday party, a new character appearing on the street), the story line would link the elements of each show together, carrying the child along throughout the hour. This "story line" device for sustaining attention proved wrong, producing instead the feeling of sameness. Brief reports from the research staff (Reeves, 1971) documents this observation for two shows as follows:

> "Show 262: Pet Show. The children were very interested in this theme at the beginning. They were attentive, responsive, and loved Slimy the worm. But, by the time first prize was awarded, the children were restless and inattentive.
>
> "Show 265: Ice Cream Machine. Much of the street action revolved around the installation of an ice cream machine on _Sesame Street._ By the time the ice cream man quit, hardly any children were still watching these segments." (Reeves, 1971, p. 2)

Also, a program tends to have the feeling of sameness if too many programming elements within it are similar in character (no matter how attractive the performer may be), content, style, or pace.

> "Show 274. Theodore Bikel. Nearly half of this program revolved around Bikel. This included his singing of six complete songs and snatches of several others. By the end of the program, only three of the six viewing groups were still intact and few of the children in these groups were watching anything.
>
> "Show 267. Animal Films. In this program, five animal films were programmed into the last half of the show: Mandrill Mother and Baby, Tree Kangaroo and Baby, Baby Reindeer, Animal Coverings, and Koala. In such a case, it is difficult to judge how attentive the children might have been to the individual films had they not occurred in the same program." (Reeves, 1971, p. 3)

The need for diversity, therefore, is readily apparent in sustaining young children's attention.

Diversity of characters

No production or writing technique ever works effectively if the characters shown (adults, children puppets, animated figures, animals, etc.) are not appealing to children or do not portray a variety of distinctive and reliable personalities.

Among the earliest inhabitants of Sesame Street were several distinctive adult characters: Gordon, a strong Black male-identification figure; Susan, Gordon's wife, but an independent female-identification figure as well; Bob, amiable, low-keyed, helpful; Mr. Hooper, slightly mean and abrasive but with a poorly hidden nice streak; Buddy and Jim, two adult blunderers who confront a series of simple problems (easy enough to be solved by the viewing child) but who can never seem to get the obvious solutions quite right. Among the earliest animated figures was, for example, Baby Alice Braitewaithe Goodyshoes, an arrogant, sanctimonious know-it-all (her standard introduction of herself is: "Hello. This is Alice Braitewaithe Goodyshoes, the most clever girl in the world.") whose cockiness and composure dissolves only slightly when her expertness is called into question. Although all these and other Sesame Street characters are designed to be distinctive and different, perhaps the range of personalities among the several puppet characters (from James Henson's repertory company of "muppet" puppets) best illustrates the needed diversity of characters in television for children:

> Oscar the Grouch: firmly and insistently contrary; from personal preference, he despises the standard virtues (friendliness, cleanliness, consideration for others, gregariousness, etc.) and thrives on what others reject (disorder, dirt, surliness in dealing with others, total privacy, etc.)
>
> Big Bird: naive; easily flustered and confused; prone to making obvious mistakes while remaining cheerfully undefeated and accepted (but not patronized) by others around him.
>
> Kermit the Frog: half-pitchman, half-courtly gentleman; tries hard to remain cool in the face of gathering chaos and usually succeeds with only minor, but visible cracks in his composure.
>
> Ernie (most often, but not always, appearing in Bert's company): an appealing tease; often trapped

by his own craftiness and cunning; retains a true sympathy and fondness for his would-be victims.

Bert: usually Ernie's straight man, but more intelligent and less innocent than most straight men; long-suffering and put-upon but retains a personal integrity and refinement that allows him to confront the intrigue and chaos gracefully; capable of delicate double-take and slow-burn acting.

Cookie Monster: voracious; sly in satisfying his incessant appetite yet aware of others and willing to understand their reasons for frustrating him; usually succeeds despite their efforts.

Grover: cordial and accommodating in a slightly gruff way; seeks opportunities to be helpful even when this places great physical and mental burdens upon him; often ends up in total exhaustion as he amiably extends himself to the utmost to cooperate.

Herbert Birdsfoot (often appearing in Grover's company): a careful and knowledgeable pedant; courteously accepts Grover's offers to assist in demonstrating Herbert's lectures by manipulating physical materials, visibly resulting in Grover's overworking and consequent exhaustion.

Professor Hastings: verging on senility; gives comically confused lectures, interrupting each at unpredictable occasions for short naps; sporadically capable of remarkable insights that stand in marked contrast to his general muddlement.

Sherlock Hemlock: a not-quite-competent detective who constantly searches for crimes to solve and prides himself on his detecting prowess; succeeds in deciphering certain clues but never quite arrives at a crime's final solution without assistance.

The Salesman: archetypical trickster who trades on the vanity and greed of others; often ends up as victim of his own avarice.

In addition to these distinctive puppets, an infinitely expandable troupe of Anything Muppets comes in all sizes, shapes, and appearances and can play any role from local grocer or postman, to members of a group of small boys and girls, to varied forms of monster, to a hip but somewhat seedy and disheveled musical group.

Beyond responding to puppets and animated figures, children generally prefer watching and listening to other children rather than adults. If the televised children are involved in some activity, especially when they are trying to solve a problem that the viewer can work through with them, attention is especially strong. Also, viewers particularly enjoy hearing other children's voices; several films that originally evoked only mild interest were much more appealing when children's voices were added to the sound track.

These televised children also should display distinctive and reliable personalities, but this is difficult to achieve. On Sesame Street, it seems especially important that the televised children be spontaneous and unrehearsed; nothing is more stilted and unnatural than child actors reciting lines from a prepared script. But when the televised children do respond freely and spontaneously, their behavior often is unpredictable and difficult to construct into a set of distinctive personalities. Here then distinctiveness of character is sacrificed for spontaneity and naturalness. (Incidentally, this unrehearsed quality of the children's behavior on Sesame Street often raises difficult problems for the adult cast.) If unpredictable behavior by children raises problems for teachers within the classroom and parents within the home, this same unpredictability presents continuous, unplanned crises for the on-screen Sesame Street cast to resolve. Since these cast members are not professional educators, the televised children's spontaneity of expression poses a constant threat of the cast's public embarrassment. The adult cast's early reaction was to restrain children by restricting their opportunities to initiate or respond -- much like the inexperienced university instructor who does not call upon students who threaten to interrupt his lectures with questions or comments. Slowly, some relaxation is being achieved as the cast learns to respond to the children's spontaneity with spontaneity of their own, even when this forces a radical departure from the planned televised lesson.

Watching adults or listening to them talk -- especially when they are presenting "message monologues" -- is much less appealing to children than watching other children. For example, in the early planning of Sesame Street, we developed a continuing series of episodes called "The Man from Alphabet," featuring a bumbling adult detective hero and a super-reasoning child who unravels the clues and solves the crimes. Although these episodes seemed appealing to the educators and producers, they never held the attention of young children and the approach was dropped. Apparently, "The Man from Alphabet" simply talked too much.

Some attention to adults can be sustained under certain conditions:

1. If, instead of showing the adult speaker on the screen, what he is speaking about is shown.

2. If the adult shares the screen with children, directing his talk to them. Here, the adult seems to use language that the child viewer can understand because he is talking directly to a child. Also, when an adult is on the screen by himself, viewing children interpret this as part of the majority of television that is not intended to be understood by them; when children share the screen with adults, the viewers receive the idea that the episode is intended for them.

3. If the adult makes mistakes and provides opportunities to be corrected by children, children's attention can be held.

Presenting a diversity of distinctive characters inevitably means presenting the diversity of language dialects natural to them. Although some misgivings were voiced during the early planning of Sesame Street about presenting any other language models than "correct" standard English, we do present the full range of dialects, accents, and informal street language appropriate to the range of characters on Sesame Street. We have found no evidence that children are confused by this or learn "incorrect" language practices. The natural diversity of language simply reflects the natural diversity of characters. For example, Roosevelt Franklin, the Black child puppet, speaks a Black English dialect; Gordon -- the adult Black male-identification figure -- speaks both standard English and Black English on different occasions, depending upon the situation and the other characters he is with.

Diversity of content

Although the Sesame Street curriculum is not designed to provide a comprehensive program (it is inconceivable that television possibly could teach everything that preschoolers might find useful to know), it does contain diverse subject matter, ranging across a large number of cognitive and noncognitive skills. This gives the producers and writers the necessary latitude to vary program content and to avoid the "feeling of sameness" that apparently reduces children's attention.

Trying to tie content together within a plot will reduce the range of subject matter that could be presented within a program, but the "story line" approach does not enhance learning; indeed, attention seems sharply reduced as the later phases of a running plot unfold. The effort to develop story lines was abandoned and the writers were free to include content from all curriculum areas within any single program.

Diversity of style

The mixing of several visual styles also helps to sustain attention or to retrieve it when it is lost. Sesame Street mixes four main ingredients: (1) puppets, (2) the cast of live adults and children on the set, (3) animation and pixilation, and (4) live-action films. All these styles are embedded in appropriate music and sound effects, and are supplemented with the appearance of guest celebrities, "mystery drawings," spoofs of game shows and soap operas, "sky-writing," stop-action techniques, etc. All this variety of style permits the mixing of fantasy (puppets, monsters, animated figures, etc.) and reality (live adults and children, live-action film, etc.). Again some early misgivings that combining fantasy and reality might create confusion between them did not materialize. For example, when the puppet characters Oscar the Grouch, Big Bird, and Bert and Ernie joined the adults and children as inhabitants of Sesame Street, viewers took this as one natural expression of the magical incongruity created by television. This mixing of fantasy and reality holds considerable appeal for young children, an appeal apparently shared by some adult cartoonist observers as well.

Diversity in pace

Beyond these useful diversities in characters, content, and style, varied pace and mood are critical in sustaining attention. The appeal of any single segment is tied closely to the contrasts provided by the episodes preceding and following it. Both fast-paced and slow-paced material will hold children's attention (the common criticism that Sesame Street is continuously frenetic simply is inaccurate), but a slow, peaceful episode is more appealing when surrounded by fast-moving episodes than when it follows another slow, quiet piece. Interest in any particular episode is higher if it creates a pace and mood that looks, sounds, and feels different from the one that preceded it. The principle that visual action and contrasts appeal to young children need not mean that the action must always be rapid or frenetic to be effective; instead, the pace of the action should be varied.

This observation has several other implications for children's programming:

1. The arguments by psychologists (e.g., Kagan and Kogan, 1970), p. 1300 ff.) for a dramatic increase around ages six and seven in the ability to sustain attention suggests that, for children below these ages, only television programs of short duration would be suitable. But, on the premise that only a program of sufficient total length would stand any chance of providing educational benefit, Sesame Street was designed to be one hour in length and the most common misgiving of educators was that this would be too long to hold young children's attention. This misgiving turned out to be wrong; when the segments within a program are varied in character, content, style, pace, and mood, young children's attention holds well over a one-hour period.

2. Some educational objectives require that the viewers be provided with a long look at the material to be taught. Varying the pace within the program, instead of insisting upon a constantly rapid pace, leaves considerable opportunity to inject slower-paced episodes that allow the viewer more time for inspection and contemplation.

Production Limitations

The list of things that television cannot do -- and should not be expected to do -- probably is far longer than the list of learning and teaching potentialities discussed in this paper. If television has some potential strengths that deserve experimentation, its inherent weaknesses perhaps are even more apparent and have received at least their fair share of attention from critics. The grievances range from relatively mild views that television teaches children the wrong lessons (e.g., physical passivity) to more strident attacks on television as the major social evil that is burying our society in violence, drug abuse, and dehumanization.

Although these strident attacks may be exaggerated, television indeed may teach aggression to some children and induce a physical passivity in others. It indeed may be severely limited as a teaching tool (one-way communication, inability to sequence material, failure to induce active responding, etc.). It indeed may cause us to lose contact with each other and instead to seek and accept solitary, vicarious spectatorship as the normal course of human activity. While we should test television's upper boundaries in providing useful learning and teaching opportunities, we also should test its potential negative consequences as well and not distort television's potential positive values by forcing its contributions into areas beyond its inherent limitations.

Conclusion

This paper has discussed (1) some informal principles of learning and teaching, and (2) some production and writing methods that have been used experimentally in television for children. Since we have only vague, beginning glimpses both of these principles and of these production possibilities, our understanding of the relationships between them is entirely tenuous and uncertain. Surely the principles of learning and teaching discussed here do not dictate directly the proposed production and writing strategies: All that these informal principles accomplish is to suggest conditions of learning and teaching that, at least, should not be violated in televised presentations for children.

Even this more cautious conclusion, however, is shaky. Developing television materials for children -- and then observing children's responses to them -- has been full of surprises and mysteries both for the producers and for the researchers using the visual medium to learn about how children learn. But for those of us who are experimenting in the effects of visual media upon children, a hidden impulse operates. Suppose we fail completely to discover anything more about how children learn; suppose television's capabilities and limitations remain a mystery despite our best efforts. Even so -- once in a while, with a little luck -- we connect with the child and get to hear him laugh. That is worth most of life's satisfactions rolled into one.

REFERENCES

Arlen, M. J. Living-room war. New York: Viking, 1966.

Broadbent, D. E. Perception and communication. New York: Pergamon Press, 1958.

Brown, L. Television: the business behind the box. New York: Harcourt Brace Jovanovich, 1972.

Cole, M., Gay, J., Glock, J., and Sharp, D. W. The cultural context of learning and thinking. New York: Basic Books, 1971.

Collins, W. A. Learning of media content: a developmental study. Child Development, 1970, 41, 1133-1142.

Connell, D. D., and Palmer, E. P. Cooperation between broadcasters and researchers. Leicester, England: International Seminar on Broadcaster/Researcher Cooperation in Mass Communication Research, 1970.

Day, H. I., and Berlyne, D. Intrinsic maturation. In G. S. Lesser (ed.), Psychology and educational practice. Glenview, Illinois: Scott Foresman, 1971. 294-335.

Deutschmann, P. J., Barrow, L. C., Jr., and McMillan, A. Efficiency of different modes of communication. Audio-Visual Communication Review, 1961, 9, 263-270.

Gibbon, S. Y., and Palmer, E. L. Pre-reading on Sesame Street. New York: Children's Television Workshop, 1970.

Hovland, C. I., Lumsdaine, A. A., and Sheffield, F. D. Experiments in mass communication. Princeton, New Jersey: Princeton University Press, 1949.

Kael, P. Going steady. New York: Little Brown, 1970.

Kagan, J. The determinants of attention in the infant. American Scientist, 1970, 58, 298-306.

Kagan, J. Cognitive development and programs for day care. In Edith

H. Grotberg (ed.), Day care: resources for decisions. Washington, D.C., Office of Economic Opportunity, 1971a. 135-152.

Kagan, J. Change and continuity in infancy. New York: Wiley, 1971b.

Kagan, J., and Kogan, N. Individuality and cognitive performance. In P. H. Mussen (ed.), Manual of Child Psychology. New York: Wiley, 1970. 1273-1365.

Lumsdaine, A. A. Instruments and media of instruction. In N. L. Gage (ed.), Handbook of research on teaching. Chicago: Rand McNally, 1963. 583-682.

Maccoby, E. E. Selective auditory attention in children. In L. P. Lipsett and C. C. Spiker (eds.), Advances in child development and behavior: Vol. III. New York: Academic Press, 1967. 99-124.

Maccoby, E. E. Early stimulation and cognitive development. In J. P. Hill (ed.), Minnesota Symposia on Child Psychology. Minneapolis: University of Minnesota Press, 1969. 68-96.

Maccoby, E. E., and Konrad, K. W. The effect of preparatory set on selective listening: developmental trends. Monographs of the Society for Research in Child Development, 1967, No. 112.

Moore, K. C. The mental development of a child. Psychological Review Monograph Supplement, 1896, 1, No. 3.

Piaget, J. The origins of intelligence in children. New York: International Universities Press, 1952.

Reeves, B. F. The first year of Sesame Street: the formative research. New York: Children's Television Workshop, 1970.

Reeves, B. F. The responses of children in six small viewing groups to Sesame Street Shows Nos. 261-274. New York: Children's Television Workshop, 1971.

Segall, M. H., Campbell, D. T., and Herskovits, M. J. The influence of culture on visual perception. New York: Bobbs-Merrill, 1966.

Stevenson, H. W. Television and the behavior of preschool children. Minneapolis, Minnesota: University of Minnesota, 1971.

Travers, R. M. W. Transmission of information to human receivers. *Audio-Visual Communication Review*, 1964, 12, 373-385.

Travers, R. M. W. *Man's information system*. Scranton, Pennsylvania: Chandlers, 1970.

White, B. L., Watts, J. C., et al. *Major influences on the development of the young child.* Englewood Cliffs, New Jersey: Prentice-Hall, 1972.

Woodworth, R. S. *Experimental psychology*. New York: Holt, 1938.

Yamamoto, K. Stimulus mode and sense modality: what's in it for education? *Teachers College Record,* 1969, 70, 513-521.

FORMATIVE RESEARCH IN EDUCATIONAL TELEVISION PRODUCTION: THE EXPERIENCE OF THE CHILDREN'S TELEVISION WORKSHOP

By Edward L. Palmer, Vice President for Research
Children's Television Workshop

The Children's Television Workshop (CTW), in producing its two children's educational television series, Sesame Street and The Electric Company, has made extensive use of formative research. This is a type of field research designed to help improve the quality of educational products and practices during the actual course of their development. It is typically contrasted with "summative" research, which is concerned with follow-up testing to determine the educational effect of new products and practices when actually put into use.

With both program series, a period of approximately a year and a half was devoted to prebroadcast research and planning. In the case of Sesame Street, the first of the two series produced, it was not at all clear at the outset just what role formative research could play. There were no precedents, either from the field of educational television production, or from the field of educational research in general, sufficient in scope or well enough documented to provide useful guidelines or models. By the time planning for the production of The Electric Company was initiated, the usefulness of formative research had been well established. The procedures followed in producing Sesame Street had come to be viewed as a model, and essentially the same model was reapplied in undertaking this new series. The effectiveness of the approach is borne out in reports of summative evaluations carried out independently by Educational Testing Service of Princeton, New Jersey, in order to assess the educational impact of the first and second seasons of Sesame Street (Ball and Bogatz, 1970; Ball and Bogatz, 1971).

This paper has been adapted in part from a presentation prepared for the International Symposium on Communication: Technology, Impact, and Policy, the Annenberg School of Communications, University of Pennsylvania, 1972.

What has been learned by CTW about the formative research process has come about under quite unusual circumstances. Accordingly, it remains to be seen which of its approaches will be found useful elsewhere, and what sorts of new or modified approaches will be required in order to suit new situations. Among the unusual circumstances associated with the Workshop's productions, some no doubt had a direct bearing on the effectiveness of the formative research. For instance, the two projects were well funded, each being budgeted at upwards of seven million dollars for production, research, and related activities. This made it possible to recruit high-level production talent, and to make extensive use of expert educational advisers and consultants. In addition, both projects enjoyed unusually long periods of time -- in each case, approximately 18 months -- for prebroadcast research and planning. This made it possible to plan the curriculum for each show very carefully and to define it very explicitly, so that all members of the production staff, as well as the independent evaluators who were undertaking the summative research, could proceed without ambiguity, and in a coordinated fashion. Other unusual conditions no doubt were significant also, including the fact that the researchers and producers were committed to a process of empirical evaluation and revision, and that the research staff involved the producers directly in the research. Research methods were continued in use only on the condition that the producers themselves found them useful.

The success of the Workshop's experiments in researcher-producer cooperation also has hinged to a substantial degree upon the point of view taken by the producers, who understood that formative research results were simply one more source of information among many, including their own past experiences with children, inputs from expert advisers and consultants, and intuitive impressions. In the Workshop's approach, it was always understood on both sides that the producers had to make the final production decisions, based upon the best information available to them, from whatever source. It was also understood that formative research would become useful, if at all, only gradually, as methods were developed for more accurately addressing the producers' information needs.

This paper will deal with methods and procedures of formative research, and with some of the types of program design decisions illuminated by each of various formative research methods, but it will not be a report of research results. Results now available from CTW's formative research are in the main not well validated, because allocations of time and resources for that purpose would have detracted from the objective of addressing the widest possible range of significant production issues. Far more generalizable at this time are the formative research methods, procedures, strategies, functions, and the like, which can be adapted by other production groups to suit their own unique program formats, educational objectives, target audiences, and viewing contexts. One precaution for anyone contemplating the use of the methods and procedures described here is that there are no perfectly dependable recipes, and no assurance that successful productions will result.

As experience with formative research procedure begins to accumulate and the conditions making for success or failure become more clear, many of the factors considered significant in the work carried out at CTW must almost certainly receive prominent continuing attention. Those here considered most significant are the subjects of the sections which follow. In brief overview, these include the overall operational framework within which CTW's formative research proceeds, the strategies and rationale for the design of formative field research methods, organizational and interpersonal conditions, and similarities and contrasts between the functions and the methods of formative research on the one hand and those of more traditional research approaches on the other.

The CTW Operational Model

The principal activities undertaken in the production of *Sesame Street* have come to be viewed by CTW as a model, and this model was again applied in the production of *The Electric Company*. If there is a single, most critical condition for rendering such a model of researcher-producer cooperation effective, it is that the researchers and the producers cannot be marching to different drummers. The model is essentially a model for production planning. More specifically, it is a model for planning the educational (as opposed to the dramatic) aspects of the production, and the formative research is an integral part of that process. In the case of *Sesame Street* and *The Electric Company*, at least, it is hard to imagine that the formative research and curriculum planning could have been effective if carried out apart from overall production planning, either as an isolated a priori process, or as an independent but simultaneous function.

The activities included in the model are presented below in their approximate chronological order of occurrence.

Curriculum planning

As the initial step toward establishing its educational goals,

CTW, in the summer of 1968, conducted a series of five three-day seminars dealing with the following topics:

1. Social, Moral, and Affective Development
2. Language and Reading
3. Mathematical and Numerical Skills
4. Reasoning and Problem-Solving
5. Perception

The seminars, organized and directed by Dr. Gerald S. Lesser, Bigelow Professor of Education and Developmental Psychology at Harvard University, were attended by more than a 100 expert advisers, including psychologists, psychiatrists, teachers, sociologists, film-makers, television producers, writers of children's books, and creative advertising personnel. Each seminar group was asked to suggest educational goals for the prospective series and to discuss ways of realizing the goals on television.

Behavioral goals

The deliberations of the seminar participants and the recommendations of the CTW Board of Advisers were reviewed in a series of staff meetings from which a list of instructional goals for the program emerged. These goals were grouped under the following major headings:

I. Symbolic Representation

- A. Letters
- B. Numbers
- C. Geometric Forms

II. Cognitive Organization

- A. Perceptual Discrimination and Organization
- B. Relational Concepts
- C. Classification

III. Reasoning and Problem-Solving

- A. Problem Sensitivity and Attitudes Toward Inquiry
- B. Inferences and Causality
- C. Generating and Evaluating Explanations and Solutions

IV. The Child and His World

A. Self
B. Social Units
C. Social Interactions
D. The Man-made Environment
E. The Natural Environment

Specific goals under each of these broad headings were stated, insofar as possible, in behavioral terms so that they might serve as a common reference for the program producers and the designers of the achievement tests. Appropriate coordination of production and evaluation thus was assured.

Existing competence of target audience

While the statement of goals specified the behavioral outcomes the program hoped to achieve, it was necessary to ascertain the existing range of competence in the chosen goal areas among the target audience. The Workshop research staff therefore undertook as its initial "formative" research effort a compilation of data provided in the literature, as well as some testing of its own, to determine the competence range. The resulting information helped guide the producers in allocating program time and budget among the goal categories and in selecting specific learning instances in each goal area.

Appeal of existing materials

To be successful, CTW had to capture its intended audience with an educational show whose highly attractive competition was only a flick of the dial away. Unlike the classroom teacher, the Workshop had to earn the privilege of addressing its audience, and it had to continue to deserve its attention from moment to moment and from day to day. At stake was a variation in daily attendance which could run into millions. Measuring the preferences of the target audience for existing television and film materials was therefore crucial in the design of the new series.

Experimental production

Seminar participants and CTW advisers had urged using a variety of production styles to achieve the curriculum goals adopted. Research had confirmed the appetite of the target audience for fast pace and variety. Accordingly, the CTW production staff invited a number of live-action and animation film production companies to submit ideas. The first season of Sesame Street eventually included the work of 32 different film companies.

Prototype units of all film series produced by or for the Workshop were subjected to rigorous preliminary scrutiny and empirical field evaluation. Scripts and storyboards were revised by the Workshop producers on the basis of recommendations from the research staff; further revisions were made after review by educational consultants and advisers; and finished films were tested by the research department with sample audiences. Some material never survived the process. Four pilot episodes were produced for a live-action film adventure series entitled "The Man from Alphabet," but when the films were shown to children they failed to measure up, either in appeal or educational effect, and the series was dropped. Sample video-taped material went through the same process of evaluation, revision, and occasional elimination.

By July of 1969 a format for the program had been devised, a title had been selected, a cast had been tentatively assigned, and a week of full-length trial programs had been taped as a dry run.

Completed prototype production elements were tested by the research staff in two ways: (1) appeal for the CTW material was measured against the appeal of previously tested films and television shows, and (2) the CTW material was tested for its educational impact under a number of conditions. For instance, field studies were conducted to determine the effect of various schedules of repetition and spacing, of providing the child with preliminary or follow-up explanation, of presenting different approaches to a given goal separately or in combination, and of the relative effectiveness of adult vs. child voice-over narration. Extensive observation of viewing children provided information regarding the child's understanding of various conventions of film and television technique. Upon conclusion of each research study, the results were reported to the producers for their use in modifying the show components tested and for guidance in the production of subsequent elements.

Production, airing, and progress testing of the broadcast series

The evolution of Sesame Street did not end with the first national broadcast on November 10, 1969. Formative research studies conducted throughout the six-month broadcast period continued to guide the development of new production techniques, format elements, and teaching strategies. As before, these studies had two foci: (1) the holding power of entertainment techniques and (2) the effectiveness of educational content.

Earlier and continuing studies of individual program segments, while useful, were necessarily limited in scope. With the onset of the broadcast season, it was possible to examine the impact of continuous viewing of entire shows over a period of time. Accordingly, the research staff instituted a program of progress testing of the show's effectiveness. Using the instruments designed by Educational Testing Service of Princeton, New Jersey, for a national summative evaluation of the series, a sample of day-care children, predominantly four- and five-year-olds, was pretested prior to the first national telecast. One-third were tested again after three weeks of viewing the show; the first third and a second third were tested after six weeks of viewing; and the entire group was tested after three months of viewing. Comparisons between experimental (viewing) groups and control (non-viewing) groups at each stage of the testing gave indications of strengths and weaknesses both in the execution of the curriculum and in the production design. Appeal measurement and informal observation of viewing children also influenced production decisions during this period.

Summative evaluation

The summative research and evaluation carried out by Educational Testing Service (see Ball and Bogatz, 1970; and Ball and Bogatz, 1971) followed a plan developed in consultation with CTW staff and advisers. Participation of ETS representatives in all main phases of pre-broadcast planning helped to ensure coordination between program development and follow-up testing.

ETS developed and administered a special battery of 11 tests covering the major CTW goal areas to a sample of children from Boston, Philadelphia, Durham, and Phoenix. The groups included three-, four-, and five-year-olds in urban and rural settings, from middle- and lower-income families, in both home and day-care situations. A special side study related to children from Spanish-speaking homes. The 11 tests were as follows:

1. Body Parts Test
2. Letters Test
3. Numbers Test
4. Shapes and Forms Test
5. Relational Terms Test
6. Sorting Test
7. Classification Test
8. Puzzles Test
9. What Comes First Test
10. Embedded Figures Test
11. *Sesame Street* Test

Other measures assessed home conditions, parental expectations for the children, and the like. Where the results of the first season's summative research feed into production decisions for the second season, they take on a formative function.

Writer's Manual

As the producers and writers began to develop scripts, animations, and films addressed to particular behaviorally stated goals, it became apparent that the goal statement was not a wholy adequate reference. After having been given several successive assignments in the same goal area, they began to express the need for extended and enriched definitions which would provide creative stimulation. Gradually, through trial and error, a format for a *Writer's Manual* was developed which the producers and writers themselves found useful.

Suggestions for the *Manual* were developed according to a number of criteria. One was to emphasize the psychological processes involved in a particular form of behavior. Another was to exploit and extend the child's own experiential referents for such behavior. Still another was to prompt the creation of various similar approaches by the producers and writers themselves, by presenting them with highly divergent examples. Another yet was to provide suggestions free of any reference to particular characters or contexts from the television program, so that the ways in which the suggestions could be implemented would be left as open and flexible as possible. These features of the *Writer's Manual* may be highlighted through an example. In the broad area of Symbolic Representation, the word-matching objective is stated as follows: "Given a printed word, the child can select an identical printed word from a set of printed words." To implement this objective, the *Manual* would encourage the producers to use words with different numbers of letters; to vary the location within the word of the letter or letters which fail to "match"; to present various matching strategies, such as comparing two given words letter by letter, moving initially separated words into superimposition, or spelling out each of two given words and comparing to see if one has made the same sounds both times. Another recommended approach was to make use of the "sorting" format already familiar to viewers, wherein three identical things (in this case, words) and one odd thing are presented simultaneously, along with a standard song which invites the viewer to find the one which is different. Still another was to construct a letter-by-letter match for a given word by choosing from a large pool of letters. To encourage still further divergent approaches, another recommendation was to present pairs of words which matched in one sense but not in another, e.g., a pair in which the same word is presented in different type faces, or in which one member of the pair is the upper- and the other the lower-case version.

Similar suggestions were developed for other goal areas, as requested by the producers and writers. Involving advisers and consultants in the creation of these suggestions afforded one more opportunity for making use of expert input. In addition, the Manual provided a place and a format for collecting the ideas of the in-house research staff and a channel for helping to ensure that these ideas would be seen and used.

Formative Research Methods

A great deal of information useful to educational television producers can be acquired through the use of a few quite inexpensive and informal methods of field observation. More sophisticated methods can provide considerable additional information in some cases, but often add little to that which can be obtained more simply and economically.

The selection of research methods is particularly critical, because the attributes focused upon by these methods tend to become prominent among those focused upon by the producers. This is particularly the case when the producers themselves have participated in selecting the methods, and thus in identifying the attributes deserving of their special attention.

CTW's formative research methods presently focus upon four principal program attributes, all considered instrumental in producing lasting instructional effects, namely: (1) appeal, (2) comprehensibility, (3) internal compatibility, and (4) activity eliciting potential. These will be discussed in more detail below. First, however, it is important to note that these attributes are identified and used at the Workshop and are presented here strictly for their heuristic value. It is convenient for the producers and researchers to have a small number of highly significant program attributes with which to associate both the host of related program design features and the many similarly related field research methods. Not only does reference to a limited number of attributes provide a manageable check list for evaluating materials under production, and a convenient categorial system, but it also invites researchers and producers alike to identify new attributes, and for each attribute, additional field research methods and program design features.

For each of these four attributes, there is not one but a family of research methods, each typically yielding somewhat different information than the others. In some cases, a single method yields information related to more than one of the four attributes. Also, more than one method can be used in assessing any one of the four attributes. In practice, where more than one method is used in studying a single attribute, it is done either for cross-validation of results, or in order to provide complementary sources of information. For example, the appeal of intact programs or program segments may be tested by direct observation of the visual orienting response of viewers; by questioning the viewers outside the viewing context about most-liked program elements; or by dealing in preference comparisons between intact programs or program types. Finally, it is very often useful to combine the results from research focusing simultaneously upon two or more attributes. As an example, for a poor segment, the reason for its failure to produce post-tested achievements may be illuminated by an investigation of its appeal, its comprehensibility, or the possibility that its entertaining and educational elements are incompatible. Incidentally, this particular type of analysis appears virtually nowhere in the standard educational research literature, in spite of its obvious value.

Formative research on program appeal

The appeal of a program has to do with its ability to capture and hold the attention of the intended viewer. In the case of both *Sesame Street* and *The Electric Company*, there was "captive" audience. The programs were designed to attract the largest possible number of at-home viewers. This meant they needed to be sufficiently high in appeal to draw the children back to the set from day to day and week to week, and to compete with popular entertainment programming available on other channels.

Because the viewer could turn away at any time, and because the two programs were designed according to a magazine format, with successive brief segments addressed to very explicit educational objectives, it was important to maintain high program appeal on a moment-to-moment basis. Accordingly, research methods capable of focusing on appeal from moment to moment throughout the course of a program were developed and used. Some of these will be discussed in more detail below.

Appeal research bears upon a wide range of program design decisions. It reveals the effects of various forms and applications of music, and of music as compared with other types of elements. It indicates the most and least popular forms of live-action films, animations, puppets, and live performers. It indicates the attention-holding power of various types of individual or interpersonal activities, such as showing one person guiding another through a difficult task in a supportive versus demeaning manner; presenting conflict resolution through the arbitrary use of power versus cooperation; revealing the simultaneous perspectives of different characters; and portraying the struggle of an individual toward an achievement goal or toward improvement upon his own past performance to mention a few.

Appeal research also helps to indicate for various conditions the amount of time over which attention can be maintained; the optimum amount of variety and the optimum pacing of events; the relative holding power of program elements which are and are not functionally relevant to the action; the ability of a segment to bear up under exact repetition; the most and least salient (memorable) characters; and the effectiveness of special techniques such as pixilation, fast and slow motion, and unusual camera angles. In addition, research on appeal can show growth or decline in the popularity of specific program elements over time; the most and least effective uses of dialogue, monologue, and the voice-over technique; the relative effectiveness of ordinary or caricaturized voices; and the effect of sparse and pointed versus sustained verbalizations. It also can reveal the effects of incongruity, surprisingness, or fantasy, as compared with straightforwardness, predictability, and realism; the effect of different motives or intentions on the part of characters; of episodic versus linear styles of continuity; and also of familiar versus unfamiliar conventions and symbols dealing with time, sequence, interpersonal relationships, and the like. Finally, this type of research can be used to investigate characteristic individual or group preferences vis-à-vis such program design features.

As in the case of other methods, those used in measuring appeal were designed to direct the attention of the producers toward particularly significant program features. For instance, because the Sesame Street program was going to make use of many brief segments, and because a viewer could at any time freely turn away, turn the set off, or turn to a different channel, it was important to keep the moment-to-moment appeal of the program high. Accordingly, a method was introduced which yields data on the appeal of a program for each successive 7.5-second interval over its entire length. The method, referred to as the distractor method, consists of placing one child at a time in a simulated home-viewing circumstance while a black-and-white video-taped recording of a television program is presented simultaneously with a color slide show flashed on a rear-projection screen, which is approximately the same size and height from the floor as the television screen, is placed at about a 45 degree angle from the child's line of vision to the television set. The child himself is seated in a chair three to four feet away from and facing the television, but is free to move about within the confines of the room at any time. A continuous record indicates when the child's eyes are directed toward or away from the set. For each viewer, the 80-slide carrousel is started at a different slide, so that the stimulus competing with a given 7.5-second interval of the televised presentation is different for each viewer. Composite graphs of the results are studied by the researchers and producers in various ways in an attempt to identify the elements of program content responsible for high and low appeal.

A frequently used complementary form of appeal testing consists of taking observations upon successive sets of viewing groups, where each group typically contains from three to five viewers. Usually, four to six such groups are observed in testing a program. A detailed record is kept according to predefined categories of visual, verbal, and motor behaviors. The visual behavior of children in viewing groups provides a cross-check on the distractor results. The record of verbal and motor responses, in addition to reflecting upon program appeal, helps to identify program approaches most and least effective in eliciting active participation. The fruitfulness of this particular approach is very much a function of the training and the creative interpretive skills of the researcher.

Audience surveys can provide much additional material on program appeal, as can structured interviews, in which the salient and lasting as opposed to the immediate appeal of various program features can be determined. The salient appeal of an element is particularly important where it is necessary to attract a voluntary audience.

Formative research on program comprehensibility

The comprehensibility of a program or segment concerns the manner in which it is interpreted or construed by its viewers during the actual course of its presentation -- what they grasp of the intended instructional points, how they view the motives or intentions of the characters.

Comprehensibility testing, while useful in evaluating a viewer's understanding of the dramatic action, is undertaken primarily for the purpose of pointing up program design features involved in the presentation of the instruction. As such, it focuses upon the qualities of the televised message as these interact with learner characteristics. It is instructive to the producers to have an empirical check on their own assumptions about the comprehensibility of program design features they are employing, and even limited amounts of field research can help them to maintain a generalized sensitivity to this important attribute.

Although CTW's research in the area of comprehensibility has just begun, and although the ultimate objective is to identify and set down specific program design principles, it may be useful at this time to mention a few of the program features to which these principles could relate. Among these are the production approaches which can help to clarify the relationship between an event occurring on the screen and the theme, the plot line, or the logical progression of the dramatic component, or between the instances and non-instances of a concept, the referents and nonreferents of a term, or the most and least effective of a set of proposed solutions to a problem.

The unique conventions and capabilities of the television medium are frequently used to convey special meanings. The manner in which these conventions are presented will determine their comprehensibility to the viewer, and thus their effectiveness in communicating the meanings intended. These include the use of the flashback technique, of special lighting effects or special combinations of music and lighting, the use of various camera perspectives, of fast or slow motion, of pixilation, and of the matched dissolve between objects. They also include the close juxtaposition of events in order to establish a metaphoric or analogic relationship between them, and the use of conventions having to do with fantasy, such as presenting puppets and cartoon characters who move and talk like humans. Still others include the creation of "magical" effects, such as making an object instantly appear or disappear from a scene, or grow smaller or larger, and the use of exaggerated motions and consequences, as with slapstick and "banana peel" humor, to mention a few. Other conventions which can be used in more or less comprehensible ways are the speech balloon, the rules of games presented for instruction or entertainment, and rules involved in reading, spelling, mathematical operations, the interpretation of maps, and the like.

Still other facets of comprehensibility relate to timing, sequencing, and the use of redundancy, as in repeating an event exactly or with an illuminating variation, in restating a point from alternative perspectives, and in making use of introductions or reviews. The list could go on indefinitely, a fact which itself suggests the significance of this attribute in educational television research.

Again, as with the appeal testing, this area employs not one but a family of complementary research methods. One very useful approach is to present a program via a portable video playback system to an audience of one or more children, to stop the presentation at predetermined points so as to "freeze the frame," and then to ask viewers about events leading up to or likely to follow from the pictured situation.

If the research concern has to do with a character premise or with a character's motivation, the viewer might be asked, "What kind of person is he?" or "Why did he do (say) that?" or "What do you think he will do next?" "Why do you think that?" and so on. In one segment designed for The Electric Company, the Short Circus, a musical rock group made up of children, was shown singing a song which contained the letter combination "ow" several dozens of times. As the "ow" song was sung, the printed "ow" was shown a number of times simultaneously. The intention was to provide repetitive practice in associating the spoken and printed forms of this particular letter combination. By using the method of freezing a single frame, it was possible to evaluate the extent to which members of the target audience actually perceived the speech-to-print correspondence. In this case, the letter combination was frozen on the screen at a point late in the song, and as the experimenter pointed to the printed letter, the subjects were asked a question of the form: "Why is that there?" "What does it mean?"

In a related method, also used frequently in CTW's formative research, a program or segment is played once or twice through. It is then presented once again, but this time without the sound (or, in a variation upon the method, with the sound but without the picture), and the viewer is asked either to give a running account of what is happening or to respond to specific questions.

Other methods useful for evaluating comprehensibility include observing the spontaneous responses of children in viewing groups, and testing for achievement gains following their exposure to a program or segment.

A strength of comprehensibility testing relative to traditional forms of summative evaluation is the opportunity it provides for discriminating between the most and least effective of the many individual segments devoted to a particular achievement objective. A potential but largely surmountable limitation is the tendency for these methods to produce biased results. Because comprehensibility testing is performed as the program is being viewed, and because the viewer knows he will be questioned, there is typically an overestimation of a segment's effectiveness. In practice, this bias can be subjectively discounted, at best, and must further be weighed against the possibility that segments which produce no measurable learning when presented in isolation may be effective in combination or when presented along with an appropriate introduction or review. However, these limitations do not detract seriously from the usefulness of such methods. The bias can in fact be turned to an asset, as when it can be shown that a segment of questionable value fails to make its point even when evaluated by means of a liberally biased method.

Internal compatibility

Internal compatibility is a program attribute which has to do with the relationship of different elements appearing within the same segment. The basic strategy underlying both Sesame Street and The Electric Company is to attempt to effect instruction through the use of television's most popular entertainment forms. To this end, it is essential that the entertainment and educational elements work well together. Without the entertainment, attention strays, and without the education, the whole point of the presentation is lost. In segments where these elements are mutually compatible, the educational point is an inherent part of the dramatic action and often is actually enhanced in its salience as a consequence. In others, the entertaining elements override and thereby actually compete with the educational message. Other cases in which the relationship of elements becomes a concern have to do with auditory-visual, auditory-auditory, and visual-visual compatibilities.

The objective of formative research in this area is to shed light upon the program design features which make for a high or low degree of compatibility. As in the case of the other major program attributes discussed here, internal compatibility can be evaluated by means of a number of different research methods. In one, a panel of judges is asked to rate each segment of a program according to a predetermined set of categories defining the extent to which a segment's entertainment either facilitates or competes with the instructional content. Working from each segment's compatibility score, which is a composite of the ratings given by the various judges, it is possible to identify sets of high-rated and low-rated segments, and to present the producers with an interpreted list of each type. The interpretations identify program design features to be emulated, revised, or avoided.

Another method involves eye-movement research, which is especially useful in the case of The Electric Company, because of the extensive presentation of print on the screen and the desire to find ways of motivating the child to read it. In most segments, the print appears on the screen along with competing stimuli. By using the well-known technique in which a beam of light is reflected from the cornea of the eye of the television-viewing subject and recorded on a photographic device for later interpretation, it is possible to identify the conditions under which the print is and is not read. Once again, the results indicate program-design features worth emulating and approaches which need to be revised or avoided.

Among the important program features focused upon by this method are the location of the print on the screen; the effectiveness of various ways of animating print; the effect of the exact repetition of segments upon the elements attended to; and the usefulness of special motivational devices, such as telling all but the punch line of a joke, and then presenting that in print.

Methods for measuring eye movement obviously have implications for the evaluation of program appeal, and in particular may be used to complement other methods of appeal measurement discussed earlier. They are also related to the category of methods taken up immediately below, those concerned with the assessment of a program's activity eliciting potential.

Activity eliciting potential

A widely expressed point of view about television as an instructional medium holds that due to the passivity of the viewer, the medium is virtually powerless to produce learning. There is no question that the medium has limitations in this regard. However, since it is patently obvious that television can and does teach, a more constructive point of view is to examine conceptually ways in which this capability comes about, and operationally, ways in which it may be exploited. The position taken here is that the activity eliciting potential of the medium, no matter how limited, is nevertheless the chief basis for whatever effectiveness it has.

One significant form of activity television can elicit is intellectual activity. Others include verbal behavior and gross physical acts, ranging from television-modified performance on tests of attitudes and achievements to the imitation of televised models. It is important to note that the concern of the medium can be either to exploit these effects as instruments of instruction or to foster them as instructional objectives.

Intellectual activities include integrating separately presented items of information, anticipating upcoming events, forming new concepts, imputing the motives and intentions of characters, following progressively developed dramatic and instructional presentations, and guessing answers to questions. The viewer also actively evaluates relationships between premises and conclusions, between information given and interpretations made of it, and between codes of behavior and the actual behaviors carried out by the performers. The viewer also frequently relates new information from a televised presentation to his own prior experiences and to his future plans. These are only a few of the many possible instances.

No review of the capabilities of television vis-à-vis imitation and modeling will be given here, since those effects already have been the subject of considerable research and conceptualization.

It is understandable that from a superficial look at television's potential as an instructional medium many educators underestimate its ability to recreate the conditions known or presumed to be essential for learning. Tentative indications from formative conceptualization and research on the activity eliciting capabilities of the medium suggest that many of its presumed limitations may be at least partially surmountable. For example, it is often assumed that learning through trial and error or through trial and reinforcement cannot occur through one-way televised presentations, on the basis that there is no opportunity for reinforcement or information feedback to be tied to an action of the learner. This is not a trivial issue, from a practical standpoint, since vast amounts of money may yet be spent studying the use of two-way communication systems in connection with televised instruction. It turns out that conceptually it is possible to effect trial-and-error learning through one-way television, simply by the use of "if" statements. That is, the viewer may be offered a choice among provided alternatives, given time to make his choice (his point of most active involvement), and then given reinforcement, or an accuracy check, of the form: "If you chose thus and so, you were correct (incorrect)." Empirical studies may or may not support the viability of such an approach, but it certainly deserves further investigation.

Similarly, the notion that certain activities containing a motoric component can be learned only through direct experience is in many instances questionable. For example, direct experience in the construction of alphabetical characters may have its most significant effect upon learning by controlling the scan of the eye over the configuration of the letter, by providing extended or repeated exposure to the letter, or by providing an occasion for the most common errors to be made and corrected. But all of these are features one-way television can either duplicate or simulate. We need to know more about the effectiveness of such features when produced by one-way television. We also need to know more about the entry skills required under such conditions in order for learning to occur, and about possibilities for the facilitation of subsequent learning.

All this is not an argument in favor of unduly widespread substitution of television for physical activity among children, by the way, nor is it intended to deny the great importance of extensive direct experience in learning, especially in early learning. It is intended, rather, to urge more open and positive consideration of some of the potential but not yet systematically explored capabilities of the television medium.

Organizational and Interpersonal Factors

As technologically sophisticated forms of instruction come into increasing prominence, it will be necessary to make increased use of production teams whose members possess a diversity of highly specialized talents. In anticipation of this trend, we need to know more about related organizational and interpersonal conditions. These conditions deserve attention in any attempts to establish a working partnership between television research and production groups, and they play a strikingly more prominent role in the formative research context than in the context of more traditional approaches to educational research. To illustrate briefly the many and different types of factors involved, a major one in CTW's case has been the opportunity afforded by an 18-month pre-broadcast period for the members of the two groups to learn about each other's areas of specialization. Another has been the attitude that every new formative research approach is an experiment, to be continued or discontinued depending on its merits as evaluated by the producers themselves.

The fact that CTW's researchers and producers possess not the same, but complementary skills is also significant, largely because it provides for clear and distinct functions on the part of each group. Still another factor is that the producers, before joining the project, made the commitment to try to work with formative research. This prior commitment helped to support the cooperative spirit through the early, more tentative period of the effort. Also, research never takes on the role of adversary, to be used against the producers in winning a point or pressing for a particular decision. The producers hold the final power of decision and are free to ignore research suggestions if production constraints require it.

In all, the factors consciously dealt with in the interests of researcher-producer cooperation have ranged from the careful division of labor and responsibility to housing the two staffs in adjacent offices, and from patience and diplomacy to occasional retreat.

Formative Research with Low-Budget Projects

With low-budget productions, the cost of sophisticated formative research can be so costly as to discourage its use altogether. However, a great deal of useful field data can be obtained quite economically if cost-effective research methods are employed, if favorable production conditions are established, and if considerable interpretive ingenuity is exercised by the researchers and producers. Experience with low-budget projects, both in the United States and abroad, suggests a number of research strategies and production conditions which are conducive to maximal effectiveness at minimal cost. As the examples below will make clear, most of these have shortcomings -- but tolerable shortcomings -- relative to more costly alternatives.

The non-empirical check list. Well-trained specialists who are experienced with a program's curriculum and target audience can provide many useful production suggestions simply by examining scripts, storyboards, or completed productions, and making judgmental observations for subsequent production guidance according to a predesigned check list of significant program attributes. The check list can include attributes and related program design features such as those listed earlier in the Formative Research Methods section. The strength of this method lies in the fact that for minimal cost, a great number of attributes may be evaluated quite regularly and explicitly. The drawbacks include the fact that experts can be wrong, or will themselves often feel the need for an empirical test of their hunches. Also, they may fail to detect important patterns which only sophisticated forms of data analysis typically reveal.

The segmented format. While the segmented format can be relatively expensive to produce, it is ideal from the standpoint of evolving a program series -- with or without rigorous formative research -- over the course of a season or over successive seasons. One advantage is that it provides the greatest possible opportunity for production experimentation, although some set formats permit considerable variability, as well. Production approaches which prove to work well can later be used more extensively, and those which work poorly can be dropped. In the case of a series with a highly varied format, formative research carried out between production seasons can provide particularly high payoff, for at that time, there is a great deal of material to test and usually ample time to test it. Another strategy made possible with the segmented format is that of distributing production resources unequally over segments so as to produce a pool of higher-than-average quality material each season for replay in the next. The advantages of this approach are that it yields an ultimate level of quality not otherwise attainable, and also that it makes possible an early demonstration for funding purposes of the additional effectiveness which can be achieved with the higher level of quality.

The visual, verbal, and motor responses of viewing groups. Group observations made during selected intervals over the course of a televised presentation can provide gross but useful information about a segment's appeal, its comprehensibility, and its activity eliciting potential. This method also provides the well-trained and ingenious observer with an occasion and an opportunity to observe a program very closely, to maintain an observational check list, to accumulate quantifiable data for special analyses, and to make in-depth probes of subjects' responses either with predesigned follow-up questions or on-the-spot interviews. The cost/effectiveness ratio for this approach is as favorable as for almost any other conceivable approach.

Pilot production and evaluation. Preseason pilot production deserves special consideration for a number of strategic reasons, one being the fact that extensive revisions are possible before the season begins airing -- at a time when extensive revisions present no threat to the integrity of the series. Another is that the producers are at that time most receptive to valid suggestions and most in a position to make use of them.

The formative use of summative data. Traditional forms of postseason testing, of the sort typically carried out in order to evaluate the educational impact of a program series over an entire broadcast season, can provide a great deal of information for revising subsequent productions. The value of this approach can be enhanced by maintaining a careful record of the amount and type of production treatment given to each objective or to the subject matter of each test item, and by then relating this record to magnitudes of tested effects. In this manner, it is possible to identify the quite specific instructional strategies which are most and least effective. Where it is possible to include in the interpretation further data on the comprehensibility of the different production approaches, on their appeal, or on the internal compatibility of their various elements, the results can be more useful still. The obvious drawback to the use of summative data for formative purposes is that the results are not available until well after a full season's broadcast.

The Distinctive Role and Functions of Formative Research

The most important factor underlying the distinctive form and style of product developmental research is its role as an integral part of the creative production process. It is important to maintain a clear distinction between this type of research, on the one hand, and that undertaken in order to test the validity of a theory or the measurable impact of an educational product or practice, on the other. Research undertaken in the context of scientific validation is concerned with effects which have been hypothesized, a priori, within the framework of a broader deductive system; with the use of empirical and statistical procedures well enough defined so as to be strictly replicable (at least in principle); and with the highest possible degree of generalizability across situations. In contrast, while research carried out within the formative context can possess all these same characteristics, it need not necessarily, and does not, typically. The only pervasive criterion for formative research recommendations is that they appear likely to contribute to the effectiveness of the product or procedure being developed. It is neither expected nor required that they be validated by the research out of which they grew. Establishing their validity is the function of summative research.

As this view implies, to achieve the objectives of formative research it is often necessary to depart from traditional research practices and perspectives. This is not to say that experimental rigor has no place in the formative context. However, for example, even where strict experimental and control conditions have been maintained, there is seldom anything to be gained by using tests of statistical significance. The creative producers often prefer to work directly with information about means, dispersions, and sample size. Also, whereas matching of experimental and control groups on the basis of pretest scores is discouraged where inferential statistics are to be used because of the conservative effect upon the significance of the results, such matching can be very useful, for efficiency, to maximize the reliability of information based on small samples.

In the area of sample selection, it also can be useful to depart from the traditional practice of including all age and socioeconomic groups for which the educational materials are intended. Time and effort often can be saved by selecting a sample of average performers, or performers from the high and low extremes, or, where the intent is mainly to upgrade the lowest performers, a sample only of those. In general, where biased methods of sampling and biased methods of testing are more efficient than unbiased methods, and where the objective is not to make accurate population estimates, it is often useful to exploit the very biases which quite properly would be avoided in other research situations.

In practice, it tends to be difficult for researchers trained and experienced in traditional approaches to adopt an appropriate formative research point of view. In the formative situation, their first responsibility is to improve a specific product or practice, and not to contribute to a general body of knowledge (although the two objectives certainly are not incompatible). Studies must first address the information needs of the product designers and not primarily the individualistic or special theoretical interests of the researchers. Covering a wide range of empirical questions may deserve priority over rigorous reporting or establishing careful experimental conditions, where it is economically impossible to achieve both, and where the usefulness of the results is not unduly compromised as a consequence. Quantitative indices such as percentages, and highly detailed item-level data, if they communicate most effectively with the creative producers, are to be preferred over those which conform to standard practice for research reports. Broad, speculative interpretations of empirical results are typically more useful than interpretations limited to the more strict implications of a study. And, as indicated earlier, biased methods of sample selection and testing often can be employed to good advantage. However, in following these departures from standard research practice, there is a risk of producing misleading results. Accordingly, it is essential that the production recommendations be very carefully qualified.

Formative research, in the view taken here, is properly eclectic and pragmatic. In these respects, it is highly compatible with the current trend toward the very explicit definition of instructional objectives, followed by the development through systematic trial and revision of instructional systems for achieving them. This approach, incidentally, in no way diminishes the traditional role of the behavioral sciences in education or the usefulness of existing theory and knowledge. Rather, it holds that a useful step between basic research and educational practice is additional research of a formative sort, far more directly concerned with specific combinations of educational objectives, instructional media, learners, and learning situations. This is not to say that formative research is exclusively concerned with putting theory into practice. An equally valid function is that of starting with practice and transforming it into improved practice. Still another is that of providing hypotheses for further research and theoretical development.

One long-standing point of view in education holds that theories and results growing out of the "mother" disciplines of psychology, sociology, anthropology, and the like, will filter into effective educational practice if enough educators have been trained in these basic disciplines. While this approach has been useful to a degree, it has not produced broadly satisfactory results. Meanwhile, creators of new educational products and practices have proceeded largely without the benefits of measurement and research. This is partly because skill and training in these areas have been linked to the process of theory construction and validation, and partly because of an inappropriately rigid adherence to traditional research practice within the product developmental context. Formative research procedure promises to help in creating a mutually constructive relationship between these two overly isolated realms -- the science and the technology of learning.

REFERENCES

Ball, S., and Bogatz, G. A. The First Year of Sesame Street: An Evaluation. Princeton: Educational Testing Service, 1970.

Ball, S., and Bogatz, G. A. The Second Year of Sesame Street: A Continuing Evaluation. Vols. I and II. Princeton: Educational Testing Service, 1971.

IV

TELEVISION OR SOMETHING ELSE?

For a meeting on television, a surprising amount of attention was devoted to other media. This was because the belief was so widely and strongly held, among the conferees, that instructional television must be viewed as only one of a number of tools of learning, each one of which should be used to do what it can do best and should only be used when an educational system can afford to use it well.

One visiting producer showed a program to the conferees and was asked, "Why did you do this on television?" He answered, "Because my job is to produce television."

This point of view did not get very far in the meeting, however. Lundgren, as we have indicated, introduced quite a different viewpoint when he described how Sweden decided what particular teaching and learning tasks, within a given course, should be assigned to television, radio, print, radiovision, or other learning aids. Alan Hancock, of BBC and UNESCO, who had served as a senior producer during the beginning years of the Open University, discussed how that institution had decided to divide its broadcasts between radio and television. In the first-year courses, each student has available one 30-minute television program, one 30-minute radio program, per course, per week. The television is typically used for an illustrated lecture or a documentary directed to the central subject matter of the week and to the study and writing the student is expected to be doing at home. The science and mathematics courses are more often lectures; the social science, documentaries. Radio, on the other hand, is used more informally -- often to discuss questions sent in by students, to guide them through their homework, and, of course, to handle topics where the spoken word and music, rather than illustrations, are the essence of the communication.

Both Sweden and the British Open University, of course, can afford to program multi-media courses. There was considerable discussion of the under-use of radio in situations when a country can afford only _one_ instructional medium, and feels it must decide between television and radio. Usually the choice is television, even at ten times the cost of radio. Why? Because of considerations of prestige, because of exaggerated ideas of the advantages of television, and because of the lack of recent research on instructional radio that will clarify what it can accomplish when optimally used. There was a general feeling among the conferees that radio has been by-passed too quickly, before its full potential as a tool of learning can be realized or tested, and that it, as well as others of the less expensive media, may be coming into a second summer.

To represent this topic of discussion, we are reproducing in the following pages a paper on the "smaller media," by C. Ray Carpenter, Professor of Psychology and Anthropology at the University of Georgia. He is one of the most experienced of all American scholars on instructional technology, and during his long career at Penn State as well as at Georgia has contributed studies of fundamental importance to the research on teaching by film, television, and radio.

Finally, we are including one other product of Professor Carpenter that proved interesting to members of the meeting. This was a form for evaluating the probable instructional effectiveness of a film or television program. It was developed in its present form in 1968, and has proved useful in many places.

THE APPLICATION OF LESS COMPLEX INSTRUCTIONAL TECHNOLOGIES

By C. Ray Carpenter, Professor of Psychology and Anthropology, University of Georgia

Purpose and Objectives

The purpose of this essay is to outline strategy considerations judged to be essential for introducing and using successfully the small, less-complicated, and less-expensive instructional technologies for developing countries. This document will reflect information and experience gained over 20 years of research, development, and application (R. D. & A.) work in American education. Experiences will be extracted, furthermore, from work with instructional and educational technology in India, Japan, Guam, Spain, and developing regions of the United States.

The objectives are limited and clear, but important: to provide practical information and suggestions that will aid developing countries and regions in selectively introducing appropriate educational and instructional technologies as a means of advancing their planned development.

Selection and Introduction Strategies

Definitions

Technologies of small scale are those that are relatively the least complicated, expensive, and difficult to operate. They are those means and procedures for use in designing and creating learning environments which effectively encourage the learning and acquisition of basic skills and essential concepts and attitudes for successfully responding to demands/needs of the indigenous country or region. Examples of demands/needs processes are those related to health, sanitation, and nutrition; and those of reproduction and socio-sexual behavior and social interactions.

A definition of educational and instructional technology is

essential at this point to indicate the nature and scope of treatment in this essay. The Commission on Instructional Technology decided after lengthy discussion and debate (1) that the principal function of such technology was to aid the teaching instructional processes to design and create favorable learning environments and conditions, and (2) that such technologies included the components of instruments or apparatus, methods and procedures, and the people who operated these things. We will extend this definition to include both formal and informal learning situations.

Selection criteria

The assumption is made that rational, logical, and objective approaches can be made to the selection of the best fit of small technologies to the targeted country or region. It is clearly evident, however, that objective and rational procedures which should be used to engineer the educational technologies of an institution or region will need to be adapted and accommodated to the sociopolitical realities and value systems of the target population. To determine the limits of the minimum necessary compromises between the rational blueprint for technologies and the sociopolitical realities and requirements puts severe demands on those who plan and implement strategies for adaptive educational innovations in developing regions and ecosystems. Let it be assumed, nevertheless, that the basis and foundation must be laid in rational objective planning before the demands of compromise with the inevitable are considered.

Scanning of educational technologies broadly and functionally defined shows a very wide range of types of things and operations in the domain of communication media that could be useful, in varying degrees, in advancing the basic developments of emerging countries like Colombia, Zaire, and Indonesia. The large number of alternatives from which selections can be made creates the necessity to have an ordered set of criteria for use in guiding the selection of those media to be applied in defined regions. Therefore, the following briefly defined selection criteria may prove to be practical and useful.

1. The necessity for research, development, and application work: A logical and rational selection approach must be based on adequate, reliable, and valid evidence that is appropriate to the target country or region. Some sources of this kind of evidence are results of research and development on communication media conducted in advanced countries like the United States, Great Britain, Italy, and Japan. The systematic observation of relevant conditions in the targeted region can provide additional evidence, along with records of the previous history of what has been tried, like educational radio

and television in Colombia, and did or did not work satisfactorily. Even with the best logical assessments of these kinds of evidence, unacceptable errors and faults of large dimensions are inevitable without the benefit and guidance of appropriately scaled and sustained indigenous programs of research and evaluations. Therefore, it is suggested that along with the efforts to introduce and use small instructional technologies, such lines and programs of research of adequate scope and variety be conducted as a basic part of the media introduction-operation procedures.

2. The expectation is that even small technologies like sound-strip film or short, limited, cassette-mounted 8mm film, even though field tested and proved in one country, will require field testing in the area or country of application. The concept of proving-ground organizations and operations for educational and instructional communication technologies is 20 years old, but it has never been applied rigorously enough, or on a scale of significance, to guide significantly and improve the economies of innovations in developing regions.

The demonstration/proving-ground mechanisms could be established, first: by cooperative efforts of industries and governmental agencies; and second: They could be established on a regional or multinational basis. A demonstration/proving ground at Kinshasa, Zaire, or Bogotá, Colombia could have a wingspread of usefulness that would extend over neighboring and somewhat similar areas, regions, or countries. Incidentally, shared demonstration/proving-ground resources could possibly instigate and advance desirable international cooperation as well as desirable joint efforts of industries and governmental agencies.

3. Field tests of equipment and procedures as well as determination of human factor requirements of acceptability and operation skills would, in addition, check out the following:

Practicability and ease of operations. The small technologies will probably score higher on this criterion than complicated systems like computer-assisted instruction and educational television.

Durability and ruggedness of equipment.* Most communication

---

*Ruggedness and durability are often related to simplicity of design. Recently in a tropical area I was using both a Bell and Howell spring-driven camera and an Arriflex power-driven camera. The main connection of the Arriflex with the power cable had nine pins of media are developed in temperate zones. Large portions of many of the developing countries like Colombia, the Congo, and Indonesia are tropical. Hence, it is essential that equipment be designed, constructed, and protected for tropical climates; otherwise fungi and high heat and humidity may seriously interfere with dependable operations.

Ease and Simplicity of Operations

Equipment, however small, should be selected for target countries using this criterion. The self-threading 8 or 16mm motion picture projectors have high preference values by users over those that need to be hand threaded. Simple, rugged, and easy to operate sound tape recorders and replay equipment should be selected, and when selected will be preferred by users to the multiswitched and more complex recorder-players. Desirably, in brief, simplicity of design, ruggedness of construction, and ease and dependability of operations can be provided all together.

Training for Operating and Servicing Equipment

Failures of equipment can seriously affect acceptability of instructional technologies by educators, teachers, and students. This has been repeatedly demonstrated during R & D efforts to apply instructional television in American universities. Therefore, good technical services must be made available, and these should be provided as near as possible to the places of use. Surely, services should be provided by training technicians of the target countries in the schools and program centers and at other places of use. Even with tape machines, slide and filmstrip projection, operating and servicing skills cannot be

---

contacts. One of these pins, micrometers in diameter and four centimeters long, broke at a solder point, and the camera was put out of commission. A day's time only was lost, but in remote areas this small fault of complex equipment could have been disastrous to the photographic mission.

In the same tropical climate, equipment with optical components, binoculars, and cameras, is attacked by lens fungi and light transmission qualities are affected. Both tropical climate proofing and humidity-controlled storage, even for equipment of small technologies, are necessary correctives.

assumed, and they must be provided for the equipment and technologies selected for use in target areas. Fortunately, it is possible to prepare and package servicing, maintenance, and simple repair instructions that are programmed and displayed or presented by the audio-pictorial media themselves. A slide or motion picture projector can have packaged with the equipment by manufacturers and/or distributors and instructions provided on slides or films of how to service and repair the equipment. Even when properly prepared written instructions can not be read, clear, understandable instructions can be given on sound tape in the country's spoken language and accompanied by still or motion picture diagrams and illustrations. Actually, full courses in "audio-visual" equipment and its operation and servicing administered on a self-instruction basis have been proved to be as effective as teacher-dominated lecture-demonstrated courses.

It is self-evident that different levels of training and skills are required ranging from those needed by the user, to local assistance and service, and to more remote and long-distance service. In conclusion on this criterion, even when small technologies are used, training and instruction in their servicing and uses cannot be neglected and to the greatest extent possible these should be provided by local people near points of use. And, finally, it is essential that sets of spare parts are selected, made available and maintained, and that parts reserves will be appropriately provided for equipment selected.

Appropriateness of Technology Scale and Scope to Educational Needs and Requirements

Ideally, the technologies selected in a technologically developing country should be related precisely in degree of complexity, scale, and scope to the educational need/demand estimates. There is a strong tendency for highly industrialized countries like the United States or West Germany to try to accomplish, in developing countries and with overly complex equipment, what they have not succeeded in doing at home. Spain is advised to go all-out for computer-assisted instruction and micro-video tape teacher training before radio or simpler, more adaptive sound slide, sound tape, and motion picture technologies have been explored. Satellite relays of educational television programs are recommended for India by advanced industrial countries before All-India Radio and very feasible expansions of audio radio facilities have been committed and applied for educational purposes. The pressures and goals for industrial growth and foreign markets, and perhaps as well, the frustrations of fully applying proved but less-glamorous technologies in education often lead to "leap-frogging" over the proved and practical to high-risk adventure with the latest great complex technological system. In addition, there are prospects of more profit in the large than the small technologies.

The other side of the coin should not be neglected in solving the equation of the appropriate scaling of technologies to educational requirements and functions, for technologies can also be under-scaled. The cheap and the small may not always be the best and most efficient. The book needs to be supplemented by sound tape and/or radio for *spoken language* instruction, where literacy is limited and where practice opportunities are essential for perceptual-motor skills and vocational training. The problem is to match with precision the media with the learning demands.

There is another dimension to the difficult task of providing technologies for target countries in *precise scale*. This is the *amount* dimension. The task is to provide enough but not too much of the selected equipment, and not only must enough be available in the country, but it *must be distributed* to match the educational needs and population dispersion patterns. In other terms, availability in a country may or may not mean *accessibility* to the fieldworker and learner where and when needed.

Cost Factors: Capital, Operation, and Maintenance-Service Costs

Selection of small technologies should include realistic estimates of original or capital costs, maintenance and repair costs, operation costs, and antiquation-replacement costs. The balance sheets are very different, for example, between these sets of costs for sound filmstrip with still photography and the same sound with motion pictures; and the balance sheets are vastly different between one-inch video-tape operations and two-inch tape systems. *Super-8 motion picture systems including wages and salaries for personnel are estimated to cost one-twentieth of even 16mm sound motion picture systems*. Corresponding additional or auxiliary costs are low.

There is probably greater availability of parts and maintenance for the smaller technologies than the large or complex. When one considers costs, both of human energy and dollars, the "down time" of the equipment must also be evaluated, a serious cost of breakdowns.

The area of communication media is one where antiquation rates are usually high. The market is very competitive on an international level and hence new developments and "improved models" are marketed frequently. Selectors of *instructional* media should be keenly aware of the antiquation rates of equipment and consequently of methods, procedures, and trained personnel. They should also be cautious and skeptical about accepting technologies or equipment which are being cast off by industry and replaced with new developments. These cautions apply equally to complex and small educational technologies, particularly since the unit volume of less complex technologies is dispersed and large.

The basic accounting and economic principle that costs interact with utility should be considered. Since it will be found difficult to apply cost/effectiveness accounting in education in developing countries, it may be necessary, in selecting technologies, to use estimates of costs (which can be "hard" estimates) *to units of instruction times the number of learners that will be served*. Costs should ideally be related to such behavioral effects as improved and measured levels of nutritional standards in the population, or indicators of changed food preferences, or reductions in birth rates in sample populations. The valid products of educational technologies are gains and contributions to serving the defined educational functions or to the achievement of specific and describable or measurable purposes and objectives.

Operation Strategies

Functions and objectives

The operation of small technologies, like all educational efforts, needs to be given direction and shape, scale and scope by the analysis of the instructional/learning functions to be served by the media, and analysis and explication of the objectives to be achieved by the media technologies. These analytic operations are obvious but difficult.

Educational-instructional-learning functions, processes, or operations which are to be mediated by small technologies are the following:

- -- recording and storage of information, instructional-learning units, courses, and programs;
- -- the selection and reproduction of instructional-learning units and programs;
- -- the distribution and display or presentation of the stimulus materials for learning or attitude change to the learner;

-- and, finally, the assessment and feedback of the results of the operations to those who need them.

The use of technologies involves these and perhaps other definable functions.

The kinds of functions to be served, the manner and style of this service, the characteristics of the content, and the numbers and kinds of dispersion patterns of the people (learners) to be served should determine how instructional technologies are used.

Populations of people

It is important to build into strategies of media operations much dependable knowledge about the people involved. The role includes the decision-makers; "gatekeepers" of public power and the peoples' welfare; those who provide logistical support both within and outside the country; the managers at national, regional, and local levels; educational authorities and experts including especially subject-matter and methods specialists; the media operators; the program and effects evaluators; and, most importantly, the working teachers and the responsible learners. One deduction from this list is clear: A large number of people of different kinds taking different roles and having different conceptual structures and vocabularies urgently needs to be informed and even instructed.

Traditionally, in communication practices emphasis is given to fitting the "message" to the "target audience." Effective uses of instructional media require extensive analysis and refinement of the processes of fitting, preparing, and developing the instructional or stimulus materials for learning for "targeted audiences" of learners. Details of these processes need not be described here, but let us outline other considerations of very practical import.

Let us assume that (1) analyses have been made of the instructional requirements necessary for achieving an educational mission over time, and the specific learning or behavioral effects subsumed over the general mission. Let us assume, furthermore, that the necessary analyses have been made of the audiences of learners and their characteristics. Let it be recalled that the analysis of learner characteristics -- interests, motivation, aspiration levels, extant relevant skills, etc. -- is a much more precision and individualized reference job than the corresponding audience analyses tasks and practices of even good journalism. Indeed, the task is so formidable that actual test-and-fit operations are parts of modern advanced methodologies for producing effective instructional programs. This job cannot be avoided without jeopardizing the effectiveness of the communication-teaching operations.

There is the practical necessity to use small media technology in a manner that is appropriate to the peoples' geographic dispersion and grouping patterns. Where are the people who will be served as learners? Where must designed learning environments be anchored, whether they are carrels; classrooms; mobile units, land or water-born; pocket and portable cassette players -- that is, the places to read, listen, talk, or write? One operational procedure is to use that technology that has the capabilities of spanning space between information sources to wherever the learning points are located in space. The mails, postage or carriage, radio broadcast, and other means such as wire or cable and point-to-point microwave transmission: Any or many in combination may need to be used to reach dispersed populations of learners. There must be physical linkage from sources of learning materials with learners. The principle to be implemented is both simple and demanding. These things are especially true in densely populated countries like Indonesia, especially Java, but also in sparsely settled regions like the riverine Congo or mountainous Colombia. The operational principle is to move information and learning materials to the people and reduce as much as possible the travel of people to the places where learning materials originate or are displayed. It is both more economical and often more effective to use the information-dissemination strategies rather than the assembly of people strategy. However, both in due proportions may be useful. Not only is the process more economical, but it produces the learning stimulus in a more natural and meaningful behavior setting.

Strategies of use need to be developed for optimizing the grouping of people for learning. Sizes of grouping need to be determined which are optimized for learning the kinds of desired behavioral changes. The extremes of mass instruction and individualization of instruction alone need not be used. All learning is individual, but the conditions of learning can be varied in terms of group size. Some learning requires isolation and privacy; other learning and learners require the social reinforcement which exists in small groups; still other learning for economic and feasibility considerations can occur without decrement in large and very large audiences. Clearly the small technologies are most useful most often in individual, small-group, and home instruction. It is clear, also, that the learning strategists, especially when managing sensitive instruction where barriers of cultural values and emotional blocks may be involved, need to use a wide range of alternative designs of learning conditions and technologies.

The time dimension is involved with populations of learners. Learning induces changes in behavior, if the learning operations are effective, and therefore the target population of learners is a changing or moving target. Accordingly, the aims and objectives, the levels of content, and the encouraged practices of skills should change as learning rates and directions change.

Let us recall that our defintion of small technology is that size and complexity which are necessary to serve well the essential educational-learning functions without excess or waste of resources.

Instructional Strategies

There is an extensive information base on the use of media for instigating and reinforcing learning, and the literature on instructional film research has been reviewed recently (Carpenter, 1971, Journal of Instructional Technology, England). The emphasis in this section will be on the often neglected factors in using media for educational purposes and for changing attitudes and social norms of human populations. There are several major tasks: (1) using media appropriately for recording, storing, distributing, and displaying information to targeted populations of learners; (2) avoiding the frequently committed errors that are made in employing media for learning; (3) using the correct communication modes within the selected media; and (4) providing reinforcing "feedback" and assessment of specific mode and media effects.

The central task is, as has been said before, the precision matching of media and modes to instructional functions and objectives; to content characteristics; to target audience characteristics; to the logistics and strategies of designing and creating learning environments; and to providing for evaluations relative to learning or behavioral change needs and anticipated results. More generally, there must be a matching of communication power (human and physical energy input requirements) with the requirements for producing desired behavioral changes. Particularly with the emerging societies and cultures, the making of estimations of the CP (communication power) requirements is most difficult but very important. Likewise, this task is especially complicated when basic and deeply embedded attitudes and cultural norms are targets of behavioral change efforts. These two conditions are involved in food raising, in buying food and its preparation, in food preferences of populations, and especially in the modifying of traditional patterns of reproductive behavior, child rearing, and family life.

A very commonly committed error is revealed by the often heard comment following discussion of an information or training-need problem, "Oh yes, we need a film." This remark reveals gross underestimation of the resistance of attitudes and social norms to the effect of change agents and influences. Not a film but a film series of many units used as part of an intensive and sustained program is required even to produce limited changes in attitudes and social norm behavior. Particularly is this true when the existing standard behaviors and affective norms are supported and frequently reinforced by the constant pressure of sociocultural patterns.

One advantage of small technologies is that they are usable in local situations and with varied but reiterated frequencies. Provided interest and learner appeals are features of these small technologies, the people who are to be affected by them may regulate their frequency of use and the timing and social context of their conditions of use.

Avoiding Biases

There are important biases which intrude into the planning and uses of media for whatever purposes in influencing peoples of emerging cultures.

There is the observable bias of conceding to or complying with adverse sociopolitical pressures rather than solving the difficult problems of convincing decision-makers to accept and support engineered and rationally designed plans. The reality of political fabrics into which educational changing processes are to be intruded must be accepted and taken into account in the designs of learning strategies. There is often a most delicate task required to adjust or compromise the logical plan with this political fabric. Often, too, such compromises strain and challenge professional ethics. No simple formula can be proposed for compromising the plan that should be projected with political forces which distort, conflict, and even vitiate the plans. It is suggested, however, that clearly formulated agreements and definitions of roles, tasks, and responsibilities at the beginning are sound steps whether complex or small technologies are to be used.

A related bias has to do with selection and definition of media, selection areas and patterns of applications, and evaluation of programs. Political biases and partisan interest often intervene in assessments and evaluations. This bias takes its most extreme form when, regardless of actual and demonstrable results, projects, programs, and educational developments are either condemned or declared to be great successes.

The bias of media myopia should be avoided. Oftentimes a kind of medium such as printed materials, radio, television, teaching machines and programmed instruction, and now the computer-regulated learning is proposed and projected as the sweeping solution to complex and difficult-to-achieve educational demands. Such proposals are often developed and projected by media specialists from highly industrialized countries who are fixated on a particular medium.

Small technologies are not so likely to be put forward as comprehensive cure-all solutions as are the more complex media systems, and hence the multi-media systems concept which was so strongly urged by the U.S. Commission on Instructional Technology is most likely to be accepted with these small technologies.

It would seem to be both sound and wise to avoid commitments to a single or limited medium, small or large, until detailed studies have been made of the needs and demands for it and the objectives that are to be achieved. A commitment should not have been made solely to "educational television" for American Samoa or Guam before an analysis was made of matching possibilities of a wide spectrum of media and learner characteristics coordinated with profiles of learning requirements.

Sometimes expensive biases are brought into the processes of introducing and using educational media by high pressure and very effective industrial marketing. This can lead both to the wrong or inappropriate media being introduced with failure and dissatisfaction assured and to the introducing of excessively complex and expensive technology.

A general and completely defensible principle for guiding the introduction and uses of media for sociocultural change would seem to be: Examine and test adequacy and appropriateness of technologies on a continuum of small to large, the lesser to more complex, and select the "media package" that is adequate but not excessively complex relative to the required performances.

Selecting Modes of Communication: The Crucial Problem

Distinctions are not often made between media and modes of instructional communication. This distinction is not only necessary, but the use of the correct mode of sign-symbol semantics is equally important with the use of the right medium or combination of media. Consideration of modes of communication and efforts to match them with practical needs may lead directly to uses of small technologies. For example, if print and print alone is *matched with precision to the essentials of the communication task*, then print as a mode, when designed into a suitable format and shown on an appropriate carrier base, will be the mode to be used. If, however, print needs to be supplemented by *picture* or sound, a solution other than print is required. Clearly along with the practical considerations of *media* uses, analysis of *mode* uses is important because the kinds and combinations of *modes* are critically related to learning and behavioral changes.

Two points of information are relevant: Adding one mode to another, or a third mode to two, does not ensure increases in the amount or rate of learning. Indeed single-mode displays may be most effective under some conditions. Some research results show *interference* with learning of some types when additional *modes* of stimulation are added to the information displays. There is, also, the related phenomenon of *information overload* when too much information is presented too fast for assimilation and thus does not contribute but may actually interfere with information learning. A third kind of interference is the "pollution" of communication channels with information noises, i.e., redundant, useless, or irrelevant elements and programs.

The effective uses of small technologies in developing countries may be related to new concepts of *literacy* in the target populations. This definition includes receptivity to many different channels through which may flow information for learning. This includes not only the sensory-perception processes but also the literacy of observing skills which are basic to seeking and accepting *new* information. It may be useful, in addition, to be aware that populations of people observably vary in their "openness for learning" and in the eagerness, interest, and initiative taken in seeking and searching to learn. This problem of defining characteristics of *prevailing learning sets of populations* is worthy of new research. In brief, what may be termed cultural patterns of learning styles need study in order to relate them appropriately to small technologies applied in developing countries to modify and improve the adaptiveness of peoples' behavior.

FORM FOR EVALUATING THE INSTRUCTIONAL EFFECTIVENESS OF FILMS OR TELEVISION PROGRAMS

By C. Ray Carpenter, Professor of Psychology and Anthropology, University of Georgia

Name of film or
Name/number of program ______________________________

Title of Series ______________________________

Produced by ______________________________

Distributed by ______________________________

Date of viewing ______________________________

This form has been designed to study the factors and elements in a unit of instructional material which contribute most significantly to its achievement of excellent quality. For the purposes of this evaluation, quality is defined as those factors which produce the desired behavioral changes in the target population.

Please circle the term which represents your best judgment of the degree to which the program satisfies each criterion. Feel free to add any comments which will help to describe the reasons for evaluation. If you believe the criterion does not apply, please encircle DNA.

I. OBJECTIVES

1. Are the instructional objectives as stated or implied in the lesson clear to the viewer?

   Very clear Clear Adequate Unclear Very unclear DNA

   What are the objectives? ______________________________

   ____

   How are they stated? By whom? ______________________________

COMMENTS:

2. Does the content of the program relate closely to the main objectives, or are there many irrelevancies?

Very closely	Closely	Adequately	Some irrelevancies	Many irrelevancies	DNA

COMMENTS:

II. CONTENT

3. Does the amount of time taken to develop each concept, procedure, or example seem appropriate or inappropriate for the intended audience?

Highly appro-priate	Appropriate	Acceptable	Somewhat inappro-priate	Highly inappro-priate	DNA

COMMENTS:

4. Is the content organized and so structured as to facilitate learning?

Very well	Well	Adequately	Poor	Very poorly	DNA

COMMENTS:

5. Is the material based on expert, up-to-date professional information?

Contains latest knowledge	Very up-to-date	Adequately up-to-date	Contains obsolete information	Very obsolete	DNA

COMMENTS:

6. Is the vocabulary level appropriate for the intended audience?

Highly appro-priate	Very appro-priate	Appro-priate level	In-appro-priate	Very in-appro-priate	DNA

COMMENTS:

III. PRESENTATION OF MATERIAL

7. Does the presentation provide for optimum repetition of the main ideas? (e.g., Summaries of main points from time to time and at end; repetition with variation.)

Optimum repe-tition	Adequate repe-tition	Some repe-tition	Too little or too much	Far too little or far too much	DNA

COMMENTS:

8. Does the program effectively use appropriate pictures, film clips, demonstrations, diagrams, and other graphics? (Number and kinds of visuals are not as important as the way in which they are used to support the instruction.)

Highly effective	Above average	Moderately effective	Below average	Ineffective	DNA

COMMENTS:

9. Is the video-photographic presentation clearly perceivable by use of good lighting, appropriate camera shots, sharpness of details, pointers, suitable backgrounds, etc. ? (This does not require a highly technical or engineering evaluation but rather a judgment as to whether or not the program or film is perceptually clear.)

Highly perceiv- able	Clearly perceiv- able	Accept- able	Barely perceiv- able	Un- perceiv- able	DNA

COMMENTS:

10. Is the audio intelligible?

Satisfactory	Unsatisfactory	DNA

COMMENTS:

11. Is there an appropriate integration of visual and audio?

Excellent integration	Good integration	Adequate	Poor integration	Very poor integration	DNA

COMMENTS:

12. Does the presentation give the impression of authenticity?

Authentic	Lacks authenticity	DNA

COMMENTS:

13. Do the personality and appearance of the teacher or teachers add to or detract from the effectiveness of the presentation?

Adds greatly	Adds somewhat	Neutral in effects	Detracts somewhat	Detracts greatly	DNA

COMMENTS:

14. Do the characteristics and quality of the instructor's or commentator's voice add to or detract from the effectiveness of the presentation?

Adds greatly	Adds somewhat	Neutral in effects	Detracts somewhat	Detracts greatly	DNA

COMMENTS:

15. Does the teacher appear on camera for an appropriate amount of time?

Optimum amount of time	Too much	Too little	Approximate percentage of time	DNA

COMMENTS:

IV. LEARNER STIMULATION

16. Are the techniques designed to provide viewer participation successful or unsuccessful? (Participation means students using work sheets, devices, and other ways of actively involving them in the instruction.)

Highly suc-cessful	Moderately suc-cessful	Barely suc-cessful	Partially unsuc-cessful	Totally unsuc-cessful	DNA

COMMENTS:

17. Does the presentation motivate the student to do supplementary work and study on the problem? (If so, specify under COMMENTS what the learners might do.)

Very high motivation	High	Adequate	Low	Very low motivation	DNA

COMMENTS:

18. Is any testing incorporated into the presentation or presented by the classroom instructor to the students following the telecast to measure the learners' achievement? (Note under COMMENTS how testing is included.)

Appropriate testing procedure	Too much testing	Too little testing	No testing	DNA

COMMENTS:

19. Is there a procedure for reporting the knowledge of test results? (Under COMMENTS, specify what type and to whom reported.)

Yes No DNA

COMMENTS:

VI. GENERAL EVALUATION

20. What is your overall evaluation of the unit?

Outstanding	Above average	Average	Below average	Very poor	DNA

COMMENTS:

21. What other criteria are applicable to this unit? Use these criteria for further evaluation of the unit. If information is available, note here facts on utilization, i.e., number of schools presently using the lesson or series, how often, etc.

V

COMMON GROUND

In point of fact, whenever the scholars and the broadcasters talked about actual programs they sounded surprisingly alike. They had little trouble, for example, agreeing that an effective program should begin, so to speak, with a child and an objective. It must begin _where the child is_ -- what he knows and is interested in, his level of ability, the culture he lives in, and the ways of learning to which he has become accustomed. It must begin with a clear objective, preferably stated in behavioral terms, and pre- rather than post-determined. It must seize and hold the child's interest. It must be clear. It must provide as much repetition (with variation) as the child needs in order to learn what is intended to be learned. It must be sequenced smoothly, and move the child from his starting point to the kind of behavior or understanding that is the objective of the program. And it must provide an opportunity to practice the desired behavior, and offer a bridge to practice and application after the program is over. There was no trouble with general statements of that order.

Furthermore, no one disagreed with the idea that an instructional program might -- should -- be fun. One of the conference papers asked: Why should a learner not learn to smile? Other people said: Why should not the experience be pleasant, challenging, exciting? The conferees saw a film of television in Niger and were impressed with the joy that was so evident on the faces of the children watching the TV program. Why should this not happen more often in American classrooms? they asked.

Broadcasters and scholars agreed, as we have said earlier, on the importance of _active_ learning from television, on the questionable advantages of embellishments and "fanciness," and on many other major points. Perhaps the best way to indicate the breadth of agreement among different groups and different backgrounds is to set down in three parallel columns three viewpoints all derived from conference papers. The first of these is a shorthand list of "principles to guide production," prepared for the writers and producers of _Sesame Street,_ and reported to the conference in a paper by Lesser. Lesser's own background is in child development, and the guidelines come out of the psychology of learning and the study of children, and have been affected by the long experience in television of some of the chief program people of the Television Workshop. The second column is taken from Lundgren's paper, derived from a lifetime in educational broadcasting. The third column is put together from several documents presented to the conference by Carpenter, who has been for many years a leader in research on instructional technology. His guidelines derive from research.

This comparison, of course, is made after the fact. None of these men knew they were heading for a comparison, and would doubtless have done their job somewhat differently, and perhaps at greater length, if shown what they were being compared with. Furthermore, we have begun with Lesser's list, and tried to make the others fit; if we had begun with Lundgren's or Carpenter's outlines, the scheme would have looked somewhat different. But the very fact that the three lists came from different backgrounds and were designed for different purposes makes all the more impressive the degree of agreement among them.

Wherever possible, we have tried to use the actual words of the three authors, although of course we do them an injustice by not presenting their ideas in full. Readers of this volume will want to go back to the original documents, to flesh out the shorthand report in the following table. (See pages 213-217.)

Considering that the papers we have drawn upon were done quite separately, at different times, thousands of miles apart, and for quite different purposes, the amount of agreement is striking. These men, from their different backgrounds, obviously were thinking along the same lines.

To put this table in perspective, however, let us ask the kind of question that might be put by a reader who has never made instructional television programs. If we have guidelines worked out in such detail, and as much consensus on them as our table indicates, why is there so much trouble in making effective ITV? Why can't we hit the bulls-eye oftener? Why can't any producer win the Japan Prize?

The answer, sad to say, is that there is a wide gap between general ideas and superlative broadcasts. Clearly, there is more known about effective ITV than most programs make use of. But <u>someone</u>, if he is aware of the guidelines in the table just presented, must make use of them. Someone has to take the ideas and turn them into concepts, action, color, sound, learning activity, and, ultimately, programs -- all based on a given set of instructional goals and designed

WHAT MAKES FOR EFFECTIVE ITV?

	LESSER	LUNDGREN	CARPENTER
Starting points			
	Behavioral objectives: "make the goal statements clear and concrete"	Concrete objectives	Are the instructional objectives clear?
	Estimates of initial competence of children	Producer must know the situation of the audience	Timing, vocabulary, level of complexity must be appropriate for performance capability of students
Assumptions about children's learning			
	Motivation	Motivation	Motivation
	Practice	Activity	Effective learning requires active and persistent responses (and) reinforcement in terms of satisfying rewards, social approval, knowledge of success, etc.

LESSER	LUNDGREN	CARPENTER
Assumptions about children's learning (continued)		
Learn from format as well as from content		
Modeling -- give learners behavior to imitate		
Narrow focusing -- the less "noise," the better	Avoid distractions	Need clear and focused perceptual fields
Cross-modal reinforcement -- messages through two modalities (e.g., words and pictures) more efficient if the two sources are well coordinated	Should have "complete coordination between video and audio"	Appropriate integration of audio and visual
		Learning most effective when materials are "meaningful" and have personal relevance for students
Assumptions about teaching		
Entertainment and education -- "make entertainment instrumental to learning"	Good ITV programs should have an element of humor	"Sometimes the materials need to be dramatic in form, enlarged, made vivid by color, motion, etc."

Use the familiar as a bridge to the unfamiliar		
Direct and indirect teaching -- employ full range of direct and indirect teaching methods	Instructional television at its best when it does not instruct, but gives students food for thought, material to work with	
Showing the world -- "Television's great power is the capacity to transport, to show the world to children."	Good ITV program makes use of the unique possibilities of the medium. It tries to give students subject matter they would otherwise not get, and forms of presentation they would otherwise not meet.	Should give "impression of authenticity"
No preaching No trivializing ("talking down" to children)	Presenter should have right sort of personality -- great interest in, liking for, what he is talking about, able to transmit his own feeling to his audience; and be brave enough to oversimplify matters.	Do personality and appearance of teacher add or detract from effectiveness of the presentation?

LESSER	LUNDGREN	CARPENTER
Assumptions about teaching (continued)		
	A good program is one that does the job it has been given as a component in a multi-media project.	Instructional materials and media of many kinds will be needed.
		Is the content organized and structured so as to facilitate knowledge?
Catching attention		
An expensive appearance (to compete with other TV)	ITV programs must be of the same professional standards as a country's general programs.	
Music and sound effects	A good program will make good use of musical and sound effects.	Stimulus materials must attract and sustain attention.
Repetition	A good ITV programs says the same thing more than once, in different ways.	Optimum repetition, with variation, of the main ideas

<u>Directing attention</u>		
Incongruity	Using screen to full potential, working with close-ups that are close enough, using camera angles to attract attention to information you want your picture to impart, etc.	Is content organized and structured so as to facilitate learning?
Action		Effective use of pictures, film clips, demonstrations, diagrams, etc., to support the instruction
<u>Sustaining attention</u>		
Humor	"Do try to make us smile sometime."	
Anticipation-participation	An ITV program should start students working . . . free their creative energy . . . be open-ended	Should make use of techniques to provide viewer participation, motivate the student to work and study on the problem. Among these variables, bet on practice, participation, involvement
Diversity of characters, content, style, pace	Variety	Variety Rate of development must be appropriate to hold attention and facilitate learning.

for a given set of learners. This is the responsibility of the writer and the producer. Whenever he reads in the outline "optimum repetition," "estimates of initial competence of students," "appropriate rate of development to hold attention" -- whenever he seeks to apply statements like that, he must seek additional information. Usually, he depends upon his insight and experience. Very seldom does he have the advantage (as the Children's Television Workshop does) of research assistance to help him understand in detail the initial competence of the students he seeks to instruct, or to tell him whether his use of repetition is indeed optimum in that situation, or whether the rate at which his program develops does indeed hold attention. Very seldom does he have that help available, or can he afford to call it in.

One member of the conference said: "You may have a mental picture of what is the perfect ITV system, but that ideal will always have to be modified according to the hard facts of life, such as budgets, and technical and staff facilities." Time, talent, money may be lacking, and in almost every ITV project they represent serious constraints. Money, for example. Sesame Street cost $40,000 an hour, whereas the budget for ITV in many developing countries is not more than $1,000 per hour.

Precepts, rules, principles, guidelines are therefore only the dry bones on which the flesh of excellent programs must be placed. But it is clear that in the last ten years we have built a considerable skeletal structure for effective instructional television. This is cause for hope. The fact that we do not accomplish more with it is cause for humility.

Instructional Television in Its Setting

One of the points to which the meeting returned again and again was that instructional television is always a part of larger universes of policy and action. It is, for example, almost always a part of a larger learning system -- whether 5 per cent of the prescribed learning activity of the British Open University, as Hancock described it to the meeting, or an integrated and changing part of the highly sophisticated combination of teaching media in Sweden, as described and illustrated by Lundgren. Out of this arise many questions of great interest: What can television do best? What combinations of media, print, and broadcast, audio or visual, are best for a given task, a given condition, a given child? How can instructional television be designed so that its learning activities carry over to, reinforce, and are reinforced by, learning experiences derived from other parts of life?

Instructional television is also a part of an economic and social system, and usually a system in process of change. Change brooded over the conference. Over and over again members returned to it -- the changes in ITV and the imminence of cable, the great swells of social and economic change throughout the world, the future pathways research will follow. This, too, was something for which time did not permit sufficiently detailed discussion. But quite enough examples were presented to indicate that a "good" program at one stage and condition of development may not be quite the same as a good program in another; that a good program in one culture may not be quite the same as a good program in another. There may in different situations even be a different premium on program quality. As Lumsdaine said, there may well be conditions in which 10,000 bicycles are preferable to 100 Rolls-Royces.

All this relativism left all too little time to talk about which guidelines are general and timeless, applicable across conditions and cultures. However, the need to interpret even the most general theory -- given the present state of research and theory -- in terms of conditions, was one of the pervading themes of the conference. And consequently, whereas the conferees had begun by talking about research, writing, and production, as the week went on there was an increasing proportion of talk -- perhaps somewhat to the surprise of the conferees themselves -- about policy and management.

Some of the more memorable sessions were, in effect, case studies presented orally with programs to illustrate them. The case of the Children's Television Workshop was reviewed at length. Tadashi Yoshida and Shigeo Ouchi talked about some of the experiences of the Japan Prize Contest, and of Japanese instructional television in general. Peter Seow talked about ITV in Singapore. Hancock described the problems of making television programs for the Open University in Britain, and Lundgren how Sweden puts together its multi-media instruction. And one of the most memorable days of the meeting brought together representatives from three "flagship" ITV projects in the developing countries -- Samoa (represented by Ivan Propst), Niger (Max Egly), and El Salvador (Stanley D. Handleman).

This was apparently the first time that representatives concerned with production in these three large projects had come together to discuss the problems they had faced and the constraints on their programming. They had much information to exchange, and the other conferees -- who were thus able to eavesdrop, and occasionally kibitz, on a historic occasion -- found the experience completely fascinating. It is too bad that the reports and discussions from that day cannot be included in this book. They were given, however, under the promise of confidentiality. In any case, descriptive reports of the projects will be available within the next year.

A major project in a developing country operates under special restraints. It has invested so much that it cannot afford to stop and start over, or write off two years as a mistake. As Handleman said, success -- or at least continuance -- must be built into it. Therefore, certain initial decisions, as Propst pointed out, tend to be irreversible, and take on a crucial importance in shaping the project as a whole, and its use of television in particular.

Niger, for example, decided to make use of the expertise provided by the French government. The highly talented people who came from France set up an experimental project, separate from the standard curriculum and free of the educational bureaucracy, in order to be able to create a truly innovative project. They by-passed the existing classroom teachers and used monitors who had only primary education, had never taught or received any teacher training (and therefore, from the viewpoint of the project managers, had nothing to unlearn). They succeeded in building something new in the educational world and used television in a way that has drawn the admiration of every visitor to Niamey. But this did not endear them to the educational establishment. The entrenched educators ignored the experiment and waited for it to fail. When it did not fail, they became hostile and resistant, and prevented it from expanding beyond 22 classrooms, 800 students, rather than the hundreds of thousands it had hoped to bring into the school system.

In a sense the Samoa project, like the Niger experiment, was "imposed," rather than growing from within -- although, to be sure, with the best of intentions. Samoa came to a decision at the outset that had profound effects. It decided to introduce the educational reform in all eight primary grades in the first year, and in the four years of high school in the second year. Both Niger and El Salvador began more cautiously, one grade at a time. The Samoa decision, dramatic and public-spirited as it was, placed an almost unbearable burden upon human resources. The schools were required to change the curriculum and the level of teaching each year as new students moved through the system and old students tried to adjust to it. By the same token, they felt they had to remake their television programs to keep up with system changes. By the second year, Samoa's tele-teachers and producers were making 180 programs a week. Last year, 6,000 live television programs were produced in Samoa. Obviously, this rate of production left little time to think about quality, or even to rehearse, and no time at all to make, test, and remake.

El Salvador made the initial decision to do the job itself. It had financial assistance and some technical advisers from outside, but unlike Niger, which brought its chief personnel from France, and Samoa, which brought teleteachers, producers, and supervisory personnel from the American mainland, it chose to depend on its own personnel and to keep the project closely integrated into the national educational system. It retrained its own teachers and provided in-service training for Salvadorans who were learning the skills of television. Consequently, it set the stage for acceptance of the educational reform, and was able to depend to a larger degree on its classroom teachers, less on its television, than the other two projects. But the use of inexperienced teleteachers and producers placed certain constraints on program quality.

Each of these projects experienced some political turmoil, and the way these political problems were resolved depended to a great extent on the strength of support at the top. Samoa had a strong governor, devoted to the educational reform; when he left, the turmoil began. El Salvador has had a strong Minister of Education, devoted to the educational reform, and his political influence has been a key factor. Niger had the support of its president, but an almost solid wall of resistance below him, and particularly in the Ministry of Education. If educational change is to go forward at the rate it moved in places like Niger, Samoa, and El Salvador, there had better be strong, supportive leadership.

Out of the discussion of the role of television in educational and social change emerged the only truly Hawaiian principle of the conference. It was promptly named the Surfing Principle: When used as an instrument of educational reform, television, like a surfer, must ride the forward edge of the wave. If it falls behind the wave of general change, it will miss the ride; if it starts too far ahead, it risks being knocked off the board. Or, in the terms most used at the meeting, the problem is to select the right wave within education where television can best be used, the right timing, the task it can do better than any media or methods can do. If we do that, it can go a long way. If not, it can founder in a sea of dissatisfaction and boredom.

Finally

The diversity of conditions under which ITV has to operate was illustrated by the conferees themselves -- Propst in Samoa, assigned to make 6,000 programs a year with an average of one hour total studio time per program; Egly, trying to make new and imaginative programs and use them in new, imaginative ways in the classroom, while the Ministry of Education looked suspiciously on; Japan and Sweden, rich in talent and equipment and network time, accepted completely by the educational system; the makers of Sesame Street, deliberately setting out to compete with commercial programs for children's attention, aiming at an out-of-school audience; the BBC, contracting to use its great skills and long experience to produce about 150 (not 6,000!) television and 150 radio programs a year by which to carry a high-quality British university education to home viewers and listeners who work by day and become college students by night.

Clearly, ITV is not one thing, but a spectrum; and what is known generally about it must be applied to a wide spectrum of conditions and audiences and goals. That is one of its greatest challenges both to science and to art.

No one at the meeting was inclined to claim that either the scholars or the broadcasters had all the answers. Everyone agreed that the making of truly effective instructional programs must be partly science, partly art. The science of instructional technology can offer a small body of general guidelines, and methods for examining the conditions under which they are applied and for testing their performance under given conditions. The art of broadcasting offers insight, creativity, skills, and a sense of how to translate precepts into programs for people. Neither science nor art can do it all alone.

A NOTE IN ACKNOWLEDGMENT

The conference took no official stands, passed no resolutions, signed no conclusions. That was not its job. However, this is not to say that there was not a high level of agreement on some of the things that might be done in support of more effective ITV. More research, of course, and more use of formative research in making programs. More training of broadcasters in the theory and research findings of instructional technology. Training of at least a limited number of persons for leadership and planning posts who combine art and science; who are experienced in broadcasting, can read and if necessary do research, and are grounded in the theory and technology of instruction. These, and other concrete suggestions, which will surface elsewhere, need not be explicated here.

Perhaps the most general point of consensus was on "sharing." It was interesting to watch that concept broaden as the week passed. The conferees began by sharing their own professional experience and insights, not, as usually, with their professional colleagues, but with persons from the other side of the professional wall. This was useful. It began to suggest other levels of sharing. Programs -- a number of people wanted to see some Niger programs, or a program like the excellent Japanese "One to One Correspondence," or a new approach like *Sesame Street,* in their home settings for a more leisurely study or for showing to program staffs. Papers -- a number of people wanted copies of research papers mentioned during the meetings, for study and use at home or for training purposes. It was suggested that each region of the world should have a library or depository of high-quality ITV programs, where these programs could be viewed or perhaps borrowed, and become the basis for teaching, in-service training, and self-assessment. More than once the conversation turned to the question of how the experience of viewing and discussing the extraordinary collection of instructional programs now entered in the Japan Prize contest might be shared, not only with the 50 or so persons who now attend the contest and view those programs, but world-wide with thousands rather than tens of ITV broadcasters, scholars, teachers, and persons in training for those roles. It was suggested that a series of traveling libraries might be assembled from the best programs entered every year in the Japan Prize. These collections might be tailored somewhat to the needs and interests of a region. I am happy to say that this suggestion is being considered most seriously by the Japan Prize Secretariat, and may be put into effect within the year.

The nearest the conference came to an official action was at the farewell luncheon, after the final sessions, when the chairman was authorized to express the deep gratitude of the conferees to the East-West Center and its Communication Institute for hospitality and support, to NHK for its cooperation in supplying a number of programs from the Japan Prize contests, to the Institute for Communication Research at Stanford for its support and planning of the meeting, and to all the other organizations and individuals who had lent programs and materials to help make the week more productive and more pleasant. Among them is the Center for Research in International Studies, at Stanford, whose generous grant to the Institute for Communication Research helped defray some of the costs. Special appreciation should be expressed also to Mr. Cuyler Shaw, who handled a multiplicity of details as an administrative assistant to the conference; Mr. Don Hatch, who was in charge of the film and television presentations; and to Mrs. Linda Miller, who has so beautifully typed this copy.

The members of the Honolulu conference have now, through this book, taken one further step toward "sharing" the resources and ideas of the field of instructional television. They hope it will share the flavor, if not the entirety, of their meeting.

Wilbur Schramm

PARTICIPANTS

in the Honolulu Seminar, 24-29 January, 1972

Gilda Benstead
Department of Education, ETV Branch
Honolulu, Hawaii

Graeme Bond
Department of Speech Communication
University of Hawaii, Honolulu, Hawaii

Walker G. Buckner
Ken Foundation Inc.
New York, N.Y.

C. Ray Carpenter
Professor of Psychology and Anthropology
University of Georgia, Athens, Georgia

Max Egly
Director, Tele-Niger
Niamey, Niger; Montmorency, France

Alan Hancock
UNESCO Regional Broadcasting Planning Adviser for Asia
Kuala Lumpur, Malaysia

Stanley D. Handleman
Principal Adviser, El Salvador ETV Project
San Salvador, El Salvador

Geoffrey Z. Kucera
Chairman, Department of Educational Communications
University of Hawaii, Honolulu, Hawaii

Arthur A. Lumsdaine
Professor of Psychology and Education
University of Washington, Seattle, Washington

Rolf Lundgren
Director of Instructional Programming
Swedish Radio and Television, Stockholm, Sweden

Shigeo Ouchi
Assistant Professor of Psycholinguistics and Audiovisual Instruction
Tokyo University, Tokyo, Japan

Edward Palmer
Director of Research, Children's Television Workshop
New York, New York

Ivan Propst
Department of Education
Pago Pago, American Samoa

Wilbur Schramm
Professor of Communication and Director, Institute for Communication Research
Stanford University, Stanford, California

Peter Seow
Head, Educational Television Service
Singapore

Robert Steiner
Director of Broadcasting
University of Hawaii, Honolulu, Hawaii

R. Lyle Webster
Director, East-West Communication Institute
East-West Center
Honolulu, Hawaii

Tadashi Yoshida
Special Assistant to the President, NHK, and Secretary-General, Japan Prize
Tokyo, Japan